Silent Fire

Harper Forum Book

Silent Fire

An Invitation to Western Mysticism

Edited by

Walter Holden Capps
and Wendy M. Wright

Published in San Francisco by
HARPER & ROW, PUBLISHERS
New York, Hagerstown, San Francisco, London

To Virgil Cordano, O.F.M.,
with love and gratitude

FIRST EDITION

Designed by Patricia Girvin Dunbar

Library of Congress Cataloging in Publication Data
Main entry under title:
Silent fire.
(A Harper forum book)
Bibliography: P. 000
Includes index.
1. Mysticism—Addresses, essays, lectures.
2. Mystics—Biography—Addresses, essays, lectures.
I. Capps, Walter H. II. Wright, Wendy M.
BV5072.S54 1978   248'.22'0922 [B]   78-03366
ISBN 0-06-061314-9

---

78 79 80 81 82   10 9 8 7 6 5 4 3 2 1

Contents

Preface

There are a host of reasons for a new book on Western mysticism. For one, the Western world is experiencing a significant shift in its religious orientation. The prevalence of schools of meditation, the adherence to disciplines that enrich the life of the spirit, the application of ancient religions as living psychologies, and the turn to the resources of the monastery are signs of a widespread upheaval. Then, too, the recent large exposure to Asian religious traditions in the West has taken an intriguing turn. Having "turned within" and toward the East simultaneously, some Westerners now seem to be facing the West. But it is not as if this has happened before. This time the West is facing the West from the East. And the turnabouts have focused new attention on resources within Western religious literature that can sustain and nurture such dramatic readjustments. Finally, from within its primary environment, the monastic milieu, Western mystical literature is being given new and fresh appraisals. Attempts are being made to reconstruct Western religious history through the perspectives of interests and traditions that, for a long time, have been neglected or underemphasized. From all sides, Western mystical religion is being viewed with eyes from which large scales have been removed. This book is an attempt to facilitate such efforts.

The format is simple and straightforward. The book consists of two sorts of material: an introductory essay on the biography and significance of the individual mystic, and one or more selections from that individual's writings. The book begins with an excerpt from Augustine's *Confessions* and proceeds to representative samples of mystical literature through the centuries from Augustine's time to the current era. The introductions to the selections contain three elements: a brief biographical sketch of the writer, a résumé of the particular contribution of the writer, and an expanded statement regarding the place the writer enjoys within the history of Western mysticism. The interpretation we, the editors, offer consists of the Introduction: The Mystic Way, and an abbreviated Historical Sketch (which emphasizes Western mysticism's nurturing conditions in its formative period).

The intention is to let the material of the book speak for itself. But before we will allow it to, without interruption, we want to record our thanks to persons who have been of special assistance to us. We think first of all the colleagues and students at the University of California, Santa Barbara, especially those students who have taken RS 100, 187, and 188. Along the way, there were numerous persons outside the university community, monks and spiritual teachers, with whom we became acquainted, from whom we learned, and with whom we consulted. We trust that the book will serve as an expression of our gratitude, especially to Mother Myriam and the community at Redwoods, Father Bruno and his confreres at New Camoldoli, Abbot Bernard and Father Paschal in Lafayette, Brothers Luke and Peter at Mt. Saviour, Abbot Thomas and Father Basil at Spencer, Abbot Thomas in Vina, Father Vincent Martin in Valyermo, John and Patricia Sommerfeldt and Rozanne Elder in Kalamazoo, the Poor Clares, Franciscans, Holy Cross fathers, and those at the Center for Spiritual Renewal in Santa Barbara.

We are very grateful to Marie Cantlon and Sarah Rush of Harper & Row, for their patience and encouragement. Finally, we thank those persons closest to us who helped make the book, in the fullest sense, an enjoyable corporate undertaking.

February 14, 1978

Introduction: The Mystic Mode

This is a book about mystical religion, specifically mystical religion as it has developed and is known in the Western world. As editors of the volume, we take the position that mysticism is not necessarily exotic or eccentric. Instead, it denotes a fundamental way of being human. It is a way, or mode, of relating to the world.

Distinct from a host of other ways, the mystic way does not approach the world primarily as though it were a problem to be solved. Nor does it view it as a puzzle to be pieced together, or even as an entity that can be penetrated by a formula or an idea. But sometimes it pictures the world as though it were a mirror, a reflector, that could be counted upon to provide an accurate portrayal of the self. Simultaneously, it often exposes reality as a mystery, deep but trustworthy, a very large portion of which will always remain unknown, uncharted and resistant to human probing.

In the mystic way, reality is neither seized nor deciphered. Nor can it be committed to ideational formulation. Instead, it is *engaged*—delicately, knowingly, and passionately. It is engaged by being loved. And in being loved, it is also given an interior place. This intricate relationship between person and world implies that the person become one with that to which he is related: one becomes like (and what) reality is. It holds too that reality is both unitary and multidimensional. The world is supple. It is also dynamically formed.

Accordingly, the mystic way seeks less to change this or that aspect of the world than to penetrate its depth and richness. It desires always that things remain in their intrinsic and unitive state. It is commited to an immediate and wholistic discernment. It tends to approach the world by way of intuitive perceptions. This is not to suggest that the mystic temper is insensitive to detail, fine features, minute parts, and special nuances. On the contrary, one of its fundamental characteristics is to allow each thing to be whatever it is—uniquely, individually, as it stands, in its own right. Yet its goal is to disclose the deeper structures, to reach the hidden ground, to find the center, to abide at the source, to locate the point of origin.

In the highly symbolic and metaphorical language of the mystics, the center is depicted as a poignant and awe-inspiring rhythm, an indelible pulsation, a majestic pathos, sometimes as cadenced as heartbeat or as spontaneous as wind, unruly as fire, and still as silence. But always it is approached as the heart of the heart of it all. Simultaneously, it is portrayed as the life of the life of the world, and, in the words of Augustine, "the Life of the life of my soul."

Those who speak from within the tradition, the mystics themselves, describe the primary compulsion as being both fearsome and inciting. They view its source and end as being something more than a magnificent and fecund origin mysteriously giving birth to all things. It is also a dynamic presence for which one yearns. In this sense, it stretches the furthest limits of one's capacity to know. It elicits the most exquisitely anguished moments of love. It is a presence experienced both as source and as final resting place, beyond time and space as well as being most deeply within them. Although it pulls the person who would experience it away from the common attachments of human life, it also draws him into a deeper life by teaching him a new perception: the perception of what has traditionally been called the "sacramental world view."

The sacramental vision describes a capacity to perceive more than one level or dimension of reality at a time, and to know that all levels or dimensions are available to any event or experience. Drawn by the hunger of love and the thirst for knowledge, mystics enter so deeply into their own inner lives that they discover a reality, as it were, "on the other side of themselves." Abandoning themselves to a transformation by the presence they discover both within and outside their own selves, they become the voice of humankind articulating its awestruck perception of God. It is as if, finding themselves at or near the vital center, they begin to hear the heart's rhythmic beating, sense its pulsing life, and little by little experience the heart as receiving its vitality from the greater heart. Here the mystic is most profoundly alone and most intimately related to every other living being. Mystics in the West have described this experience as the discovery of the image of God (*imago Dei*) within.

Those who speak from within, the mystical writers, describe the primary experience as "a tranquil abiding in the presence of God." They attest that the experience finds its culmination in "the loving gaze of the soul at God." The choice of words indicates that the mystical experience pertains first of all to what is loved, adored, and thus worshipped. It deals with the ways in which love is motivated, redirected, magnified, and enraptured toward fulfillment. The writers refer to this devotional disposition as "the way" (as in "pathway"). They sometimes call the pathway truth, as in the spirit of Augustine's counsel, "Do not go abroad, but turn within; in the inner person dwells truth." Such truth registers not when the ordinary cognitive limits have been surpassed, but when the self is made profoundly present to itself. Thus, mystical expressions tend to be personal, devotional, aspirational, frequently autobiographical, and often lyrical.

The Unitive Dimension

The documents of mystical religion resemble romantic literature much more than philosophical treatises. Throughout their pages, the dominant images and metaphors are examples of unitive patterns of relatedness. Indeed, the most prominent and consistent analogue within the tradition is the marriage covenant, the relation of male and female, bride and bridegroom, in which the relation of God and the soul is imaged and mirrored. So, too, is "spiritual friendship" offered as a prime example of how disparateness or "twoness" becomes unitive and single. The love between a man and a woman is also taken to symbolize the underlying conjunction of things, and is utilized prominently as a symbol of the eventual wedding of heaven and earth. Frequently, the holy city, the new Jerusalem, is depicted as "coming down from heaven as a bride adorned for her husband."

Mystical religion seems to exult in the bonds love creates and brings to awareness. It encourages union and wholeness. It makes communion the occasion for doxology. And, for this reason, one of the most dominant strains within the tradition was inspired and nurtured by the biblical The Song of Songs (also called The Canticle as well as The Song of Solomon), the collection of love poems spoken alternately by a man and his beloved, a book of romantic literature long associated with sacred marriage in Jewish tradition. The contemplative tradition initiated by Bernard of Clairvaux (1091-1153), sustained and elaborated by John of the Cross (1542-1591) and, along the way, by a succession of Cistercian writers, from the twelfth century on, developed as a series of commentaries on The Song of Songs.

The strong disposition toward the unitive is also expressed in cosmic or cosmological terms. The heavens, the sky, the rotation of the stars and planets, the coming of morning and evening, the silence of night, the brilliance of day—indeed, the cosmos itself—provide a range of images and materials suited to unitive inspiration. Frequently, mystical writers portray the unity of the cosmos in musical terms, as if identical harmonies ruled the celestial spheres and permeated the human heart. In revised Pythagorean form, they depict the cosmic unity liturgically, as an eternal but perennially new comprehensive choral chant.

The same tendency can accommodate the components of the natural world. Here the compelling insight is that each living thing bears resemblances to all other living things. Francis of Assisi's perception that everything alive is related to him in a personal way is the outstanding example of this conviction. But Francis is not alone in recognizing that trees, birds, rocks, water, the wind, butterflies, silk-worms, flowers, and the human heartbeat all belong to one another. Through them the life that is the life of the world is made present, as in the words of the liturgical antiphon, "O Lord, you have given every-thing its place in the world, and no one can make it otherwise. For it is your creation, the heaven and the earth and the stars. You are the Lord of all."

But this is not all, for mystical religion is preoccupied with the unitive character of silence. We refer to the deep, pervasive fullness that resonates before sounds are made, words are uttered, and quiet is shattered. This is the recurrence of "pretime," of the original harmony, when, as Mircea Eliade, the historian of religion, puts it, the creation is received fresh from the creator's hand. Sound, by contrast, can be disruptive, severing, and blatant, although there are some sounds that sustain the harmony of the original silence. The disposition recognizes silence to be full of content. It also knows that words come at a high price and must be allocated carefully, since they carry the potential of fragmenting the original unity. Silence is not simply "no-sound," but the context for the working of memory, recollection, and meditation. It also stimulates the vast worlds of the imagination. It enables one to sense interior rhythms, to hear interior melodies, to discover new patterns of coloration, and to cultivate sensitivity to words and sounds of another order. At times it also provides occasion for the cessation of thought, words, and the products of the imagination. It is within this setting that the contemplative tradition affirms that faith comes by hearing *(fides ex auditu)*. It is within the same context that mystics attest to the occurence of an "intellectual vision."

There is another prominent context within which much can be made of the unitive character of contemplative aspiration. We refer to the power of beauty. Beauty, like Goodness and Truth, has an integrative power. It is able to bring things to coherence and culmination. It bestows harmony, balance, and design. It comprehends things in their intrinsic patterns of interrelatedness, and in so doing, enunciates their radiance and splendor. The contemplative tradition holds truth and goodness in high esteem. But it is particularly open to the presence of beauty. Beauty's character is neither propositional nor axiomatic, but affective, contemplative, and visionary. Thus the term most correlative with beauty, like knowledge with truth, is love. The terms are used together. Love lends fullness to beauty and is expressed therein.

This brings us by another route to appreciate the the remarkable place of The Song of Songs in Western mystical literature. The work is formed by the themes of love and beauty. Indeed it can be understood as a hymn or ode to the world that beauty informs.

The theme of beauty also gives added vitality to the other contexts through which mystical religion is expressed. There are cultivated and deliberate ways of expressing the beauty of the earth, for example, as there are esthetically refined ways of making cosmic harmony and balance explicit. Similarly, there are definite ways prescribed for sensing and adoring the beauty of Mary the Virgin, the Mother of God, who, from time to time, in her archetypal form, is approached as the personification of Beauty, and, under Christian refinement, as Beauty Incarnate. The key adorational lines are in Augustine's *Confessions,* "Oh beauty, so ancient, so new," repeated by Dante as "Beauty, so ancient, so lovely."

There are intrinsic ties, too, as Henry Suso's verse indicates, between beauty and silence.

Beautiful are the things that are seen.
More beautiful are the things that are understood.
By far the most beautiful are the things not understood.

The things that cannot be uttered remain in the realm of silence— hidden, hushed, secret, as if expression entailed loss of beauty. Utter silence is true beauty, silence with content of its own choosing.

There is a sense, too, in which the mystical tradition understands the religious community to have a unitive capacity. We mean "unitive" in more than sociofunctional terms. For the religious community was conceived to reflect the underlying harmony that is God's will for the world. Thus the community provided a foretaste of the awaited kingdom. It sought to mirror the heavenly ideal. It was regarded as a sign of that deeper order as well as being an effective organism within this time and place. It was designed to support the cultivation of individual aspirations within a group context. The community was organized to assist the individual to become something more (and something other) than he could become if left to his own resources. At the same time, the community itself was subjected to the same transformational processes. In being subjected, it exhibited the promise of an immortality that challenged the vicissitudes of cultural change and survived the destructiveness of death.

Significant, too, is the unitive character of the individual life cycle. "Personal wholeness" is proper terminology here. Yet mystical awareness is something other than a form of personal and/or humanistic psychology, for there are very specific liturgical contexts within which the integration of the self is sought. Again, the setting is important. The tradition attests that it is through participation in life of God in the world that personal integration occurs. Because persons of mystical persuasion had examined themselves within this perspective, they learned something significant about the pulses of the interior life. They recorded their experiences. They tracked the motions of feeling, temperament, and interior aspiration. They noted the distinctions between various periods and moods in the individual's life. They were sensitive to the content of distinct moments, to periods of upheaval and transition, to the rhythms within that process by which the self finds location. Always relying upon a power beyond themselves, their experience became cumulative; they learned from one another. Their testimony indicates that the unitive character of mystical religion can be expressed vividly and forcefully in terms of psychological integration and personal wholeness. The religion of which we speak seeks to bring the self under the discipline or mastery of a unitive principle so that self-alienation might be overcome. It stimulates and nurtures the impulse toward unification and integration in the life of the spirit.

Thus the mystic way is something more than an apprehension or a set of attitudes and perspectives. It is also an interior process, a pattern of inwardness, by which the individual comes to know himself and senses that he is known. The mystic way is both an instinctual and a highly disciplined response to Socrates' challenge that "The unexamined life is not worth living."

The Transformative Dimension

So far we have emphasized the unitive tendency of mystical religion. It is necessary to add that the modality has a transformative side too. It can be transformative because of its thoroughly dynamic character. It does not refer to a fixed or finished personal state that can be achieved once and for all; instead, it refers to a perpetual process that occurs within the self. We refer to this as "the activity of the human heart." It is as though the motivated individuals were following the impulses of an interior odyssey—an inner pilgrimage that is developmental and sequential. The individuals whose interior life are principled by the impulse become something other than they would have been or would have known themselves to be. They experience, as it were, a second birth: they are born anew. By resigning themselves to the authority of the transformative process, they "find" themselves and "come" to themselves. They become both someone else and more truly themselves in the exchange. Their sense of significance is reconstructed. Their priorities are redesigned. Their loves and devotions are rearranged. Their basic instincts are rekindled. Their previous consciousness of place, position, and status is challenged, then broken, and subsequently reconceived. The entire person is affected by the transformation.

The representatives of the tradition recognize that the journey of each soul is unique and unrepeatable. Yet they also believe that the interior landscape exhibits a discernible shape and some common characteristics. In this respect, there is a strong tendency in the West to root the mystical impulse within the life of prayer. Prayer is understood to have an organic quality and to be regulated by stages of development and transformation. The basic pattern is characterized by a dying—to-self and a rising-to-new-life (in God) and is frequently described in a threefold sequence: purification, illumination, and union. Against this background, mystical religion is portrayed as deepening experience within prayer.

This is not to suggest that such interior changes occur by straight-line forward motion. For those so compelled and devoted, the general tendency is positive and developmental. Yet the evidence emphasizes that the interior life is marked by a variety of conflicting currents. There are backward and forward oscillations. Some of the impulses are in phase, some not, some on course, some otherwise. There are hesitant beginnings, bold advances, repeated shocks from overexposure, cautious retreats, withdrawals inward, movements outward: a perpetual kinetic transition and transformation.

It is important to emphasize that all interior motions are understood to belong to the range of sanctioned experience—not just the highs, the peaks, the times of ecstasy and rapture. All of it is given appropriate place. All pertains. All belongs. All, including the negative elements, the dark sides, the feelings of abandonment, the experiences of alienation, the deep suffering, even the courting of despair can and must be honored. All lend support to the practice of the presence of God.

The reason for the flexibility is that the self is multidimensional. It consists of a variety of levels of which the individual is only partially conscious. Reality too is multilayered. It is graded. In the mystical tradition, consciousness is depicted as the meeting ground of the various dimensions of the self with the various levels of reality. Accordingly, the mystical experience involves an increasingly penetrative awareness of one's truest self as reflected by a disclosure of the depths of reality.

The same images and metaphors used to evoke the unitive dimension of mystical religion are just as effective in giving expression to its transformative side. The image of marriage, for example, by which the union between God and the soul is depicted, emphasizes this transformative dimension. The parties to the sacred bond are interiorized within each other. In this interiorization there is promise of a greater joy and splendor. As John of the Cross writes in the *Spiritual Canticle*:

Love never reaches perfection until the lovers are so alike that one is transfigured in the other. And then the love is in full health. The soul experiences within herself a certain sketch of love, which is the sickness she mentions, and she desires the completion of the sketch of this image, the image of her bridegroom, the Word, the Son of God, who as St. Paul says, "is the splendor of his glory and the image of his substance."

So too with the imagery of the cosmos. The world isn't taken to be an already-finished entity, fixed, established, its coming-to-be a past and closed event. Rather the world is viewed as a dynamic organism, whose life is new every morning. To be sure, the cosmos is regulated by a series of recurrent cycles and patterns. But these cosmological cycles give new shape—and transformed possibilities—to the world they regulate.

Nature operates according to the same principle. Nature pulsates. It is alive. It is dynamic. And in the power of its dynamism lies its capacity for perpetual transformation.

Personal wholeness is the most obvious context within which the transformative element resonates. For personal wholeness is the context to which all other frames of reference can be directed. Cosmic cycles and natural rhythms—even the union of male and female—all are taken as reflections or mirrors of occurrences within the self. When the cosmic cycles and natural rhythms are interiorized, they provide impetus and energy for personal growth. They lend content to the inward odyssey. And when the interior pattern is discerned, one finds it to be consonant with the external harmony. It is sealed with a tendency toward wholeness.

The Vision

The basis of it all is that life is a supreme gift for which the most appropriate posture is the giving of thanks. Thus, when the mystics celebrate the day, without requiring that it be remade to conform to some more perfect norm, it is because they have caught the incredible truth that something—indeed, Being—is. When they take deliberate steps to monitor or influence the pulses of the interior life, it is because they have learned that the vitality which courses through their own spirits is of the same substance as that which issues from the heart of things. To acknowledge life as a supreme gift is to sense that the underlying mystery—unfathomable, ineffable, eventually unspeakable—is nevertheless benevolent. To receive it as mystery is to respect the beauty of its pathos.

And should it begin to appear at times that the mystics have invested too much, committing themselves to rigors and disciplines that seem manifestly inhuman, one should remember that, for them, the ultimate scheme of things now unfolding is so wonderfully intoxicating, overwhelming tantalizing, and thoroughly preoccupying that, no matter how great the sacrifice, they wish to be admitted to witness the final configuration.

Historical Sketch

Mysticism possesses a deep and abiding place in religion. Its manifestations are present in Eastern and Western religious traditions, more prominently in some religions, of course, than in others. A great portion of the Hindu tradition, for example, can be taken as a refined and elaborate expression of the mystical orientation. Buddhism, particularly in its Mahayana form, enunciates mystical tendencies throughout. Sufi mysticism is a prominent feature of Islam. And mystical sensitivities have a place in Jewish worship and practice.

But mystical aspirations are not restricted to the major religions of the world. They are to be found elsewhere, even outside the religious traditions. Indeed, one dominant characteristic of mysticism is its tendency, at times, to resist easy adaptation to conventional religion (with its dogmas, creeds, and institutional forms). Repeatedly, through the centuries, it has challenged the more regulatory, acculturated forms of religious life.

Since mystical awareness is intrinsic to religion, it would be a mistake to try to trace its occurrence within Christianity to a genetic root. It will prove more illuminating, instead, to look for specific nurturing conditions. Mysticism becomes explicit in Christianity, for instance, because the Jewish tradition, within whose self-consciousness and self-criticism the Christian religion arose, was open to this form of development and interpretation. Signs of this are evident in the Old

Testament, particularly in the Wisdom literature, kingship materials, New Year rituals, and in the prophetic literature. Mystical religion developed under Christian form, in part, because there had been occasion and precedent for it in the legacy Christianity inherited. The new religion simply carried that legacy forward. It can even be argued that the Christian religion is Judaic religion in mystical version.

There are many instances of mystical interpretation within the New Testament, particularly in the Gospel According to John, and the letters of Paul. The Fourth Gospel records Jesus' saying to his disciples "I and my father are one" and "If you abide in me, I will abide in you." Paul reports to the Colossians that "The mystery kept secret through all previous ages has now been disclosed," then identifies that mystery as "Christ in you, the hope of glory." Similar sayings are prominent throughout the New Testament.

Furthermore, Christian mysticism was supported by the more general and syncretistic religious context of which it was a part. The mystery religions of both Greek and Roman origin gave a prominent place to mystical sensitivities. Many of these called for the individual (identified as *mystes*) to be initiated into cultic secrets and divine knowledge. From this followed a pilgrimage by which the soul embarked on a homeward journey. All of these themes—the emphasis upon initiation as the prerequisite to divine knowledge, the pilgrimage, the journey of the soul—are incorporated within Christian mysticism, wherein they are refined, modified, reformulated, and communicated through biblical imagery.

Thus, from the beginning, the Christian faith was susceptible to mystical interpretation and expression. Such interpretation and expression has developed over the long centuries of Christian history.

Platonic Roots

In the larger context, the key integrative factor in the development of mystical religion in the West is the correspondence between the Christian religion and Platonic philosophy. Approached in this way, the specific occasion for the expression of the mystic temper lies in Plato's contention that reality is graded. By this he meant that the various components of the world are not of the same piece, kind, quality, or status.

Plato formulated his opinion on this subject in response to the question, "What abides when all else passes away?" or, as it was phrased in the "*Timaeus*, :What is that which always is and has no becoming, and what is that which is always becoming and never is?" It was the fundamental philosophical dilemma, a problem that has been posed as "the relation of being and becoming." The early thinkers discerned two orders of reality, one manifesting a sense of permanence, the other, by contrast, change and transitoriness. Plato wanted to provide a place for being, or permanence, while allowing the force of becoming, or change, to be properly acknowledged. Clearly-cut contrasting alternatives were formulated by Parmenides and Heraclitus respectively. Parmenides said that "being is, not being cannot be." And Heraclitus offered that "reality is a stream into which one cannot step twice in the same place." Parmenides understood the core element of reality to be being; being's contrary, becoming, was illusion. Heraclitus took the opposing view, calling change normative, then treating reality in process terms.

In retrospect, one recognizes that Plato found value in both contentions. He gave permanence a primacy over change, being over becoming, but without relegating becoming to mere illusion. If being were all that is, he affirmed, it would be imperceptible. The two are present together.

Plato's formulation of the relationship became paradigmatic in the west. He accorded full priority to being while insuring that a subordinated becoming wouldn't slip into a state of unreality. He used the formula to define the relation of permanence and change, eternal and temporal, ideal and particular, form and instances. He invoked it too when considering how society ought to be ordered, how education ought to be conducted, how values function, and, most frequently, how knowledge occurs.

Plato developed his response to the question by identifying two levels, dimensions, or orders of reality. He gave being, or permanence, primacy over becoming. He was unwilling to relegate becoming to illusion, or a state of unreality. If being were all that is, he affirmed, it would be unintelligible; and if becoming were all that is, it would be imperceptible. The two dimensions or orders are present together.

Certainly, Plato did not intend his formulation to have mystical import. It was a philosophical rather than a religious proposal. Soon, however, its range of applicability was extended. Eventually, it was used to stipulate the relation not only between being and becoming and between eternal and temporal, but also between supernatural and natural, creator and created, God and the world, and, in Augustine's *De Civitas Dei (Of the City of God)* between heavenly and earthly realms.

Plato's formula supplied the language, concepts, and intellectual framework by which mystical aspirations could be expressed and charted. It was appropriate that the two became conjoined. Mystical religion needs to apprehend the world in a multidimensional way, and Plato's insight attests that the world exhibits distinct levels or dimensions that can be graded and comparatively valued.

Another, more speculative side of Plato was communicated through his dialogue *Timaeus*, where he presented his views on the cosmos, or universe, including the worlds of physics, astronomy, and biology. Here he tested possibilities in an imaginative manner; he allowed conjecture to follow its own course. The product was a sketch of the nature of things in which he also developed a theory of the soul. His account, influenced by earlier Greek religion (particularly the Eleusian mysteries and Pythagorean thought), pictures the soul as having once had a home in the realm of the fixed stars. From this realm it fell through several levels of reality to earth, where it became united with a body. As it fell, it acquired the characteristics of the other levels of reality through which it descended. Its earthly task is to reverse the process: to find liberation from the body, discard the attributes and qualities it has acquired from its fall through intermediary levels of reality, and return to its original sacred place.

Plato presented both schemes, a depiction of the relation of being and becoming and a more speculative account of the journey of the soul to its celestial home through a series of cosmic levels and spheres. But he didn't synthesize the two clearly. That task was reserved for subsequent thinkers and commentators. Systematically, they placed the two schema together. They utilized Plato's ruminations and speculations as a springboard toward further cosmological postulation. And the development occurred through a series of commentaries on the *Timaeus*. Those who conducted it are referred to as Neoplatonists.

In their view, reality is inclusive of all things. It is also graded. Hence, everything that is can be placed within the hierarchical network and classified thereby. The entities most like pure being belong at the top of the scale, and the entities most like becoming nearer the bottom. All things are related to one another by means of this scale of gradation.

In Neoplatonic extension and reformulation, the supreme principle within the hierarchy of being is Mind, and, indeed, sometimes, "the One." Significantly, some authors refer to Mind as God, and some place the forms (or ideal substances) in the Divine Mind. Viewed from a subsequent perspective, this is the crucial equation. It insures that the hierarchical pattern is open to a religious interpretation. It also implies that the religious orientation so situated will be of a distinctively "otherwordly" kind. It means that religious aspiration is regulated by an ascendant tendency.

Literally speaking, Plato hadn't gone this far. He marked out the pattern and provided clues as to how the world's components might be arranged. From time to time, he acknowledged a world of religion. He made reference to "the gods" or "the deities," for example, and he gave some credence to the idea of a "creator-craftsman." But he didn't call the highest principle God, nor did he identify God with being. This fundamental equation does not appear. He didn't even identify "the Good" (the entity placed at the top of the hierarchical ladder) with God. It was enough for him to engage in cognitive and speculative work simultaneously. Subsequent thinkers, with pronounced theological interests, established the necessary correspondences.

Thus, within the Platonic tradition, the philosophical and religious schemes were fused. The relation between being and becoming was made interchangeable with the relation between God and the world. God was identified as the highest form of being. Eventually, knowledge of being was construed as knowledge of God. And in subsequent developments, knowledge of the Good was interpreted as union with God.

To trace this turn of events accurately, we need to turn our attention to the ongoing development of Platonic thought, from Plato's time forward. Specifically we refer to a tradition within Platonic understanding known as "Middle Platonism" (or Pre-Neoplatonism), which is associated with Plutarch of Chaeronea (46–120 A.D.) and influenced by Poseidonius (c. 135–50 B.C.). It was in correspondence with this strand of intellectual development that the Christian thinkers of the patristic era, notably Clement and Origen of Alexandria, Tertullian, and even Augustine, worked out their own formulations. For, by the time of the Church Fathers, Platonism was much more than a theory of knowledge and a portrayal of the universe; it had also become a fully developed world view within which one could find a self-consistent way of life.

The way had been prepared by Philo (c. 30 BCE to c. AD 40), noted Jewish philosopher and citizen of Alexandria, who had been deeply influenced by the Neoplatonic tradition. Philo's vocation was to commend the Jewish religion to the Greek world. In the process he worked out a synthesis between Jewish religion and Platonic philosophy. The synthesis was based on a supposition that all of Greek philosophy has its roots in Moses. It was expressed by means of an allegorical reading of the Hebrew Bible. It included many additional parallels between the truths of the Scriptures and the teachings of the philosphers, both Platonic and Stoic.

In Philo's view, the God made known through Jewish experience from the time of Moses on is the same God the Greeks placed at the top of the hierarchical ladder. The two traditions are making the same affirmations. They can be understood to be illuminating each other because adherents of each worshipped the same one true God.

The first comprehensive translation of Plato's philosophy into a mystical orientation was effected by Plotonius (205-270) the most famous Neoplatonist. Plotinus allowed the two dominant traditions—the theological rendition of the relation between God and world, and the philosophical portrayal of the relation of being and becoming—to become interchangeable. These schemas, in his view, were integral readings of the same dynamic interplay. In addition, Plotinus made it clear that the human being possesses a capacity for union with the highest principle. This union, he stated, was to occur through interior experience.

These interrelated themes found vivid expression in the eighth tractate of Plotinus' fifth *Ennead*. Here Plotinus asserts that the distance between God and the soul is to be overcome through inner experience.

Bring this vision before your sight, so that there shall be in your mind the gleaming representation of a sphere, a picture holding all the things of the universe moving or in repose, some at rest, some in motion. Keep this sphere before you, and from it imagine another, a sphere stripped of magnitude and of spatial differences. Cast out your inborn sense of matter, taking care not merely to attenuate it. Call on God, maker of the sphere you now hold, and pray him to enter. And may he come bringing his own universe with all the gods that dwell in it.

The unity one shares with all things, the fundamental coherence of the world, can be sensed, apprehended, intuited and experienced through interior awareness.

There were significant developments within the Platonic tradition after Plotinus, and they extended to the time of the Platonic revival in the Renaissance. But, with respect to the period we are considering, it is important to cite the intellectual work of Iamblichus, who died about 330, a century before Augustine was born. Because he codified the philosophical and religious point of view, Iamblichus is known as the first "Scholastic" of Neoplatonism. But what is more significant for our purposes is that during Iamblichus' time, assisted by his efforts, the mystical union sought for was shifted to other bases. For Plotinus, union was to be effected through personal inner experience. In Iamblichus, the same union is approached through *theurgy* (magical acts, covertly performed and sometimes involving sorcery, through which divine and/or supernatural spirits were invoked). The important implication is that the prominence of theurgy testifies to an increased lack of optimism regarding the capacities of personal experience.

Augustine, the Father of Christian Spirituality

Augustine (354-430), referred to as the father of the Christian mystical tradition, was both Platonist and anti-Platonist. As a party to Neoplatonic self-criticism, he too was mistrustful of the previous optimism. But in mistrusting that optimism, he did not abandon confidence that one could experience the presence of God. As with Iamblichus, it was a matter of approaching the goal from a proper base. The task was to find a way consonant with the nature of the goal.

Thus, for Augustine, it wasn't ascendancy that commended itself, but as thorough reorientation of the human soul. Human loves had to be cleansed and redirected. Man needed to become centered and properly oriented. The soul had to undergo a basic transformation.

Augustine formulated his contention in terms of the contrast between *superbia* and *humilitas*. He used the term *superbia* to describe the Neoplatonic expectation that union can be attained by one's own efforts. He recognized that the expectation is built on some unwarranted assumptions and that it generates a false optimism. In truth, given the nature of both man and God, union is possible only via the power of *humilitas*, the contrary disposition to *superbia*. *Humilitas* implies that self-interest will be subordinated to divine intention. It involves a self-emptying, an admission of need, a declaration of one's dependence upon divine assistance, a yearning for God's love and acceptance. *Humilitas* denotes the dispositional capacity to receive "the love of God shed abroad in our hearts."

Augustine had no lasting quarrel with the belief that the presence of God is to be experienced. He also agreed that the dominant reality is, indeed, the interior one. In these respects, his views were in line with revised, updated Neoplatonic teaching.

The change came in the understanding of the relation between divine and human. Augustine knew the gulf between God and the soul to be so great that it could be overcome only by a transforming divine power. This is the power of grace, exemplified in God's becoming human in Jesus Christ. At the same time, man is made in the image of God and carries this essential likeness to God, marred though not destroyed by sin. Because of sin and its consequences, the likeness needs to be reformed and its vitality rekindled. This too is effected by the presence of God in human form. Grace quickens and deepens the natural reciprocity between man and God. *Humilitas* describes the form of the divine action. And as God humbled himself, so is *humilitas* the appropriate disposition of the receptive interior self. It is the disposition of the human heart, bestowed and formed by the divine presence. Through it, the image of God is reconstituted and the presence of God is brought to interior consciousness.

Thus it was Augustine's achievement to blend the tendency toward divinization within mystical awareness with the Christian appreciation of the incarnation of God in Christ. He was not the first to seize upon the formula, but no one before had done it in such systematic fashion and in the language of personal, interior self-consciousness.

This delicate interweaving of elements gave the person of Christ a distinctively interior place. Born in a manager, Christ, the reality of God in human form, was also understood to be born within the soul. The soul, in turn, by virtue of the divine indwelling, is to be patterned according to the form of the life of God in Christ. Thus, the aspirations of the religious life can be realized through the power of grace, as it was said, "in Christ."

This understanding of the Christian gospel also implied that the life of Christ—his birth, suffering, death, and triumph—carries interior resonance: it describes the dispositional pattern by which the divine presence is both perceived and formed within the interior life. It also discloses the manner by which human victory over all threats to existence will occur. Drawing on this realization as the fundamental clue to the meaning of his own narrative, Augustine defined mystical awareness in developmental terms. Instead of being reduced to a profound single experience or even a number of extraordinary occurrences, mystical religion is understood to have its culmination in the silence that is recaptured at the end of time, when, having viewed all things as in a mirror darkly, the pilgrim sees God face to face.

Augustine's formulation treats the *vita contemplativa* as the distinctively Christian way of being human. It also places mystical religion within the context of autobiographical history. Appropriately, he called the recounting of this narrative *The Confessions*.

It will help us grasp the importance of Augustine's achievement to place it within the context of the dominant developmental tendency in the early history of the Church. That history consists of a series of intricate translations of fundamental religious affirmations into a variety of comprehensive frameworks. We can refer to the entire process as the "institutionalization of the faith," that is, the development of the creeds, systematic theological statements, liturgical forms and symbols, and social organization. Augustine played a key role in this process, not least in translating the articles of faith into the conceptual idiom of revised Platonic philosophy.

For our purposes, however, his most crucial translation is the interior one: the fundamental Christian outlook was communicated in the language of individual self-consciousness. It was portrayed in terms of the complicated motions, rhythms, and tendencies of the interior or spiritual life. In fact, God was understood to reveal himself in just these terms. The incarnation of God—his appearance in human form—was an interior event. And he makes himself known, Augustine attests, in a manner in keeping with the nature of disciplined self-knowledge.

The Confessions is the literary form in which this process is both traced and made self-conscious. It portrays the divine disclosure in interior terms, for personal self-consciousness is the context in which the life of God is mediated. As knowledge of the self became more extensive and sophisticated, the correspondence between divine activity and interior motion became more detailed and elaborate. Specific events in the life of Christ, as presented in the liturgy, were also viewed as moments in the interior life. They were celebrated, interwoven with events in other liturgical cycles, and made occasions for festivals. The Church year became a rich context for sensing the correspondence between events in the individual life cycle and events in the scheme through which God is made present in the world. Augustine set the process in motion. Human self-understanding, from his time forward, was influenced by this specific pattern of divine/human correspondence.

The Monastic Milieu

Our portrayal, so far, depicts mystical religion as issuing from Western intellectual history. It is appropriate to present the subject in this way. Yet, we must also recognize that the tradition was composed not primarily within academies or by philosophers, but through a specific nurturing environment, the world of monasticism. Through the centuries, those pursuing the contemplative religious life have been drawn to settings equipped to nourish the ideal. The monastery, hermitage, and desert retreat are understood to create conditions that foster interior awareness. The climate is markedly ascetic, requiring that ordinary human attachments be relinquished and personal priorities readjusted. Here religious life is fed by a daily absorption of the Hebrew Bible, particularly the Psalms, and the Christian New Testament. In the monastic setting, exposure to scriptures and to the writings of the Church Fathers and other noted authors on the religious life are part of the daily routine. This included intimate familiarity with the life and passion of Christ and, eventually, with the lives of the saints. Similarly, the atmosphere was marked by participation in liturgical worship. Some monastic communities considered the celebration of the liturgy to be the prime reason for their existence. The tradition came to recognize seven "hours" during the day—Matins, Lauds, Prime, Terce, Sext, None, Vespers, and Compline—when the psalms, hymns, lessons, and prayers were to be recited. Worship culminated in the celebration of the eucharist, the holy communion, in which bread and wine were received as the body and blood of Christ. Through the ceaseless repetition of the liturgical cycles, the cosmic acts of creation and redemption were understood to enrich and transform the lives of the participants. By actively celebrating the liturgical events, the individual was made conscious of the mystery that these same events carried interior resonance. In worship, the perennial mysteries bestowed new life in both unitive and transformative dimensions.

The climate was monastic, but this could be effected in both individual and corporate terms. The earliest form of distinctively contemplative life is that of the solitary. Beginning with Anthony (250-355), the first Christian monk, and those subsequently referred to as the Desert Fathers, a few individuals left society to dwell alone in cells, hermitages, and, gradually, in hermit communities. The founder of communal monastic life, also known as cenobitism, was Pachomius (290-346). In this form, monasticism became highly organized and followed specific guiding principles, the most famous of which is the Rule of St. Benedict, a sixth-century document that became normative not only for the Benedictines, but for other monastic communities as well. It set forth a vision of the simple life, incorporating manual labor, the communal ownership of goods, the communal practice of prayer, silence, and the avowal of poverty, chastity, and obedience.

Over the centuries the face of communal monastic life changed many times. Some groups developed into large and wealth institutions whose primary function was the continual celebration of the liturgy and the elaborate enactment of the rituals of the Church. This happened to many of the Benedictine monasteries during the Middle Ages. They were joined by other communities, particularly reform groups, the

Cistercians and the Carthusians, who sought to return monasticism to its stricter, more austere primitive state. Other offshoots of the monastic vine—the Franciscans and the Dominicans in particular—emphasized itinerant preaching. The Society of Jesus was founded as a teaching congregation. Still others found occupations as ministers to the poor and sick, as missionaries, teachers, or scholars.

The monastic stimulus came primarily from the Eastern regions within the Christian world. Among the persons responsible for the cultivation of Eastern Christian spirituality in terms that could be carried to the West were John Cassian (360-435), famous monk, abbot, and theologian, the Cappadocian Fathers (Basil, Gregory of Nyssa, and Gregory of Nazianzus,), and Macarius. The most influential of these figures, judged by subsequent developments, is the mysterious Dionysius the Areopagite. Portrayed as one whom Paul encountered, Dionysius is actually a fifth or sixth-century Syrian monk; thus the appellation Pseudo-Dionysius (or Dionysius so-called). Dionysius' work became well known, widely consulted, and frequently cited by Medieval writers. It emphasized the ineffability of God, cultivated the famous *via negative* (in which God is defined in terms of that which he is not), and provided much of the language as well as the conceptual framework employed by subsequent mystical writers in the West.

From Augustine to Bernard of Clairvaux

In the West, following directly upon Augustine, there were a number of important figures, most of whom prayed, thought, and worked within the monastic context. This was the time when the legacy of the classical world was being translated and transposed into the idiom of Medieval European culture. The monks played an important role in this transaction, particularly the Benedictines. Their founder, St. Benedict, was the subject of a biography by Gregory I (540-604), also a mystic and claimed by many to be the greatest pope. Gregory contributed to the formation of the mystical tradition primarily through his concern for practical application. He was intent on finding and recommending ways by which spiritual aspirations could be realized. Through his influence, contemplative thought and monastic practice were brought into closer correspondence.

A more dominantly intellectual form of development, via John Scotus Erigena and others, within the Augustinian tradition took lines that came to focus on the work and influence of Anselm (1033-1109) and his school. Anselm was interested primarily in tracing the process by which "faith seeks understanding" *(fides quaerens intellectum)*. The outcome was a series of theological treatises on the most important classical Christine doctrines. Significantly, instead of perpetuating Augustine's confessional and autobiographical form of expression, Anselm staged a series of theological debates. The spirit in which the inquiries were conducted led the mystical tradition in a new direction. Theology itself became a form of contemplation. Both belonged to worship, for each was a means through which the reality of God was brought to clearer enunciation.

A quantum leap forward occurred with Bernard of Clairvaux (1053-1109), who is associated with the founding of the Cistercian monastic order (although he was not the founder). In keeping with Augustine's counsel, Bernard made *humilitas* the authentic disposition of the interior life. But he turned much more deliberately to the sensitive (or affective) rather than the intellectual side of the interior life to locate the presence of God.

He stressed that when such a choice has to be made, reality should be likened to heart instead of to mind.

Appropriately, Bernard expressed much of the content of his orientation as an allegorical interpretation of The Song of Songs. He compared the relation of God and the soul to the relation of bridegroom and bride. His watchword was taken from the New Testament (from the first epistle of John): "God is love, and he who abides in love abides in God, and God in him." (Another translation of the same verse reads: "God is love; by the gift of love he dwells in us, and we in him.")

Concerning the flavor of Bernard's orientation, Etienne Gilson has written:

God is neither perceptible to our senses nor conceivable by our intellects, but he is sensible to the heart. To love him as he loves himself, to love him as he loves us, and by the gift of that very love with which he loves himself and loves us, this is to have God in us.

Bernard's allegorical reading of The Song of Songs was fitting because, in his view, God is love.

Before we trace subsequent developments, we must recognize that the Bernardian line has continued to the present time. The contemporary Nicaraguan poet Ernesto Cardenal, for example, has written a revised commentary on The Song of Songs under the title *To Live Is to Love*. Wherever the Bernardian spirit rules, the contemplative formulation exhibits the following characteristics. Not only is God approached as the very font and source of love, but communication with God is guided by the allegorical interpretation of The Song of Songs and is facilitated by the language of that Jewish love tale. The relation of God and the soul is couched in the language of love between a man and a woman.

The Medieval Flowering

After Bernard, the contemplative tradition developed in accordance with a panoply of formulations. An important chapter in its history belongs to the work of some monks of the Abbey of St. Victor in Paris, the best-known of which are Hugh (c. 1096–1141) and Richard (c. 1123–1173). At the same time, Hildegarde of Bingen (1098–1179), mystic, seer, artist, and visionary, was developing an orientation, full of apocalyptic overtones, that became the first of a series of important statements from the Rhineland region. Hildegarde is also distinguished for being the first in a line of important women mystical writers, including Mechthild of Magdeburg (1212–1299), Angela of Foligno (1248–1309), Catherine of Siena (1347–1380), Catherine of Genoa (1447–1510), Teresa of Avila (1515–1582), Marie of the Incarnation (1599–1672), and Jeanne de Chantal (1572–1641).

Richard and Hugh, the famous Victorines, were known for their intellectual acumen and for demonstrating that mystical religion could be harmonized with devotion to the liberal arts, scholarly Scriptural studies, and other activities dependent upon the exercise of rational sensitivities. The Victorines placed the possibility of mystical awareness within a comprehensive framework that marked the ascent of the intelligence from sensible perception to "the light of God's face." They exemplified the attitude that theological reflection is indeed a form of worship.

Special mention must also be made of Francis of Assisi (1182–1226) and of the religious order to which he gave his name, the Franciscans. For Francis, the imitation of the poverty of Christ was a form of living divine companionship. In addition to this day-by-day renunciatory vocation, Francis experienced extraordinary rapture, ecstasy, and encounters with God. The oneness he felt with God pervaded the entire universe and all things in it.

The Franciscan form of spirituality was continued in the development of the Franciscan order. Among the descendents was Bonaventura (1217–1274), who took the emphasis on renunciation and transposed it into a description of the journey through which the soul passes in its aspiration toward union with God.

By the fourteenth century, the English school of mysticism, represented by Richard Rolle (1300–1349), Julian of Norwich (1343–1413), Walter Hilton (c. 1396), and the author of *The Cloud of Unknowing*, had established itself as expressing a unique portrayal of the contemplative life. In the Low Countries, it was Jan von Ruysbroeck (1293–1381) who developed the most distinctive and influential position.

The Rhineland school of the late thirteenth and fourteenth centuries, whose chief authors were Meister Eckhart (1260–1327), Henry Suso (1300–1366), and John Tauler (1300–1361), also has a prominent place in the history of mystical religion in the West. One senses in their writings that the world is no longer that of Bernard of Clairvaux, and certainly not that of Bonaventura. Mystical religion is no longer the contemplative component of sanctioned theology. It is no longer the product of mainline Medieval theology conceived in a contemplative spirit. Instead, one finds it searching for its own ground. It looks to stand upon an intrinsic base. And the shift is reflected in the language. Eckhart placed great emphasis upon the unbreachable distance between divine and human realities, and, thus, upon the utter transcendence of God. He reached back to the writings of Pseudo-Dionysius to cultivate the technique that proceeds by negation: God is defined in terms of that which he is not. There are distinctions between the God Christians worship (and can name) and the Godhead. The distinction itself is a sign of a greater conceptual elasticity, but in that same intactness are new stimulants to peril.

The Reformation Era

Rhineland influences reached into the Reformation period, and not simply as recommendations regarding the nature and disposition of the religious life. The Rhineland emphasis on the majesty of God was made consistent with the nominalist philosophical position (previewed by Duns Scotus, advanced by William of Ockham, and championed by others) that all natural ontological connections between God and man have been severed. Viewed from one side, this meant that the possibility of natural knowledge of God had been destroyed. From the other side, it gave occasion to a mystical response. It was against the background of these twin assumptions that the Reformation view of the nature of the religious life was conceived.

It was a marked change. From Reformation times forward, the mystical impulse could be acknowledged and secured only with great difficulty and ambivalence. Previous centuries had witnessed mysticism's flowering in the West. It had found large and elegant expression in all quarters of Christendom—in Germany, France, Italy, Spain, the Low Countries, England, and Scandinavia. Indeed, mystical religion had provided both the outlook and language through which Medieval Christianity had been enunciated. It was supported by the Medieval synthesis.

This is not to suggest that mystical religion ceased to exist in the West after the Reformation. On the contrary, some of its most articulate expressions were advanced in post-Reformation times. It is simply to recognize that from the sixteenth century onward, mystical impulses were subjected to rigorous criticism and self-scrutiny. When they became manifest, they encountered formidable and, at times, extreme resistance. Heretofore, they belonged as components of a synthesis. They gave that synthesis its direction and dominant energies. From the mid-sixteenth century forward, they stood in contrast, always in contrast. They were no longer understood to be second nature to religious aspiration. Instead, they tended to take on an alien character, like themes out of time, tendencies out of character, an orientation both eccentric and full of personal deceptions and dangers.

The best-known reformers, Martin Luther (1483–1546) and John Calvin (1509–1564), expressed profound mistrust of the mystical impulse as well as of the monastic setting within which it was nurtured. They were acquainted, of course, with the spiritual disciplines. They were also well schooled in Medieval forms of piety. It was as a monk in the Augustinian order that Luther came to the insights that led to the Protestant Reformation. Earlier he had been greatly influenced by the mystical treatise *Theologia Germanica* and had been immersed in the spiritual tradition represented by John Tauler. Debate continues concerning the extent to which these contemplative and implicit mystical tendencies were perpetuated into Lutheran and distinctively Protestant forms of spirituality. But in some respects, the more significant mark of Luther's influence was its public dimension. It was directed toward the development of a religious orientation that could be upheld outside the cloister. This was the fundamental change. In an earlier day, under different circumstances, similar efforts might have resulted in significant spiritual or monastic reform, or even in the rise of a new religious order. But Luther's attempt at purification led to the founding of a new church—indeed, an alternative church—and, by implication, to much greater diffusion of the mystical impulse.

The clearest early mystical witnesses within Protestant Christiantity were among the radical reformers of the sixteenth century, Sebastian Franck (1499–1542) and Kaspar von Schwenkfeld (1489–1561), to name but two of the most prominent. Both Franck and Schwenkfeld utilized "religious enthusiasm" as a way of countering the tendency toward dogmatic formulation and institutionalization within Lutheranism; the "mysticism" they advocated cannot be construed as a continuation of Medieval tradition.

Some distance away was Jacob Boehme (1575-1624), whom some describe as the first Protestant mystic, but who is more accurately known as the author of very creative and original speculative mystical writings. A theosophist and seer, Boehme lived in Protestant territory, but was denounced and excommunicated by the Lutheran church. He had great influence upon subsequent thinkers—Hegel, Bergson, Tillich, Heidegger, and, most especially, William Blake.

A special chapter in the Protestant chronicle belongs to George Fox (1624-1691), founder of the Society of Friends (Quakers). Fox was critical of ineffective institutional religion, challenged it with an emphasis on the direct experience of God, and taught that God resides in every person.

Counter and Post-Reformation Responses

As a result of the Reformation, and in keeping with its own efforts toward placing Christian aspiration on a purified and authentic base, Catholic mysticism became more reflective and self-critical in the Counterreformation period. The clearest example of this turn toward rigorous restatement was provided by Ignatius of Loyola (1491-1556), the founder of the Jesuit order, whose *Spiritual Exercises* set out a methodical course by which those given to such practices might grow in holiness. Rigorous restatements of a much more lyrical character issued from Spain in the form of several compositions by Teresa of Avila (1515-1582) and John of the Cross 1542-1591). Both dedicated their lives to bringing Spanish monasticism back to its original intentions and austere conditions. In so doing, they marked out the distinctive stages in the development of the interior life. John of the Cross, while offering still another commentary on The Song of Songs, schematized the process by which the soul moves from attachment to the things of this world to the abandonment of all things. The same personal rigor mixed with attention to schematic detail is present in Teresa's *Interior Castle*, as well as in her autobiographical statement.

In seventeenth-century France, mystical religion flourished in the writings of Madame Guyon (1648-1717), Archbishop Fenelon (1651-1715), Jeanne de Chantal (1572-1641), François de Sales (1567-1622), and Jean-Pierre de Caussade (1675-1751). These writings exhibit a marked stress on the everyday character of the religious life, an emphasis on what de Caussade referred to as "the sacrament of the present moment." Compared with earlier expressions, these formulations seem simpler, clearer, more down-to-earth, less dependent upon metaphysical safeguards and philosophical sanctions and manifestly less pretentious.

But they encountered trouble. Some versions of the disposition were intermeshed with a theological viewpoint called Quietism, which counseled passivity, disinterest, and a total abandonment of the self to the mercy and providence of God. When Quietism was condemned as a heresy, those forms of mystical religion associated with it, through actual or alleged affinity, were looked upon with grave suspicion.

In Protestant lands, a large outpouring of mystical enthusiasm (called Pietism) occurred in Germany in the seventeenth and eighteenth centuries, stimulated by the writings of Johann Arndt (1555-1621), Philip Jakob Spener (1635-1705), and others. Much of the enthusiasm generated by the Pietists was centered at the University of Halle, from which it was sent in many directions. Modern Protestant theology was influenced significantly by it, not least, the position of Friedrich Schleiermacher (1768-1834) in which religion is described as "a feeling of absolute dependence." Earlier, when Immanuel Kant (1724-1804) conceived critical philosphy to "deny reason in order to make room for faith," it was by translating pietistically based religous compulsions into conceptual form.

It was a time of intense introspective analysis. Kant and other philosophers attempted to describe the process, or grammar, by which human beings think or reflect in a logically consistent manner. The custodians of the mystical tradition directed the same analytical interest toward tracing and codifying the interior process. It had always been understood, first, that the journey of each soul is unique and unrepeatable and, second, that the contours of the interior landscape exhibit common characteristics. Consequently, there was a tendency to develop a standard terminology. There were attempts to schematize the entire process, to identify the rules or grammars by which it is conducted.

Within the life of prayer, for example, the movement from meditation to contemplation—from that state in which the mental faculties are dominant to a deeper engagement of the divine presence—was traced sequentially. The interior process was also delineated according to a threefold pattern. The first of these stages, purification, focuses upon a process of self-emptying that prepares the soul by stripping away all protective barriers. The second stage, illumination, may be marked by flashes of insight and disclosures of the divine reality. The third state, union, describes a state of identification and communication between God and the soul. Both schema were viewed as bases for the acquisition of virtues. Both led to an eventual apprehension of God as being Triune, an awareness that is placed at the summit of the life of prayer. Once these contours of the interior life were identified, the pattern was consulted repeatedly by those whose experience was marked this way, to illumine the moments, stages, and sequential ordering of the religious life. The pattern is reflected in the spiritual manuals used especially in monasteries and convents. Such manuals have their roots in the spiritual exercises proposed by both Ignatius of Loyola and François de Sales. The carefully sequenced meditations are designed to lead the initiate over a series of days, weeks, and months into a progressive exploration of the life of the spirit.

The Modern and Contemporary Era

From the Reformation period on, after the Christian world became fragmented, the history of mystical religion can be recounted only as a plural and composite chronicle. There is no single trajectory, but a history interlaced with the history of the Church, the history of theological controversy, the histories of various religious orders, the intricate oscillations of a larger cultural history, and the history of the diverse and profound workings of the human imagination. In the midst of it all, there have been times of great mystical enthusiasm, and times when the impulse seems more diaphanous. Through all of it, the candle has continued to burn, but the light has been flickering.

At one time, closer to the time of origin, the *vita contemplativa* stood for a comprehensive mode through which life itself was received, interpreted, and lived. In more recent times, it has offered itself in contrast to other religious and antireligious tendencies. In times of moral decadence and spiritual bankruptcy, for example, its resources have been drawn upon to spark and guide religious reform. At other times it has come into prominence to combat excesses in other directions. And in the modern era it has served as a refuge for those seeking an alternative to rationalist-supported religion. It has come and it has gone, in recent generations, more frequently in opposition to the spirit of the age than in league with it. It has found its adherents among those for whom the modern age has provided some unease, those for whom the Medieval heritage remains alive. For, wherever the impulse is strong, it seeks to remove fragmentation and restore primordial unity. It is unwilling to allow itself to be placed alongside other interests, to compete against them. Rather, it works, silently but forcefully, to reestablish its fundamental nurturing conditions. It has a stake in the unitive and transformative capacities of the sacramental vision.

The current era is an intriguing time when viewed against the appraisal we have offered. For the mid-twentieth century seems to be experiencing a new wave of interest in mystical religion. This time the components include perennial classical and Medieval themes in combination with religious currents of Eastern or Asian derivation. The revival is related to the heightened cultural self-criticism that was launched in the West in the 1960s and early 1970s. The critical attitude was accelerated by the Vietnam War, which altered conceptions of winning and losing, and created an openness to religious currents that counseled a radically different way of engaging the world. Included in this reevaluation is a willingness, in some quarters, to come to terms with the strengths and weaknesses of the Enlightenment, a fresh appraisal of the positive and negative aspects of the scientific method, and a grand declaration that there are important aspects of human life to which few of the sanctioned approaches provide reliable access. Associated with these reassessments is a pronounced form of monastic revival, a renewed and sustained interest in Medieval religion, fresh commitments to the practice of the spiritual disciplines, a new openness to the worlds of prayer and meditation. The development has been assisted by college and university courses in comparative and world religions. The major texts of the world's historical religious traditions have become readily available, and hundreds of scholars have been trained to translate and interpret them. The knowledge and spiritual wisdom they contain and have the capacity to impart have almost become publicly accessible.

Thus, much of the excitement of the mid-twentieth century concerns the extent to which dominant patterns of spiritual growth will be confirmed, extended, and made pliable by the insights and wisdom of religious experience from non-Christian and non-Western sources. Indeed, a large portion of the contemporary crosscultural interchange is being conducted in manifestly religious terms. Simultaneously, a significant aspect of Western culture's submission to internal self-criticism is the interest this has directed toward other religious traditions, both Eastern and Western, for insights that may have become obscured, lost, or remain undiscovered.

There is no way of forecasting what new religious formulations and insights the present constellation of interests may inspire. But we can expect that a new chapter in the history of mystical religion will be written. We can be sure too that, however it is written, it will lend strength to the most fundamental assumption. Socrates said it first, then Plato, then the tradition of nearly two and a half millennia: "The unexamined life is not worth living." In paraphrase, the conviction holds that the *vita contemplativa* is to be prized most highly among all competing ways of being human. Put in a different way, the insight attests that the contemplative life is the profoundest expression of what it is to be alive. After all religious elaboration has been stripped away, this is the fundamental affirmation. The religious writers have added that the powers of contemplation are rooted in the designs and compulsions of human love. It is to working out the varieties of formulating these combinations that the literary tradition gives expression. And it is to examples of this expression that we shall now turn.

1. The Founding Fathers

Augustine of Hippo

(354–430)

Augustine of Hippo is the father of the contemplative tradition within the Christian religion, the most significant formative personality in the history of Christian self-consciousness, the person more influential than any other in giving distinctive shape, scope, direction, and range to the development of the Christian religion in the Western world. In certain respects, he is both mother and father to Christian spirituality. He can be all of this at once because he, more than any other, effected a transposition to what Krister Stendahl refers to as "the introspective conscience" in the West. Certainly there was piety before Augustine's time. The life of the spirit was being cultivated too. Spiritual religion was not without its adherents and practitioners. Mysticism had sophisticated devotees. But never before was there an effective, systematic elaboration and interpretation of the same. Neither was there the degree of self-consciousness regarding the way in which a personal psychological makeup interacts with the presence of God within the soul. It was in Augustine, in short, that the Christian faith became deliberately and comprehensively internalized.

The story of his childhood, his parentage, his devotion to his mother, Monica, and his distance from his father, Patricius, the opposition between his Christian mother and his pagan father in providing direction to his life, his fall into sin, his pursuit of the profession of rhetorician, his testing and sorting of philosophical and religious positions, his being influenced by Ambrose in Milan, his dramatic conversion—all of this is well known. It is well known because it is recounted in his famous work, *The Confessions.* This work counts as the first full autobiography in the Western world. The literary event matched the occurrence of a new development in Western self-consciousness. And some would add that the reflective and contemplative insight could not have occurred until the appropriate literary medium had been created. For the chronicle Augustine narrated was the interior odyssey, the story of the human heart, its spiritual pulse, its devotions and passions, its aspirations and self-doubts.

Was he a contemplative? The response is undoubtedly affirmative. A mystic? Here the answer depends most upon one's point of view. In the purely literal sense, Augustine had associated mystical experience with the religious recommendations of the Platonists, and these he had come to understand in terms of vertical ascent: the mind, or psychic center of the human being, working its way from things temporal and finite to the eternal, infinite, and transcendent. "The Platonists know the goal, but not the way," he concluded. And as alternative to ascent-motivation *(superbia)*, he offered the form and example of God's becoming flesh in Jesus the Christ *(humilitas)*. At the same time, Augustine always held firm to the realization that man is made in the image of God, and bears a likeness that has been injured but not effaced by human sin. This realization gave him basis to counsel, "Do not go abroad, but turn within, for in the inner man dwells truth." Augustine understood God to be "nearer to us than we are to ourselves." And, for him, the religious life is centered on the realization that God lives within the human soul. Though God is distinct from the soul, self-knowledge and knowledge of God become interdependent: to know oneself properly involves an awareness of the presence of God and this awareness can grow, by the power of grace and its consequent redirected love, from dim sensation to surer awareness to an eventual vision—from "viewing in a glass darkly" to "seeing God face to face."

The selection reprinted here is from *The Confessions*, Book X. It follows the completion of the narrative portion of *The Confessions*, after a description of his conversion and the death of his mother (in which, significantly, Augustine's own narrative ends too). He turns next to matters theoretical and conceptual: time, creation, and memory. And in the course of his exposition of the interior life, made partially accessible through a sensitivity to the workings of memory, he comes to offer a definition of God as "the Life of the life of my soul." This is a cardinal insight of the contemplative tradition. It was formed in Augustine's time and has been transmitted from age to age to the current era.

The Confessions

What does it profit me, then, O Lord, to whom my conscience confesses daily, confident more in the hope of your mercy than in its own innocence, what does it profit me, I ask, also to make known to men in your sight, through this book, not what I once was, but what I am now? I know what profit I gain by confessing my past, and this I have declared. But many people who know me, and others who do not know me but have heard of me or read my books, wish to hear what I am now, at this moment, as I set down my confessions. They cannot lay their ears to my heart, and yet it is in my heart that I am whatever I am. So they wish to listen as I confess what I am in my heart, into which they cannot pry by eye or ear or mind. They wish to hear and they are ready to believe; but can they really know me? Charity, which makes them good, tells them that I do not lie about myself when I confess what I am, and it is this charity in them that believes me.

*   *   *

My love of you, O Lord, is not some vague feeling: it is positive and certain. Your word struck into my heart and from that moment I loved you. Besides this, all about me, heaven and earth and all that they contain proclaim that I should love you, and their message never ceases to sound in the ears of all mankind, so that there is no excuse for any not to love you. But, more than all this, *you will show pity on those whom you pity; you will show mercy where you are merciful;* for if it were not for your mercy, heaven and earth would cry your praises to deaf ears.

But what do I love when I love my God? Not material beauty or beauty of a temporal order; not the brilliance of earthly light, so welcome to our eyes; not the sweet melody of harmony and song; not the fragrance of flowers, perfumes, and spices; not manna or honey; not limbs such as the the body delights to embrace. It is not these that I love

Augustine, *Confessions*, trans. R. S. Pine-Coffin (London: Penguin Books, 1961), pp. 209, 211–13, and 231–2. Footnotes have been omitted.

when I love my God. And yet, when I love him, it is true that I love a light of a certain kind, a voice, a perfume, a food, an embrace; but they are of the kind that I love in my inner self, when my soul is bathed in light that is not bound by space; when it listens to sound that never dies away; when it breathes fragrance that is not borne away on the wind; when it tastes food that is never consumed by the eating; when it clings to an embrace from which it is not severed by fulfilment of desire. This is what I love when I love my God.

But what is my God? I put my question to the earth. It answered, 'I am not God,' and all things on earth declared the same. I asked the sea and the chasms of the deep and the living things that creep in them, but they answered, 'We are not your God. Seek what is above us.' I spoke to the winds that blow, and the whole air and all that lives in it replied, 'Anaximenes is wrong. I am not God.' I asked the sky, the sun, the moon, and the stars, but they told me, 'Neither are we the God whom you seek.' I spoke to all the things that are about me, all that can be admitted by the door of the senses, and I said, 'Since you are not my God, tell me about him. Tell me something of my God.' Clear and loud they answered, 'God is he who made us.' I asked these questions simply by gazing at these things, and their beauty was all the answer they gave.

Then I turned to myself and asked, 'Who are you?' 'A man,' I replied. But it is clear that I have both body and soul, the one the outer, the other the inner part of me. Which of these two ought I to have asked to help me find my God? With my bodily powers I had already tried to find him in earth and sky, as far as the sight of my eyes could reach, like an envoy sent upon a search. But my inner self is the better of the two, for it was to the inner part of me that my bodily senses brought their messages. They delivered to their arbiter and judge the replies which they carried back from the sky and the earth and all that they contain, those replies which stated 'We are not God' and 'God is he who made us.' The inner part of man knows these things through the agency of the outer part. I, the inner man, know these things; I, the soul, know them through the senses of my body. I asked the whole mass of the universe about my God, and it replied, 'I am not God. God is he who made me.'

Surely everyone whose senses are not impared is aware of the universe around him? Why, then, does it not give the same message to us all? The animals, both great and small, are aware of it, but they cannot inquire into its meaning because they are not guided by reason, which can sift the evidence relayed to them by their senses. Man, on the other hand, can question nature. He is able to *catch sight of God's invisible nature through his creatures*, but his love of these material things is too great. He becomes their slave, and slaves cannot be judges. Nor will the world supply an answer to those who question it, unless they also have the faculty to judge it. It does not answer in different language—that is, it does not change its aspect—according to whether a man merely looks at it or subjects it to inquiry while he looks. If it did, its appearance would be different in each case. Its aspect is the same in both cases, but to the man who merely looks it says nothing, while to the other it gives an answer. It would be nearer the truth to say that it gives an answer to all, but it is only understood by those who compare the message it gives them through their senses with the truth that is in themselves. For truth says to me, 'Your God is not heaven or earth or any kind of bodily thing.' We can tell this from the very nature of such things, for those who have eyes to see know that their bulk is less in the part than in the whole. And I know that my soul is the better part of me, because it animates the whole of my body. It gives it life, and this is something that no body can give to another body. But God is even more. He is the Life of the life of my soul.

*   *   *

I have learnt to love you late, Beauty at once so ancient and so new! I have learnt to love you late! You were within me, and I was in the world outside myself. I searched for you outside myself and, disfigured as I was, I fell upon the lovely things of your creation. You were with me, but I was not with you. The beautiful things of this world kept me far from you and yet, if they had not been in you, they would have had no being at all. You called me; you cried aloud to me; you broke my barrier of deafness. You shone upon me; your radiance enveloped me; you put my blindness to flight. You shed your fragrance about me; I drew breath and now I gasp for your sweet odour. I tasted you, and now I hunger and thirst for you. You touched me, and I am inflamed with love of your peace.

Pseudo-Dionysius

(c. 500)

The author of the writings attributed to Dionysius the Areopagite was probably an early sixth-century Syrian monk who was familiar with Neoplatonic philosophy, particularly the tradition of Proclus (410–485). The writings were forged in the name of Dionysius, who is named as one of Paul's converts in his visit to Athens as recorded in *The Acts of the Apostles* in the New Testament. After Paul gave his sermon, in the middle of Mars Hill, the account records:

When they heard about the raising of the dead, some scoffed, and others said, "We will hear you on this subject some other time." And so Paul left the assembly. However, some men joined him and became believers, including Dionysius, a member of the court of the Areopagus, also a woman named Damaris, and others besides. (Acts 17:32–34)

Legend has it that Dionysius became the first bishop of Athens, that he went from there to Gaul and was also the first Christian bishop there. He has also been identified, at times, with Saint Denis, first bishop of Paris and patron saint of France, who was martyred during the persecution of Christians by the emperor Valerian about 258. The real author of the writings is neither Dionysius the Areopagite nor Denis, bishop of Paris. But not until the time of the Renaissance was the authenticity of the alleged authorship denied, though probing questions were raised about even during the Medieval period. The corpus is commonly referred to as the writings of Pseudo-Dionysius.

The essays had large influence both in Eastern Orthodox regions and in the West. Many of the major Medieval figures—among them John Scotus Erigena, Hugh of St. Victor, Albertus Magnus, Thomas Aquinas, Bonaventura, Richard Rolle, the author of *The Cloud of Unknowing*, Meister Eckhart, and John Tauler—made use of them, were persuaded by them, and, in some instances, offered commentaries and/or translations. The writings had a formative influence on the development of the contemplative tradition in the West.

The corpus includes ten letters and four theological treatises. The latter were dedicated to Timothy, Paul's apostle and companion, to keep the presumed first-century apostolic context intact. The first treatise, *Divine Names* deals with the scriptural appellations of God as indices regarding his nature. The second, *Mystical Theology*, chronicles the ascent of the soul to union with God. The third, *Celestial Hierarchy*, provides a systematic classification of the levels (the divisions and subdivisions) of angels. And the fourth, *Ecclesiastical Hierarchy*, shows how the sacramental and administrative orders within the Church reflect the heavenly pattern.

Pseudo-Dionysius advances "the negative way." In its ascent to the heights, the soul must strip aside everything that hampers. This process begins with the senses, moves to thoughts, progressively, until there is recognition of "the darkness of unknowing." In that desolate place, the soul is illumined by "the light of darkness" which comes from a source "beyond all light and all being."

The selection reprinted here presents the vision in summary fashion. It consists of Chapters 1, 3, 4, and 5 of the second treatise, *Mystical Theology*.

Mystical Theology

What is the divine gloom?

Trinity, which exceeds all Being, Deity, and Goodness! Thou that instructs Christians in Thy heavenly wisdom! Guide us to the topmost height of mystic lore which exceeds light and more than exceeds knowledge, where the simple, absolute, and unchangeable mysteries of heavenly Truth lie hidden in the dazzling obscurity of the secret Silence, outshining all brilliance with the intensity of their darkness and surcharging our blinded intellects with the utterly impalpable and invisible fairness of glories which exceed all beauty! Such be my prayer; and you, dear Timothy, I counsel that, in the earnest exercise of mystic contemplation, you leave the senses and the activities of the intellect and all things the senses or the intellect can perceive and all things in this world of nothingness or in that world of being and that, your understanding being laid to rest, you strain (so far as you may) toward a union with Him whom neither being nor understanding can contain. For, by the unceasing and absolute renunciation of yourself

Translated by the Editors from *Dionysius the Areopagite. The Divine Names and The Mystical Theology*, trans. C. E. Rolt (London: S.P.C.K., 1920), pp. 191-96, 199-201.

and all things, you shall in pureness cast all things aside and be released from all, and so shall you be led upward to the Ray of that divine Darkness which exceeds existence.

These things you must not disclose to any of the uninitiated, by whom I mean those who cling to the objects of human thought and imagine there is no superessential reality beyond and fancy that they know by human understanding Him that has made Darkess His secret place. And if the Divine Initiation is beyond such men as these, what can be said of others yet more incapable thereof, who describe the Transcendent Cause of all things by qualities drawn from the lowest order of being, while they deny that it is in any way superior to the various ungodly delusions that they fondly invent in ignorance of this truth? That while It possesses all the positive attributes of the universe (being the universal Cause), yet in a stricter sense It does not possess them, since It transcends them all, wherefore there is no contradiction between affirming and denying that It has them inasmuch as It precedes and surpasses all deprivation, being beyond all positive and negative distinctions?

Such at least is the teaching of the blessed Bartholomew. For he says that the subject matter of the Divine Silence is vast and yet minute, and that the Gospel combines in itself both width and straitness. I think he has shown by these words how marvelously he has understood that the good cause of all things is eloquent yet speaks few words or rather none, possessing neither speech nor understanding because it exceeds all things in a superessential manner and is revealed in its naked truth to those alone who pass right through the opposition of fair and foul and pass beyond the topmost altitudes of the holy ascent and leave behind them all divine enlightenment and voices and heavenly utterances and plunge into the Darkness where truly dwells, as the Scripture says, that One Which is beyond all things. For not without reason is the blessed Moses bidden first to undergo purification himself and then to separate himself from those who have not undergone it; and after all purification hears the many-voiced trumpets and sees many lights flash forth with pure and diverse-streaming rays and then stands separate from the multitudes and with the chosen priests presses forward to the topmost pinnacle of the Divine Ascent. Nevertheless, he meets not with God Himself, yet he beholds—not Him indeed for He is invisible—but the place wherein He dwells. And this I take to signify that the divinest and the highest of the things perceived by the eyes of the body of the mind are but the symbolic language of things subordinate to Him who Himself transcends them all. Through these things His incomprehensible presence is shown walking upon those heights of His holy places which are perceived by the mind; and then It breaks forth, even from the things that are beheld and from those that behold them, and plunges the true initiate into the Darkness of Unknowing wherein he renounces all the apprehensions of his understanding and is enwrapped in that which is wholly intangible and invisible, belonging wholly to Him that is beyond all things and to none else (whether himself or another), and being through the passive stillness of all his reasoning powers united by his highest faculty to Him that is wholly Unknowable, of whom thus by a rejection of all knowledge he possesses a knowledge that exceeds his understanding.

*   *   *

What are the affirmative expressions respecting God, and what are the negative?

Now I have in my *Outlines of Divinity* set forth those conceptions which are most proper to the affirmative method, and have shown in what sense God's holy nature is called single and in what sense triune, what is the nature of the Fatherhood and Sonship which we attribute to It; what is meant by the articles of faith concerning the Spirit; how from the immaterial and indivisible Good the interior rays of Its goodness have their being and remain immovably in that state of rest which both within their Origin and within themselves is coeternal with the act by which they spring from It; in what manner Jesus being above all essence has stooped to an essential state in which all the truths of human nature meet; and all the other revelations of Scripture whereof my *Outlines of Divinity* treat. And in the book of the *Divine Names* I have considered the meaning as concerning God of the titles Good, Existent, Life, Wisdom, Power, and of the other titles which the understanding frames, and in my *Symbolic Divinity* I have considered what are the metaphorical titles drawn from the world of sense and applied to the nature of God; what are the mental or material images we form of God or the functions and instruments of activity we attribute to Him; what are the places where He dwells and the robes He is adorned with; what is meant by God's anger, grief, and indignation, or the divine inebriation and wrath; what is meant by God's oath and His malediction, by imagery of allegoric symbolism. And I doubt not that you have also observed how far more copious are the last terms than the first for the doctrines of God's nature and the exposition of His names could not but be briefer than the *Symbolic Divinity*. For the more we soar upward the more our language becomes restricted to the compass of purely intellectual conceptions, even as in the present instance plunging into the Darkness which is above the intellect we shall find ourselves reduced not merely to brevity of speech but even to absolute dumbness both of speech and of thought. Now in the former treatises the course of the argument, as it came down from the highest to the lowest categories, embraced an ever-widening number of conceptions that increased at each stage of the descent, but in the present treatise it mounts upward from below toward the category of transcendence, and in proportion to its ascent it contracts its terminology, and when the whole ascent is passed it will be totally dumb, being at last wholly united with Him Whom words cannot describe. But why is it, you will ask, that after beginning from the highest category when one method was affirmative we begin from the lowest category where it is negative? Because when affirming the existence of that which transcends all affirmation, we were obliged to start from that which is most akin to It and then to make the affirmation on which the rest depended; but when pursuing the negative method, to reach that which is beyond all negation, we must start by applying our negations to those qualities which differ most from the ultimate goal. Surely it is truer to affirm that God is life and goodness than that He is air or stone, and truer to deny that drunkenness or fury can be attributed to Him that to deny that we may apply to Him the categories of human thought.

*   *   *

That He Who is the Preeminent Cause of everything sensibly perceived is not Himself any one of the things sensibly perceived.

We therefore maintain that the universal Cause transcending all things is neither impersonal nor lifeless, nor irrational nor without understanding: in short, that It is not a material body and therefore does not possess outward shape or intelligible form or quality or quantity or solid weight; nor has It any local existence that can be perceived by sight or touch; nor has It the power of perceiving or being perceived; nor does It suffer any vexation or disorder through the disturbance of earthly passions or any feebleness through the tyranny of material chances or any want of light; nor any change or decay or division or deprivation or ebb and flow or anything else that the senses can perceive. None of these things can be either identified with It or attributed unto It.

* * *

That He Who is the Preeminent Cause of everything intelligibly perceived is not Himself any one of the things intelligibly perceived.

Once more, ascending yet higher we maintain that It is not soul or mind, or endowed with the faculty of imagination, conjecture, reason, or understanding; nor is It any act of reason or understanding; nor can It be described by the reason or perceived by the understanding, since It is not number or order or greatness or littleness or equality or inequality, and since It is not immovable nor in motion or at rest and has no power and is not power or light and does not live and is not life; nor is It personal essence or eternity or time; nor can It be grasped by the understanding, since It is not knowledge or truth; nor is It kingship or wisdom; nor is It one, nor is It unity, nor is It Godhead or Goodness; nor is It a Spirit, as we understand the term, since It is not Sonship or Fatherhood; nor is It any other thing such as we or any other being can have knowledge of; nor does It belong to the category of nonexistence or to that of existence; nor do existent beings know It as it actually is, nor does It know them as they actually are; nor can the reason attain to It to name It or to know It; nor is It darkness, nor is It light or error or truth; nor can any affirmation or negation apply to It; for while applying affirmations or negations to those orders of being that come next to It, we apply not unto It either affirmation or negation, inasmuch as It transcends all affirmation by being the perfect and unique Cause of all things, and transcends all negation by the preeminence of Its simple and absolute nature—free from every limitation and beyond them all.

Gregory the Great
(540–604)

One of the most versatile figures in the history of Christendom, Gregory was a monk, the author of books and many letters, the holder of several governmental positions, the Pope from 590 to his death in 604, and a prime stabilizer of the Western world during a period of great political, cultural, and religious upheaval.

He was born the son of a Roman senator and seemed destined for a career in public life, becoming prefect of the city in 573. Yet he had ambitions that public life alone could not satisfy. Selling his property and donating the proceeds to the poor, Gregory soon afterwards entered a monastery (St. Andrew's Abbey in Rome), giving himself over to a life of great austerity. After several years this retirement was interrupted by the Pope, who compelled him to leave the cloister by creating him a deacon of Rome. Not long after, he was sent to the Imperial Court at Constantinople.

There he gained the experience and practical wisdom which was to serve him well during his pontificate. Accepting the papal position only after an intense period of self-searching, Gregory was faced with devastating problems. Italy was in the grip of flood, famine, disease, and invasion by the Lombards. Moreover, the Roman Church was threatened by the claims of the Imperial power in Constantinople. It was due to Gregory's personal humility and his firm but gentle administration that many of these problems were alleviated. In addition, he was responsible for the conversion of England and for strengthening the Church in Spain, Gaul, and northern Italy. He rightly gained the reputation of bringing dignity to the office while expanding its authority.

As an author, this remarkable man left a legacy that profoundly influenced the temper of Christendom. His directives for the pastoral lives of bishops became the textbook of the Medieval episcopate. Similarly, his *Dialogues* exerted influence on the future. This book tells of the lives and miracles of early saints, especially of Benedict of Nursia, the formative figure in the development of Western monasticism. The example Benedict upheld was one that Gregory greatly admired, being himself an ardent promoter of monasticism. He was responsible not only for founding monasteries, but for granting monks privileges that exempted them from much episcopal jurisdiction. Thus he laid the foundation for the later exemption of religious orders that brought them under direct papal control.

Gregory was concerned that, as Pope, he be a shepherd as well as an administrator of souls. Many of his extant writings are sermons. The extract reprinted here from his *Homily on Ezekiel* shows him as a religious leader actively seeking to lead his flock to a greater awareness of the life of God within. It also reveals him as an individual of religious depth and one of the masters of the contemplative tradition.

With respect to the development of that tradition, Gregory stands as a mediator and formalizer. Living between the time of Augustine and Bernard, he both perpetuated a portion of the former's outlook and anticipated a portion of that which was to follow. Dom Butler describes his views as lacking "the elevation of the former [Augustine] and the unction of the latter [Bernard]." His mystical writings are characterized by a personal and practical quality as well as by an attempt to employ psychological insights in exploring the dynamics of the interior spiritual life. Both personal and psychological dimensions are explicit in his attention to the progression of steps within mystical awareness.

More specifically, Gregory stressed that the capacity for mystical apprehension is born and trained within the world of asceticism. He regarded mystical awareness as belonging to a process of spiritual training in which the entire person is made fit for the reception of the divine presence. This process includes the practice of self-denial, a relinquishing of interest in worldly fortune, and persistent, comprehensive interior cleansing. The individual must submit to the process by which the desires of the flesh are put to death, appropriate good works are fostered, and the capacity for contemplation is nurtured.

Gregory employed the terminology of "the ladder of ascent," but he gives it a distinctive turn. For the soul in process of formation, ascent is not understood as climbing the ladder; rather, the soul in self-reflection appears to itself as a ladder, "whereby in ascending from outward' things it may pass into itself, and from itself may tend unto its maker." Thus the process of ascent is effected by a simultaneous process of interiorization—a coming to oneself. And this becomes synonymous with an eventual union with God.

Light imagery abounds in Gregory's writings. He refers, for example, to "the eternal brightness of God." When speaking of beholding God's face, he describes a "boundless and unencompassed light." And yet he makes it clear that no one ever sees God's essence. The rays of light emanating from the source are perceptible, but one cannot gaze upon the source of that radiance. The perception is likened to "seeing the sun through a cloud." It is at once accessible and distant.

Through his reformulations, Gregory brought mystical awareness into closer correspondence with the day-to-day activities of persons committed to the monastic life. It would be overstating the case to suggest that he is responsible for institutionalizing the contemplative temper. But he did give spirituality an expanded and vital working context. In the process, union with God lost something of its "special" character and became more and more a practical religious ideal.

All but the final two paragraphs of the selection following is taken from Gregory's *Homily on Ezekiel*. The rest comes from *Moralia in Job*.

Homily on Ezekiel

In the cognition of the Almighty God our first door is faith and our second is sight, to which, walking by faith, we arrive. For in this life we enter the door of faith, that afterward we may be led to the other. And the door is opposite the door, because by the entrance of faith is opened the entrance of the vision of God. But if anyone wishes to understand both these doors as of this life, this by no means runs counter to a sound meaning. For often we desire to contemplate the invisible nature of Almighty God, but we are by no means able. The soul, wearied by these difficulties, returns to itself and uses itself as a ladder by which it may mount up, that first it may consider itself, if it is able, and then may explore, as far as it can, that Nature which is above it. But if our mind be distracted by earthly images, it can in no way consider either itself or the nature of the soul, because by how many thoughts it is led about, by so many obstacles is it blinded.

And so the first step is that it collect itself within itself (recollection); the second, that it consider what its nature is so collected (introversion); the third, that it rise above itself and yield itself to the intent contemplation of its invisible Maker (contemplation). But the mind cannot recollect itself unless it has first learned to repress all phantasmata of earthly and heavenly images, and to reject and spurn whatever sense impressions present themselves to its thoughts, in order that it may seek itself within as it is without these sensations. So they are all to be driven away from the mind's eye, in order that the soul may see itself as it was made, beneath God and above the body, that receiving life from What is above, it may impart life to that which it governs beneath. . . .

When the soul, stripped of bodily images, is the object of its own thought, it has passed through the first door. But the way leads from this door to the other, that somewhat of the nature of the Almighty God may be contemplated. And so, the soul in the body is the life of the flesh; but God, who gives life to all, is the life of souls. And if life that is communicated (vita vivificata) is of such greatness that it cannot be comprehended, who will be able to comprehend by his intellect of how great majesty is the Life that gives life (vita vivificans)? But to consider and to grasp this fact is already in some measure to enter the second door; because the soul from its estimate of itself gathers what it should

Dom Cuthbert Butler, *Western Mysticism* (London: Constable and Company, 1922), pp. 66-67, 69-71, and 81.

think concerning the unencompassed Spirit, who incomprehensibly governs what He has incomprehensibly created.

When the soul raised up to itself understands its own measure and recognizes that it transcends all bodily things, and from the knowledge of itself passes to the knowledge of its Maker, what is this, except to see the door opposite the door? However much it strive, the soul is not able fully to fathom itself; how much less the greatness of Him who was able to make the soul. But when, striving and straining, we desire to see somewhat of the invisible Nature, we are fatigued and beaten back and driven off: and if we are not able to penetrate to what is within, yet already from the outer door we see the inner one. For the very effort of the looking is the door, because it shows somewhat of that which is inside, although there be not yet the power of entering.

In slanting, or splayed, windows that part by which the light enters is narrow, but the inner part that receives the light is wide because the minds of those that contemplate, although they have but a slight glimpse of the true light, yet are they enlarged within themselves with a great amplitude. For even the little they see, they are scarcely able to hold. It is very little indeed that those who contemplate see of eternity; but from that little the fold of their minds is extended unto an increase of fervor and love.

He who keeps his heart within, he it is who receives the light of contemplation. For they that still think immoderately of external things know not what are the chinks of contemplation from the eternal light. For that infusion of incorporeal light is not received along with the images of corporeal things because while only visible things are thought of, the invisible light is not admitted to the mind.

Moralia in Job

When the mind is suspended in contemplation; when, exceeding the narrow limits of the flesh, with all the power of her ken she strains to find something of the freedom of interior security, she cannot for long rest standing above herself because though the spirit carries her on high, yet the flesh sinks her down below by the yet remaining weight of her corruption.

Not even in the sweetness of inward contemplation does the mind remain fixed for long, in that, being made to recoil by the very immensity of the light, it is called back to itself. And when it tastes that inward sweetness, it is on fire with love, it longs to mount above itself; yet it falls back in broken state to the darkness of its frailty.

2. The Twelfth Century: Spiritual Formation and Monastic Reform

---

Bernard of Clairvaux

(1090–1153)

One could find strong support for the contention that Bernard—nobleman, monk, and abbot of Clairvaux—is the founder of Christian mysticism. This does make him the first Christian mystic nor even the founder of the Christian contemplative tradition. We have suggested that Augustine had more influence than anyone else in giving shape and direction to the contemplative tradition within Christianity. And we recognize that there was a mystical tradition within Christianity from the time of Pseudo-Dionysius. Some would claim that both traditions have roots in Paul's exposition and interpretation of the faith of the primitive Church, a faith that was expressed in mystical terms even within The Gospel According to St. John.

Yet, given these qualifications, there are very important senses in which Bernard was founder: Bernard included all of the components that made the dominant mystical strain possible. That strain was monastic in both origin and sponsorship. It approached reality's unifying principle in affective rather than theoretical terms. And it based the exposition of mystical experience on an allegorical application of a specific biblical book, The Song of Songs.

Born to a well-to-do family near Dijon in Burgundy, Bernard seemed destined for a career in the Church from the beginning. The biographies describe him as a timid child, deeply drawn to his mother, Aleth, a woman of remarkable virtue who died in 1107 when Bernard was seventeen. Bernard entered the monastery at Citeaux in 1112, did his formal studies in theology and spirituality between 1112 and 1115, and was asked to establish a new monastery at Clairvaux in 1115. So committed was he to the monastic vocation and so persuasive in influencing others that, eventually, thirty members of his family and friends—including two uncles, two cousins, and four of his five brothers—joined with him. (His father subsequently joined another religious order.) Under his direction, the monastery enjoyed remarkable growth and resilience despite its abbot's chronic ill health. Bernard soon became known as one of the most powerful personages in Christendom. It was in keeping with this reputation that he traveled on missions for popes and potentates, gave support through eloquent preaching to the Second Crusade, controlled bishops, popes, and councils, and was constantly embroiled in the theological controversies and ecclesiastical politics of his day. In recognition of his extraordinary influence over the life and affairs of his time, he has been called "the conscience of all Europe."

Bernard's mystical propensities were congruent with the viewpoint he had taken concerning the relation of faith and reason. Following the pattern established by Augustine, Anselm had championed the slogan, *Credo ut intelligam* ("I believe in order to understand"). For Anselm it was necessary to grasp religious truths by faith before one could probe their meaning. Abelard, on the other hand, Bernard's arch-enemy, reversed Anselm's formula. Finding it necessary that belief be in harmony with reason, Abelard said that "he who believes quickly is light-minded." In his elaboration of this contention, Abelard explained that he did not want to make understanding an absolute condition of faith, and conceded that there were truths of faith that surpassed the power of human reasoning. Bernard, in opposition to Abelard and more radically than Anselm, wanted the truths of faith to rest on their own intrinsic ground. His version of the formulation was, "I believe though I do not comprehend, and I hold by faith what I cannot grasp with the mind." And then in clarification he added that "union with God [the mystical experience] makes truth self-witnessing and self-evident." In short, Bernard attested that many of the most significant and profound religious truths are accessible only through personal mystical experience. Such experience constitutes its own validational base and is an independent source of certitude.

The shift from the powers of the intellect to human sensitivities, to the affections, is in keeping with the thorough interiorization of religion—which also occurs in Bernard. Not only is he preoccupied with the conviction that the human being is made in the image of God—which image, despite sin, is retained—but he also finds the unity between God and man to be expressed most characteristically in terms of love *(caritas)*. Thus interiorization is phrased in the language of romantic love and courtship. The medium is the ancient Hebrew love song, which Bernard read and meditated upon, taken as a description of the mystical relation of God and the soul.

The first portion of the selection that follows is autobiographical. The second describes union with God in an interpretive manner.

On the Song of Songs

But bear now with my foolishness for a little. I wish to tell you, as I have promised, how such events have taken place in me. It is indeed a matter of no importance. But I put myself forward only that I may be of service to you, and if you derive any benefit, I am consoled for my egotism; if not, I shall have displayed my foolishness. I confess, then, though I say it in my foolishness, that the Word has visited me, and even very often. But although He has frequently entered into my soul, I have never at any time been sensible of the precise moment of His coming. I have felt that He was present; I remember that He has been with me; I have sometimes been able even to have a presentiment that He would come; but never to feel His coming or His departure. For whence He came to enter my soul, or whither He went on quitting it, by what means He has made entrance or departure, I confess that I know not even to this day . . . It is not by the eyes that He enters, for He is without colour; nor by the ears, for His coming is without sound; nor by the nostrils, for it is not with the air but with the mind that He is blended; nor again does He enter by the mouth, not being of a nature to be eaten or drunk; nor lastly is He capable of being traced by the touch, for He is intangible.

You will ask, then, how, since the ways of His access are thus incapable of being traced, I could know that He was present. But He is living and full of energy, and as soon as He has entered into me He has

Bernard of Clairvaux, "Sermon 74 on the Song of Songs," from H. A. Reinhold, *The Soul Afire* (New York: Doubleday, 1973) pp. 333–5.

quickened my sleeping soul, has aroused and softened and goaded my heart, which was in a state of torpor and hard as stone. He has begun to pluck up and destroy, to plant and to build, to water the dry places, to illuminate the gloomy spots, to throw open those which were shut close, to inflame with warmth those which were cold, as also to straighten its crooked paths and make its rough places smooth, so that my soul might bless the Lord and all that is within me praise His Holy Name. Thus, then, the Bridegroom-Word, though He has several times entered into me, has never made His coming apparent to my sight, hearing, or touch. It was not by His motions that He was recognised by me, nor could I tell by any of my senses that He had penetrated to the depths of my being. It was, as I have already said, only by the movement of my heart that I was enabled to recognise His presence, and to know the might of His power by the sudden departure of vices and the strong restraint put upon all carnal affections. From the discovery and conviction of my secret faults I have had good reason to admire the depths of His wisdom; His goodness and kindness have become known in the amendment, whatever it may amount to, of my life; while in the renewal of the spirit of my mind, that is, of my inward man, I have perceived in some degree the loveliness of His beauty, and have been filled with amazement at the multitude of His greatness, as I meditated upon all these things.

But when the Word withdrew Himself, all these spiritual powers and faculties began to droop and languish, as if the fire had been withdrawn from a bubbling pot; and this is to me the sign of His departure. Then my soul is necessarily sad and depressed until He shall return and my heart grow warm within me, as it is wont, which indeed is the indication to me that He has come back again.

After having, then, such an experience of the Word, what wonder that I should adopt for my own the language of the Bride, who recalls Him when He has departed, since I am influenced by a desire, not indeed as powerful, but at least similar to hers. As long as I live that utterance shall be in my mind, and I will employ, for the recalling of the Word, that word of recall which I find here in the word "Return." And as often as He shall leave me, so often shall He be called back by my voice; nor will I cease to send my cries, as it were, after Him as He departs, expressing the ardent desire of my heart that He should return, that He should restore to me the joy of His salvation, restore to me Himself. I confess to you, my sons, that I take pleasure in nothing else in the meantime, until He is present who is alone pleasing to me.

On the Song of Songs

*   *   *

When the Beloved who is thus sought for pays a visit in his merciful love to the soul that is filled with longing, that prays often, even without intermission, that humiliates itself in the ardor of its desire, that soul may fittingly say with St. Jeremiah: "You are good, O Lord, to those who hope in you, to the soul that seeks you." And that soul's angel, one of the friends of the Bridegroom, and by him commissioned to be the minister and witness of that secret and mutual exchange—that angel, I say, must be dancing with joy! Does he not participate in their gladness and bliss, and turning to the Lord, say: "I thank you, Lord of majesty, because 'you have granted him his heart's desire, not denied him what his lips entreated' "? He is everywhere the soul's tireless attendant, never ceasing to lure it on and guide it with constant inspirations, as he whispers: "Take delight in the Lord, and he will give you the desire of your heart;" and again: "Wait for the Lord and keep his way." Or: "If he seems slow, wait for him; he will surely come, he will not delay." Turning to the Lord, he says: " 'As a hart longs for flowing streams, so that soul longs for you, O God'. It has yearned for you in the night, and your Spirit within it watched for you from morning onwards." And again: "All the day this soul reaches out to you; grant what it wants because it is shouting after you; relent a little and show your mercy. Look down from heaven and see, and visit this desolate spirit." This loyal groomsman, watching without envy over this interchange of love, seeks the Lord's glory rather than his own; he is the go-between for the lover and his beloved, making known the desires of one, bearing the gifts of the other. He quickens the soul's affections, he conciliates the Bridegroom. Sometimes too, though rarely, he brings them into each other's presence, either snatching her up to him, or leading him down to her: for he is a member of the household, a familiar figure in the palace, one who has no fear of being rebuffed, who daily sees the face of the Father.

Be careful, however, not to conclude that I see something corporeal or perceptible to the senses in this union between the Word and the soul. My opinion is that of the Apostle, who said that "he who is united to the Lord becomes one spirit with him." I try to express with the most suitable words I can muster the ecstatic ascent of the purified mind to

Bernard of Clairvaux, *The Works of Bernard of Clairvaux*, vol. III, *on the Song of Songs, II*. Kalamazoo: Cistercian Publications, 1976, pp. 127–129.

God, and the loving descent of God into the soul, submitting spiritual truths to spiritual men. Therefore let this union be in the spirit, because "God is a spirit," who is lovingly drawn by the beauty of that soul whom he perceives to be guided by the Spirit, and devoid of any desire to submit to the ways of the flesh, especially if he sees that it burns with love for himself.

One who is so disposed and so beloved will by no means be content either with that manifestation of the Bridegroom given to the many in the world of creatures, or to the few in visions and dreams. By a special privilege she wants to welcome him down from heaven into her inmost heart, into her deepest love; she wants to have the one she desires present to her not in bodily form but by inward infusion, not by appearing externally but by laying hold of her within. It is beyond question that the vision is all the more delightful the more inward it is, and not external. It is the Word, who penetrates without sound; who is effective though not pronounced, who wins the affections without striking on the ears. His face, though without form, is the source of form, it does not dazzle the eyes of the body but gladdens the watchful heart; its pleasure is in the gift of love and not in the color of the lover.

Not yet have I come round to saying that he has appeared as he is, although in this inward vision he does not reveal himself as altogether different from what he is. Neither does he make his presence continuously felt, not even to his most ardent lovers, nor in the same way to all. For the various desires of the soul it is essential that the taste of God's presence be varied too, and that the infused flavor of divine delight should titillate in manifold ways the palate of the soul that seeks him. You must already have noticed how often he changes his countenance in the course of this love-song, how he delights in transforming himself from one charming guise to another in the beloved's presence: at one moment like a bashful bridegroom manoeuvring for the hidden embraces of his holy lover, for the bliss of her kisses; at another coming along like a physician with oil and ointments, because weak and tender souls still need remedies and medicines of this kind, which is why they are rather daintily described as maidens. Should anybody find fault with this, let him be told that "it is not the healthy who need the doctor, but the sick." Sometimes, too, he joins up as a traveller with the bride and the maidens who accompany her on the road, and lightens the hardships of the journey for the whole company by his fascinating conversation, so that when he was parted from them they ask: "Did not our hearts burn within us as he talked to us on the road?" A silver-tongued companion who, by the spell of his words and manners, persuades everyone, as if in a sweet-smelling cloud arising from the ointments, to follow him. Hence they say: "We will run after you in the odor of your ointments." At another time he comes to meet them as a wealthy father of a family "with bread enough and to spare" in his house; or again like a magnificent and powerful king, giving courage to his timid and poverty-stricken bride, stirring up her desire by showing her the ornaments of his glory, the riches of his wine-presses and storehouse, the produce of his gardens and fields, and finally introducing her into his private apartments. For "her husband's heart has confidence in her," and among all his possessions there is nothing that he thinks should be hidden from her whom he redeemed from indigence, whose fidelity he has proved, whose attractiveness wins his embraces. And so he never ceases, in one way or another, to reveal himself to the inward eye of those who seek him, thus fulfilling the promise that he made: "Be assured I am with you always, to the end of time."

On all these occasions he is kind and gentle, full of merciful love. In his kisses he shows that he is both loving and charming; with the oil and the ointments that he is boundlessly considerate and compassionate and forgiving; on the journey he is gay, courteous, ever gracious and ready to help; in the display of his riches and possessions he reveals a kingly liberality, a munificent generosity in the bestowal of rewards. Through the whole context of this song you will find images of this nature to delineate the Word. Hence I feel that the Prophet was thinking on these lines when he said: "Christ the Lord is a spirit before our face; under his shadow we shall live among the nations," because now we see in a mirror dimly and not yet face to face. So it will be while we live among the nations; among the angels it will be otherwise. For then we shall enjoy the very same happiness as they; even we shall see him as he is, in the form of God, no longer in shadow.

Hildegarde of Bingen

(1098-1179)

The twelfth century was a remarkable period in the history of the Western Church. It witnessed the rise of that great monastic reform movement, the Cistercian order, under the auspices of Bernard of Clairvaux. It experienced the mobilization of European armed power that launched the Second and Third Crusades. It flowered in a literary renaissance and suffered the theological growing pains of what has become known as the debate between faith and reason embodied in the persons of Bernard and Peter Abelard. A period of such intense activity tends to coincide with the emergence of intensely creative personalities. One such was Hildegarde of Bingen, abbess of the Benedictine monastery of Rupertsberg near Bingen, poetess, playwright, musician, artist, author of a work on the physical world, prophetess, reformer, visionary, spiritual adviser, and mystic.

Hildegarde was born into a family of noble rank and from an early age was subject to supernatural visions. Entrusted for her upbringing to Jutta, a recluse in a nearby religious community, her spiritual capacities were well nurtured in the atmosphere of contemplation. At the age of eighteen she was clothed in the habit of a Benedictine nun. Succeeding Jutta as abbess of the community in 1136, she soon began to record some of her visionary experiences with the aid of her secretary, the monk Volmar. Gaining fame as seer and prophetess, Hildegarde found her visions subject to the scrutiny of a commission delegated by Pope Eugenius III. The commission proclaimed them to be of genuine divine inspiration. Two other popes as well as the Council of Trèves were later to concur with this approbation.

Yet Hildegarde was not content to merely receive validation for the authentic inspiration that guided her visions and communications. Like her contemporary, Bernard, the abbess was acutely aware of the need for reform within an all-too-worldly Church. After moving her band of contemplatives to a new site on Mount Rupert (a move at first strongly opposed by the monks of the adjoining community), Hildegarde set out on a preaching and teaching mission designed to cleanse the mystical body of Christ. Not only did she visit and advise the inhabitants of the monastic world on the value of reform but she was the valued correspondent of such twelfth-century luminaries as the Emperor Frederick Barbarossa, Henry II and Eleanor of Aquitaine. Moreover, her practical advice was highly regarded and her wisdom in matters of theological subtlety was often sought. Her letters to communities of monks, interpreting abstruse biblical passages and illuminating the delicate outlines of the spiritual life, have survived.

Hildegarde's mysticism is of a unique brand. While she can certainly be numbered among the great line of visionaries that includes Mechthild of Magdeburg and Julian of Norwich and that has given Christian mysticism a rich heritage of devotional imagery, she nonetheless stands

apart from them. For the abbess of Rupertsburg there are no loving and
tender conversations with God nor transports of desire nor elaborate
enactments of divine and human nuptials. Rather, her communications,
while highly dramatic, are less personalized and use almost no erotic
metaphors but convey in visual expression the meaning of such mysteries as the Trinity, the Last Judgment, and the hierarchies of angels. In
Hildegarde's view, humans are essentially rational beings. It is through
their intelligence that they are most closely united to the transcendent.
Indeed, the intellect is God's greatest gift to humans. The visions
Hildegarde received were of a highly rational type, conveying to
humans information of the eternal realm designed to instruct them in
the divine mysteries and show them the way to eternal splendors.

One feature of Hildegarde's writing worth noting is the grandness of
its scale. Her concerns are focused on the cosmic implications of the
Creation, the Fall, the Redemption and the Last Judgment of the world.
She tells us of the unity of the eternal plan in all its magnificence and
awesome splendor. There is much less emphasis on the interaction
between the individual soul and God. This is not to say that she passes
over the basic assumptions of the Christian inner life. Found throughout her works are the orthodox teachings that asceticism is at the
beginning of the mystic path, that one enters into the prayer of
contemplation, undergoes periods of painful purification and spiritual
dryness, and emerges with a true humility that properly evaluates and
adores the relation between God and creature. All this is there, yet the
emphasis in her writings is on the order and structure of the universe
and the mystery revealed in the unfolding drama of its history.

The selections presented here are from a work known as *The Divine
Works of a Simple Man.*

The Divine Works of a Simple Man

And I saw as it were in the mystery of God, in the southern sky, a
wonderful and beautiful image in the form of a man, whose face was so
brilliant and beautiful that I could more easily have looked into the
sun. A large ring of a golden colour surrounded His head and His face.
But in the same ring above the same head another face like that of an

Francesca Maria Steele, *The Life and Visions of St. Hildegarde* (London: Heath,
Cranton and Ousely, Ltd., 1900), pp. 204–237. Footnotes have been omitted.

older man appeared, whose chin and beard touched the top of His head, and from each side of His neck one wing proceeded, which ascending above the aforesaid ring joined together. But in the top of the arched curve of the right wing, was as it were the head of an eagle, which I perceived had fiery eyes, in which the splendour of the angels appeared as in a mirror. But in the top of the arched curve of the left wing was as it were the face of a man, which shone like the light of the stars. These faces were turned to the east. But from each shoulder of this image one wing was extended to the knees. Also He was clothed in a tunic like the shining of the sun, and in His hand He had a Lamb, like the splendid light of day.

But He trod under His feet a certain monster of a terrible and poisonous shape, and of a black colour, and a certain serpent, which fixed its mouth in the right ear of the same monster, and bending the rest of his body, in turning away his head, he extended his tail on his left side down to his feet. And this image said:

I am the high and fiery power, Who kindled all living sparks, and I breathed out no human things unless I judge them as they are. I placed that encircling wing with My wings above it rightly, that is surrounding them with wisdom. But I burn in the fiery life of the substance of the divinity above the beauty of the fields, and I shine in the waters, and I burn in the sun, and the moon and the stars, and with an aerial invisible wind, by a certain life which sustains all things, I quicken all things vitally.

For the air lives in greenness and in flowers, waters flow as if they live, the sun also lives in his light, and when the waning moon shall come to the light of the sun, it is kindled as if it were living again; the stars also shine in their light as if they were living. I created also the columns which support all the world: likewise (I created) those winds which had wings placed under them, that is to say the gentler winds, which by their gentleness hold back the stronger winds, lest they spread themselves with danger, as the body covers the soul and contains it lest it should expire.

As also the breath of the soul collects in strengthening the body, so that it should not fail, so also the stronger winds animate those subject to them, that they may exercise their office in agreement.

And so I, a fiery force, hide in them and they burn from me as the breath moves man constantly, and as in fire there is a blazing flame. All these things live in their own essences, nor are they found in death, because I am the life. For I am reason, having the wind of the sounding word through Whom every creature was made, and I breathed in all these things, so that none of them may be mortal in his kind, because I am the life. For I am the whole life which is not cut off even from stones, and it does not put forth leaves from roots, and it is not rooted in virile strength, but everything vital is rooted in Me. For reason is the root, and the spoken word blossoms in her.

By what means then, since GOD is rational, is it possible that He should not work when He breathes through every work of His, which He made in His image and likeness, and designed all creatures according to the measure of this same man? For He always was in eternity, because GOD wished His work that is man to be made, and when He had perfected that work, He gave to him all His creatures, that he might work with them; and GOD also made this work, that is man himself.

But I also am of service, because all vital things live from me, and I am the coeval life in eternity, which has neither beginning nor end, and GOD is that same life itself, moving and working, and nevertheless this one life is in three powers. And the Father is said to be Eternity, the Son the Word, and the breath connecting these Two is said to be the Holy Spirit, as GOD also signified in man, in whom are body, soul and reason.

But because I shine above the beauty of the fields, that is the earth, which is that material from which GOD made man: and because I shine in the waters, that is following the nature of the soul: for as water pours through all the earth, so the soul passes through the whole body: but because I shine in the sun and moon, this signifies reason, for the stars are the innumerable words of reason. For when by a certain invisible life which sustains all things I quicken all things, that is, because those things which increase in growing by air and by wind when grown cannot subsist apart from that influence to which they owe their primary existence.

And again I heard a voice from heaven saying to me: GOD, Who created all things, made man to His own image and similitude, and signified in him the superior creatures as much as the inferior, and had such great love for him, that He destined him for the place from which the falling angel was cast out, and ordained him to honour and glory in the beatitude which he had lost; this vision which thou seest shows that.

For that thou seest as it were in the midst of the southern sky, in the mystery of GOD, a beautiful and wonderful image in the form of a man, this is because in the strength of the unending divinity is the love of the Father on high, beautiful in election and wonderful in the gifts of secrets, showing man that when the Son of GOD put on flesh, He redeemed lost man through charity.

Then his face was of such beauty and brightness, that thou wast able more easily to look into the sun than on it, because the abundance of charity is so great in the eminence and brilliancy of her gifts, that she so transcends all understanding of human knowledge, by which divers things can be understood in the soul, that in no way can it be received through the senses. But this is shown in the signification that through charity He is known to faith, Who is not seen visibly with visible eyes.

And a large circle of gold colour surrounds the head of this same face because the Catholic faith is spread throughout the whole world, rising in the first dawn of exceeding brightness, it comprehends the excellence of the greatness of true charity with all devotion, when GOD in the humanity of His Son redeemed man, and through the infusion of the Holy Spirit strengthened him, so that he might know One GOD in Trinity, Who without time beginning, before all time was God in the Divinity.

But because in that same ring above His head, another face like that of an older man appears, that is because the excellent goodness of the Divinity which is without beginning and without end, helps the faithful in all things, so the chin of His face and His beard touch the top of His head, because the Divinity in disposing and protecting all things reaches the excellence of the highest charity, when the Son of God in His humanity brings back lost men to Heaven.

And from each side of the neck of this same figure a wing proceeded, which ascending above the aforesaid ring, were there joined together, because the love of God and of our neighbour, proceeding in the unity of faith through the power of charity, and through the highest desire comprehending that same faith between them, are not to be separated from each other, when the holy Divinity darkens the innumerable splendours of His glory, for men as long as they are in the shadow of death, are without the celestial clothing which they lost in Adam.

But in the top of the arched curve of the right wing, thou didst see as it were the head of an eagle, which has fiery eyes, in which appeared a multitude of angels as in a mirror, because in the excellency of the triumphant subjection, when whosoever will subject himself to God conquers himself and the devil, he is exalted in the happiness of the Divine protection. And when he raises up his mind inflamed by the Holy Spirit, and fixes his intention upon God, the blessed spirits will appear clearly in his mind, and they will offer to God the devotion of his heart. For in the eagle spiritual men are showed, who with all the devotion of their heart, frequently in contemplation, like the angels look upon God. Wherefore the blessed spirits beholding God constantly, rejoice concerning the good works of the just, and they show them also in themselves, and thus persevering in the praise of God, they are never wearied, because they are never able to bring it to an end.

*   *   *

Then God made to arise another life which He covered with a body, which is man, to whom He gave the place and glory of the lost angel, so that this one might accomplish in the praise of God, what that one was unwilling to do.

But in this face of a man were shown those who, given corporally to the world, nevertheless continually serve God in the spirit; neither do they on account of being detained in the world as seculars, forget those things which are of the spirit in communing with God. And these faces are turned to the east, because both religious and seculars who desire to walk with God, and to preserve their souls in life, ought to turn themselves to the bringing forth of holy conversation and sanctity.

But from each shoulder of this image, a wing was extended to his knees, because in the strength of love, the Son of God gathered together to Himself the just and sinners, and bore up those to the shoulders who had lived justly, and those to the knees whom He had called back from a life of unrighteousness, and made them companions of the citizens above, as a man sustains those things, which he carries as much by the shoulders as by the knees.

For in the knowledge of charity, man is led in body and soul to the fulness of purity, although he is many times moved from a state of unbiased steadfastness. When the gifts of the Holy Spirit pour down from above in pure and holy liberality, they educate him abundantly in celestial and spiritual things. They also teach him in another way many earthly things also, for the use of corporal necessities, in which nevertheless he understands that he is weak and infirm and mortal, although he is fortified by many of these gifts.

But that He was clothed in a tunic shining like the sun, this is because in charity He clothed Himself in a human body, without any contagion of sin, in the similitude of the beauty of the sun, for as the sun shines at such a great height above other creatures, that by no one among men is he able to be touched, so also no human knowledge unless united to faith, is able to understand the humanity of the Son of God, or in what manner it exists.

And in His hands He had a Lamb like the splendid light of day, because charity, in the works of the Son of God, brings forth the meekness of true faith, shining upon all things, when He chooses from publicans and sinners, martyrs and confessors and penitents, and when

He makes just men from impious, as Paul from Saul: and seeing that they flew above the wings of the winds, this means that they flew in celestial harmony.

Thus charity perfected its works distinctly and by degrees, so that no weakness but all perfection might be in it, which man does not do, because when he might have a moderate possibility of doing something, he scarcely bears up until he can perfect that, as truly may be seen from others. Man may consider these things within himself, because as a bird going forth from an egg and lacking feathers, does not yet hasten to fly, but after it has received its wings, it flies by that power which it had seen to be in itself.

Richard of St. Victor
(d. 1173)

Richard of St. Victor stands at the confluence of two streams of thought that merge to create the Western contemplative tradition. The first of these streams draws primarily upon the authority of Pseudo-Dionysius. The second takes inspiration from the tradition shaped by Augustine of Hippo and those who followed in his train. Like the Pseudo-Dionysian precedent, Richard speaks of supernatural modes of prayer set apart from more ordinary prayer experience, modes characterized by darkness and emphasizing the nonrational apprehension of the divine. Yet, distinct from that precedent and more in keeping with the authorities on the other side, he does not regard rational modes of knowledge as being useless tools in the search for God.

Augustine and Gregory before him affirmed the value of experimental and acquired spiritual knowledge. God, they felt, could be sought and in some sense found through the practice of love, humility, and prayer. It was not only in the divine darkness where the mind, imagination, and memory were inoperative that He was to be discovered.

Richard drank deeply from both these streams, drank deeply and went well beyond his predecessors to construct a vision of the interior life that was to have lasting influence through the centuries of Christian spirituality. To him belongs the distinction of being the first writer to create a systematic theology of the mystical process. This theology is not merely a synthesis of previous thought on the subject, it is a creation that, while drawing upon that previous thought, is distinctive, personal, and new.

It was the tendency of Scholasticism, the form of philosophical and theological inquiry that came into vogue in the twelfth century, to employ formal methods of reason in the most rigorous manner possible, even when religion is the subject being addressed. The school of theology emanating from the abbey of St. Victor, of which Richard was a part, has become known as a cradle of this nascent Scholasticism. Thus his systematic approach to the field of mystical theology can be seen within the context of the intellectual trends of his times. Yet, Richard also brought a very personal touch to his work. He was an insightful psychologist, fascinated by the processes of the human mind and anxious to explore and describe the phenomena that the mind experiences. As a consequence, his systematic description of the mystic process is marked by its immediacy and its sensitivity to the subtle workings of the interior life.

His two most famous works, *Benjamin Minor* and *Benjamin Major*, reveal him at his most perceptive. He begins with the biblical story of the patriarch Jacob and his offspring and fashions two treatises, one on the psychology of the virtues and vices and another on contemplation. The first of these is a masterful exposition of the inner dynamics of a soul preparing for the contemplative life. In order to achieve the grace of contemplation, the aspirant must subject himself to an exacting interior asceticism, conquering the vices he finds within and acquiring virtues to replace them. Richard points out the interrelationship of the various faculties of the mind and body, the senses and the reason, in order to instruct the aspirant in the self-knowledge that will prepare him for his contemplative journey.

Beyond self-knowledge, and indeed knowledge of any kind, Richard places knowledge of God. His treatise *Benjamin Major* deals with the transformation of self-knowledge into God-knowledge by the action of God Himself upon the soul, in other words, with contemplation. A note here on Richard of St. Victor's use of the word "contemplation" may be helpful. By it he does not mean solely a nonvocal, nondiscursive stage of prayer, a restricted definition it came to acquire later on. For him, contemplation has a broader sense. It is the capacity to integrate a variety of perceptions into one all-embracing intuition focused in awe upon divine things. In *Benjamin Major* he attempts to describe the respective fields of both the rational and nonrational powers in the contemplative experience. While in his view the rational faculties have a part to play, nonetheless in the heights of contemplative ecstasy they are transcended and a new type of knowledge, a love-knowledge, is received.

The framework upon which these two treatises are based is the biblical tale of Jacob and his family. By structuring his remarks in this way, Richard is basing his work on what he believed to be the biblical, and thus God-designed, exposition of his mystical theology. It was characteristic of the Medieval theologian, and this is true as well of writers on contemplation, to base his statements upon the authority of the Scriptures. This he did, accepting the axiom that the Scriptures were multidimensional and could yield not only one but several layers of interpretation. By the twelfth century, at least three levels of meaning were considered to be contained in the text of the Bible: the literal level, the allegorical level, and the moral or tropological level. In his two *Benjamin* treatises Richard utilizes both the allegorical and tropological methods of interpretation of the text. He also goes deeper and extracts what he referred to as the mystical interpretation of the text. In the words and symbols of the Scriptures he sees the pattern of the interior life outlined, and his exposition is an attempt to reveal that pattern for the contemplative.

History has shrouded the life of Richard of St. Victor. Of his origins and upbringing we know nothing. The date and place of his birth are not known, nor is the date of his reception into the abbey of St. Victor, on the outskirts of the busy university town of Paris. At that time St. Victor's was a community dedicated to the ideals of the contemplative life that had produced some of the most noted thinkers in twelfth-century theology and philosophy. Into this environment Richard came, presumably as a young man, and in this environment he lived and was formed in the ways of contemplation.

From documents we know that he served as subprior of the abbey as well as prior, a post to which he was appointed in 1162. It is only from this late date onward that we have any concrete, albeit scanty, information of the events of his life. As prior he had the misfortune to serve under an abbot who was ill-suited to the demands of his position. Apparently this abbot involved himself and the abbey in intrigues at the French court and at Rome, wasted the resources of the community on ill-conceived building projects, and conducted himself in an altogether tyrannical way. Richard, as prior, was forced to try to carry out his duties under this oppressive leadership. An appeal was made to the

Pope, who reproved the abbot. But the situation was not remedied until 1172, when the offender was officially deposed. Apparently Richard had taken an important part in all these events, marking his last years of life with the strain of interpersonal discord.

Benjamin Minor

Of the study of wisdom and a commendation thereof.

'Benjamin a youth, in ecstasy of mind'. Let the young men hear a sermon about youth, let them wake up to the words of the prophet: 'There is Benjamin, a youth, in ecstasy of mind.' Many know who this Benjamin is, some by learning and some by experience. Let those who know from teaching listen patiently, and those who know by experience, listen willingly. For he who has once come to know Benjamin by experience as a master, will never (I speak confidently), be satisfied with a sermon about him, however lengthy. But who can be fit to speak worthily of him? For he was fair of form among all the children of Jacob, even he who was worthy to be born of Rachel. For Leah, though she had many children could not have fairer ones. Jacob, as we read, had two wives. One was called Leah, the other Rachel. Leah was more fruitful, Rachel more beautiful; Leah though fruitful was blear-eyed, Rachel though sterile was well favoured. Now let us see what these two wives of Jacob signify that we may more easily understand what their sons mean. Rachel is the teaching of truth, Leah the discipline of virtue. Rachel is the search for wisdom, Leah the desire for righteousness. But we know that Jacob served seven years for Rachel and yet the days seemed few for the greatness of his love. Do you wonder at this? According to the greatness of her beauty was the greatness of his love. I should like to attempt something in praise of wisdom, whatever I shall say it will be but little. For what is loved more ardently than wisdom or is sweeter to possess? For her comeliness is beyond all beauty and her sweetness beyond all delight. For one says, 'she is more lovely than the sun and above all the order of the stars; being compared with the light she is found before it.' For the day is followed by night, but wisdom is

Richard of St. Victor. Selected Writings on Contemplation, trans. with introduction and notes, Clare Kirchberger (New York: Harper & Row, 1957), pp. 78-79, 80-81, 90-93. Footnotes have been omitted.

not overcome by evil. 'She reacheth therefore from end to end mightily and ordereth all things sweetly. I have loved her and have sought her out from my youth, and have desired to take her for my spouse: and I became a lover of her beauty.' What wonder is it then if Jacob burned with love for such a bride, if he was unable to temper the flames of such a fire, of such love? 'I have loved wisdom above health and beauty.' As we have said, nothing is loved more ardently than this wisdom, nothing is sweeter to possess. Hence it is that all men wish to be wise but very few can attain wisdom.

* * *

Of the double fountain of all good things, namely the reason and the affections.

Now if you please, we will examine carefully the subject of Jacob's two wives and manifest openly whatever our mind suggests. Every rational spirit is given two powers by the Father of lights from whom comes every good and perfect gift. The one is the reason, the other the affections; the reason for truth, the affection for virtue. . . . They are the two wives of a rational being which produce numerous offspring and are the heirs of the heavenly kingdom. Of reason springs right counsel, of affection holy desires. Of the first spiritual senses, of the second ordered affections. The latter produces all the virtues, the former all truth. Therefore we must realize that the affection begins truly to be Leah when it strives to conform to the pattern of righteousness. And reason can definitely be identified with Rachel when it is illumined by the light of the true and highest wisdom. But we shall not forget how laborious the one is, and how joyous the other. For the affection of the soul is not withdrawn from illicit things and set upon right things without great labour, so that this wife Leah is rightly called 'laborious'. Can anything be sweeter and happier than to fix the mind's eye in contemplation of the highest wisdom? Therefore when reason is direct-ed to this contemplation it deserves to be honoured by the name of Rachel. The word Rachel is interpreted as meaning 'seeing the begin-ning' or 'a sheep'. To be worthy of this name she must fulfil what is written, 'Think of the Lord in goodness, and seek him in simplicity of heart.' For he who thinks of the Lord in goodness discerns him who is the beginning of all things. And in a true sense he is a 'sheep', if he seeks in simplicity. See then that it is not any ordinary wisdom but the highest wisdom, pursued in simplicity which makes one to be Rachel. I think therefore that you will not be surprised that Rachel is so much loved when her handmaid (I speak of the wisdom of the world which in comparison with her mistress is accounted foolishness), is pursued with such love by the philosophers of the world.

How by the study of wisdom the soul is often secretly drawn to the ways of righteousness.

Those who have learned by experience rather than by hearing will easily recognize how it is that Leah is substituted when Rachel had been hoped for. It often happens that a soul not yet wholly cleansed from a low way of life and not yet fit for contemplation of heavenly things, hastening to the marriage-bed of Rachel and preparing itself for her embrace, at the moment times his praise shall ever be in my mouth'. . . . But do not think that Judah was content to praise God in his heart without praising him with his mouth. For the man Judah desires to make God known to others and to kindle them to love him whom he thinks worthy of love, and he desires that all men should love him.

This we have said of the confession of praise, but what shall we say of the confession of sins? Does Judah ignore the latter when he so well proclaims the former? I think not, for I know that both contribute greatly to God's honour. And a true lover willingly accomplishes what he knows will tend to God's glory. Not only God's generosity but also our sin, commends his goodness to us. For if it is a great thing freely to grant much to those who deserve nothing, how much greater to give good things to those who deserve evil. . . . ? Therefore let us confess our bad deeds and our good deeds. Let us confess that our sins are our own fault so that he may mercifully forgive them, and confess that our good deeds come from him that he may preserve and increase them. This is Judah's constant occupation, lest he seems ungrateful either for pardon received or for grace given. I think this son Judah, that is confession, is rightly so called, for love is always confessing love. . . . Now we have spoken of Leah's four sons. The first is fear of sin, the second sorrow of penitence, the third is hope of pardon, the fourth love of righteousness. And after that she left off bearing.

*   *   *

How the mind is moved by love for invisible things to enquire into them.

Now what will be going on in Rachel's heart? By what heated desires will she not be agitated when she sees her sister a joyful mother of sons and she herself left sterile? Let us hear what she says and understand her grief. She says to Jacob her husband, 'Give me children or else I die!' Certainly if the search for wisdom is not pursued it will soon fail. Let us look carefully why Rachel's desire for children should have grown stronger after Judah's birth. For as it is Leah's part to love since she is the affection of the soul, so it is Rachel's part to know, for she is reason. The former gives birth to ordered affection; the latter to the reason or the pure intelligence. Judah represents to us ordered love, love of heavenly things, love of God, love of the highest good. And when Judah is born, that is, when desire and love of unseen good things is rising and growing strong, then Rachel begins to desire children passionately, for she wants to know. Where love is there is vision. We like to look upon him whom we love greatly, and certainly he who can love invisible things will immediately desire to know them and to see them by the intelligence. So the more Judah grows, that is the power of loving, the greater becomes Rachel's desire to bear, that is the zeal for knowledge.

*   *   *

That the first path to the contemplation of unseen things is by the imagination.

Everybody knows how difficult or almost impossible it is for the carnal mind still untaught in spiritual studies to raise itself to the understanding of unseen things and fix its eye upon contemplating them. For so far it knows nothing but bodily things; nothing presents itself to its thoughts but what it is accustomed to thinking about, that is visible things. It seeks to see invisible things and nothing meets its eye but the form of visible objects; it desires to consider incorporeal things but dreams of the images of corporeal things only. What shall it do then? Is it not better to think somehow about these things rather than to give up and neglect them? Indeed if the soul loves truly it will not easily forget them, yet it is much more difficult to rise up and contemplate them. Let it do what it may and think of them as it is able. Let it think through the imagination since it cannot yet by the pure intelligence. This is, I think, why Rachel first had children through her handmaid before she gave birth herself; for it is sweet for her to think upon them through the imagination when she cannot yet have an intelligent understanding by the reason. As we mean reason by Rachel, so we mean the imagination by her handmaid. Therefore the reason persuades us that it is better to think about the good things in some way or other and at least to kindle the soul with desire for them through imagining their beauty, rather than to fix the mind upon false and deceptive goods. And this is the reason why Rachel wished to give her handmaid to her husband. Everybody unless he is quite inexperienced, knows that this is the first road towards contemplation of invisible things for a beginner.

How the Sacred Scriptures refer to this method of beginners.

We must not overlook the fact that the Sacred Scriptures make use of this way of thinking and condescend to human infirmity. For they describe unseen things by the forms of visible things and impress them upon our memories by the beauty of desirable forms. Thus they promise a land flowing with milk and honey; sometimes they name flowers or odours and describe the harmony of celestial joys either by human song or by the harmony of bird-song. Read John's Apocalypse and you will find that the heavenly Jerusalem is often described as being adorned with gold and silver, pearls and other precious gems. Yet we know that none of these things are in that place from which no good thing is absent. For none of these things is there in 'form' (reality) while all are present in 'likeness'. In all these things Bilhah has the where-withal to serve her mistress usefully, since she may bring them all to mind wherever and whenever she likes. And we can immediately imagine these things when we like. The imagination can never be more useful to the reason that when she ministers to it in this way.

3. The Poetic Visions of the Thirteenth Century: The Spirit of the Friars

Bonaventura

(1217–1274)

The thirteenth century witnessed the birth of one of the great religious orders spawned by Medieval Christendom—the order of Franciscans—founded and inspired by one of the most unusual and charismatic figures of religious history, the "poor man" of Assisi, Francis. The Franciscan order infused the Christian Church's essentially monastic spirituality with a new spirit, a spirit informed equally by the contemplative and apostolic visions of the Christian life. Francis of Assisi, desiring to pattern his own life after the life of Christ, sought for the outlines of that pattern in a vocation that centered upon intense interior prayer and private communion with God. But he also wanted a vocation that stressed the value of activities "in the world," such as preaching and living as the humblest of men among the poor and unimportant of the world. Throughout its complex and often turbulent history, the Franciscan order continually made attempts to realize the potential inherent in this blend of contemplative and active spirituality.

Bonaventura, a follower of Francis and a member of the Franciscan order, worked out a combination of these religious currents in a unique way. His working environment was the world of the university. Thus his particular task involved perpetuating the spirit of Francis while providing elaborate conceptual linkages between contemplative experience and theological reflection. The achievement of all of this at once

required that Francis' insights, regarding both action and contemplation, be translated into a systematic conceptual form.

Bonaventura was named Giovanni (or John) at birth, the son of Maria
and Giovanni Fidanza, of Bagnorea near Viterbo in Italy. His father
was an able physician. Early in Bonaventura's youth, he fell gravely ill
and was saved from death not by the medical ministrations of his father
but through intercessory prayers to Francis.

He entered the University of Paris in 1235, studying theology and
philosophy under Alexander of Hales and John of La Rochelle. He
received his MA in 1243, joined the Franciscan order the same year,
and received the name Bonaventura upon his admission to the order.
He began teaching at the University of Paris in 1248 and was appointed
to the chair reserved for Franciscan theologians in 1253. He became
father general of the Franciscans in 1257, declined the archbishopric of
York in 1265, and attended the Council of Lyons in 1274, during which
he died, on July 14, 1274.

These are the externals. The greater interest Bonaventura holds for
us issues from the way in which he combined the teachings of Francis
with the traditions of sophisticated theological and philosophical reflection that were being transmitted within the universities.

We recall that Francis was a simple and unlearned man who had
warned his followers about the perils of learning. Francis' attitude was
reflected in the words of Paul: "I determined to know nothing among
you except Jesus Christ and him crucified." (I Corinthians 2:2) Bonaventura was not only committed to the Franciscan way of life but also
felt a close personal affinity with Francis. Indeed, the imagery (the
personal story) that seems most influential comes from Francis' biography, particularly his experience at the mountain retreat at Alvernia,
where, in a miraculous way, he received the stigmata. Bonaventura is
biographer, recording the event when Francis perceived a figure
coming toward him from the heights of heaven as he was meditating on
the passion of Christ:

... Francis saw a seraph with six fiery wings coming down from the highest
point in the heavens. The vision descended swiftly and came to rest in the air
near him. Then he saw the image of a man crucified in the midst of the wings,
with his hands and feet stretched out and nailed to a cross. Two of the wings
were raised above his head and two were stretched out in flight, while the
remaining two shielded his body. Francis was dumbfounded at the sight and his
heart was flooded with a mixture of joy and sorrow. He was overjoyed at the
way Christ regarded him so graciously under the appearance of a seraph, but the
fact that he was nailed to a cross pierced his soul with a sword of compassionate
sorrow. . . .

...As the vision disappeared, it left his heart ablaze with eagerness and impressed upon his body a miraculous likeness. There and then the marks of nails began to appear in his hands and feet, just as he had seen them in his vision of the man nailed to the cross.*

In short, Francis received the same wounds in his hands, feet, and side that Jesus Christ received in his crucifixion.

It would not be too much to suggest that Bonaventura saw the figure of Christ through the person of Francis, or, indeed, that he understood the lives of both to exhibit the same truth about the nature of the divine reality. It was the centrality of the crucifixion that provided the correspondence, for Bonaventura, between critical philosophical reflection and the inspiration of the "little poor man." It was the same emphasis that persuaded Bonaventura that philosophical reflection finds its culmination in mystical experience. Bonaventura's vocation was to translate Francis' vision into epistemologiclal and metaphysical terms.

As was typical of most thinkers of the time, Bonaventura charged his affirmations with a marked ascendant tendency. He depicted the soul as being on a journey, the disposition of which is gradually upward-sloping. He talked about stages of ascent and identified the corporeal and spiritual levels through which persons pass in moving from the depths to the heights. Utilizing patterns of threes and sixes, he contended there were six human powers or faculties, just as there were six days of creation, six days after which God called Moses from the midst of darkness, six wings on the angel that Isaiah beheld in his vision, and "after six days" that Jesus took his disciples to the Mount of Transfiguration. Ordinarily, the sixfold pattern lends detail and refinement to the sequence of threes. The fundamental division is between the corporeal and spiritual levels, with an intermediate level designated as mixed corporeal and spiritual. That threesome can be correlated with another prominent sequence: sensual, spriritual, and mental. Bonaventura describes apprehension as traversing contemplation, faith, then reason. Theology is divided into symbolical, properly theological, and mystical; in the latter stage the penetration of the divine reality becomes most knowing.

Ultimately, the pilgrim—for whom the imagery of the exodus is interiorized and coupled with the figure of the ladder—can do no better than approximate the vision of Francis. Bonaventura has that

---

*Bonaventura, *The Life of St. Francis*, in *St. Francis of Assisi. Writings and Early Biographies*, edited Marion A. Habig (Chicago: Franciscan Herald Press, 1972), pp. 730–1.

vision uppermost in mind when he describes the goal of mystic awareness to be a discovery of "the shaft of light that flashes out from the divine, mysterious darkness." The phrase is taken from Dionysius, but the reference is to Francis on Mt. Alvernia and to Christ on the Mount of Transfiguration. The two pictures coalesce, and the personages involved are transformed into one another. Bonaventura adds that the pilgrim, like Francis, an itinerant, should seek the fire beyond the light, "a fire kindled on earth by Jesus in the fervor of his ardent passion." Appropriately, Christ is referred to as "the passion of God." And mystical union is placed within the dynamism of the crucifixion.

Through the influence of Francis of Assisi, the *caritas* (love) Bernard of Clairvaux stressed has become particularized by Bonaventura as divine *passion*, while retraining the capacity to point to the nature of the heart of things.

The Mind's Road to God

Blessed is the man whose help is from Thee. In his heart he hath disposed to ascend by steps, in the vale of tears, in the place which he hath set (lb Ps., 83, 6). Since beatitude is nothing else than the fruition of the highest good, and the highest good is above us, none can be made blessed unless he ascend above himself, not by the ascent of his body but by that of his heart. But we cannot be raised above ourselves except by a higher power raising us up. For howsoever the interior steps are disposed, nothing is accomplished unless it is accompanied by divine aid. Divine help, however, comes to those who seek it from their hearts humbly and devoutly; and this means to sigh for it in this vale of tears, aided only by fervent prayer. Thus prayer is the mother and source of ascent (*sursum-actionis*) in God. Therefore Dionysius, in his book, *Mystical Theology* [ch. 1, 1], wishing to instruct us in mental elevation, prefaces his work by prayer. Therefore let us pray and say to the Lord our God, "Conduct me, O Lord, in Thy way, and I will walk in Thy truth; let my heart rejoice that it may fear Thy name" [Ps., 85, 11].

By praying thus one is enlightened about the knowledge of the stages in the ascension to God. For since, relative to our life on earth, the world is itself a ladder for ascending to God, we find here certain traces

The Mind's Road to God, trans. George Boas (New York: The Liberal Arts Press, 1953), pp. 7–10, 34–38. Reprinted by permission of Bobbs-Merrill Co. Footnotes have been omitted.

[of His hand], certain images, some corporeal, some spiritual, some temporal, some aeviternal; consequently some outside us, some inside. That we may arrive at an understanding of the First Principle, which is most spiritual and eternal and above us, we ought to proceed through the traces which are corporeal and temporal and outside us: and this is to be led into the way of God. We ought next to enter into our minds, which are the eternal image of God, spiritual and internal; and this is to walk in the truth of God. We ought finally to pass over into that which is eternal, most spiritual, and above us, looking to the First Principle; and this is to rejoice in the knowledge of God and in the reverence of His majesty.

Now this is the three days' journey into the wilderness [Ex., 3, 18]; this is the triple illumination of one day, first as the evening, second as the morning, third as noon; this signifies the threefold existence of things, as in matter, in [creative] intelligence, and in eternal art, wherefore it is said, Be it made, He made it, and It was so done [Gen., 1]; and this also means the triple substance in Christ, Who is our ladder, namely, the corporeal, the spiritual, and the divine.

Following this threefold progress, our mind has three principal aspects. One refers to the external body, wherefore it is called animality or sensuality; the second looks inward and into itself, wherefore it is called spirit; the third looks above itself, wherefore it is called mind. From all of which considerations it ought to be so disposed for ascending as a whole into God that it may love Him with all its mind, with all its heart, and with all its soul [Mark, 12, 30]. And in this consists both the perfect observance of the Law and Christian wisdom.

Since, however, all of the aforesaid modes are twofold—as when we consider God as the alpha and omega, or in so far as we happen to see God in one of the aforesaid modes as through a mirror and in a mirror, or as one of those considerations can be mixed with the other conjoined to it or may be considered alone in its purity—hence it is necessary that these three principal stages become sixfold, so that as God made the world in six days and rested on the seventh, so the microcosm by six successive stages of illumination is led in the most orderly fashion to the repose of contemplation. As a symbol of this we have the six steps to the throne of Solomon [III Kings, 10, 19]; the Seraphim whom Isaiah saw have six wings; after six days the Lord called Moses out of the midst of the cloud [Ex., 24, 16]; and Christ after six days, as is said in Matthew [17, 1], brought His disciples up into a mountain and was transfigured before them.

Therefore, according to the six stages of ascension into God, there are six stages of the soul's powers by which we mount from the depths to the heights, from the external to the internal, from the temporal to the eternal—to wit, sense, imagination, reason, intellect, intelligence, and the apex of the mind, the illumination of conscience (*Synteresis*). These stages are implanted in us by nature, deformed by sin, reformed by grace, to be purged by justice, exercised by knowledge, perfected by wisdom.

Now at the Creation, man was made fit for the repose of contemplation, and therefore God placed him in a paradise of delight [Gen., 2, 16]. But turning himself away from the true light to mutable goods, he was bent over by his own sin, and the whole human race by original sin, which doubly infected human nature, ignorance infecting man's mind and concupiscence his flesh. Hence man, blinded and bent, sits in the shadows and does not see the light of heaven unless grace with justice succor him from concupiscence, and knowledge with wisdom against ignorance. All of which is done through Jesus Christ, Who of God is made unto us wisdom and justice and sanctification and redemption [I Cor., 1, 30]. He is the virtue and wisdom of God, the Word incarnate, the author of grace and truth—that is, He has infused the grace of charity, which, since it is from a pure heart and good conscience and unfeigned faith, rectifies the whole soul in the threefold way mentioned above. He has taught the knowledge of the truth according to the triple mode of theology—that is, the symbolic, the literal, and the mystical—so that by the symbolic we may make proper use of sensible things, by the literal we may properly use the intelligible, and by the mystical we may be carried aloft to supermental levels.

*   *   *

If you wish then to contemplate the invisible traits of God in so far as they belong to the unity of His essence, fix your gaze upon Being itself, and see that Being is most certain in itself; for it cannot be thought not to be, since the purest Being occurs only in full flight from Non-Being, just as nothingness is in full flight from Being. Therefore, just as the utterly nothing contains nought of Being nor of its conditions, so contrariwise Being itself contains no Non-Being, neither in actuality nor in potency, neither in matters of fact nor in our thinking. Since, however, Non-Being is the privation of Being, it cannot enter the intellect except through Being; Being, however, cannot enter through anything other than itself. For everything which is thought of is either thought of as Non-Being or as Being-in-potency or as Being-in-actuality. If, therefore, Non-Being is intelligible only through Being, and if Being-in-potency can be understood only through Being-in-actuality, and if Being is the name of that pure actuality of Being, Being then is what first enters the intellect, and that Being is pure actuality. But this is not particular Being, which is restricted Being, since that is mixed with potentiality. Nor is this analogous Being, for such has a minimum of actuality since it has only a minimum of being. It remains, therefore that that Being is divine Being.

Marvelous then is the blindness of the intellect which does not consider that which is its primary object and without which it can know nothing. But just as the eye intent upon the various differences of the colors does not see the light by which it sees the other things and, if it sees it, does not notice it, so the mind's eye, intent upon particular and universal beings, does not notice Being itself, which is beyond all genera, though that comes first before the mind and through it all other things. Wherefore it seems very true that just as the bat's eye behaves in the light, so the eye of the mind behaves before the most obvious things of nature. Because accustomed to the shadows of beings and the phantasms of the sensible world, when it looks upon the light of the highest Being, it seems to see nothing, not understanding that darkness itself is the fullest illumination of the mind [Ps., 138, 11], just as when the eye sees pure light it seems to itself to be seeing nothing.

See then purest Being itself, if you can, and you will understand that it cannot be thought of as derivative from another. And thus necessarily that must be thought of as absolutely primal which can be derivative neither from nothing nor from anything. For what exists through itself if Being does not exist through itself and of itself? You will understand that, lacking Non-Being in every respect and therefore having no beginning nor end, it is eternal. You will understand also that it contains nothing in itself save Being itself, for it is in no way composite, but is most simple. You will understand that it has no potentialities within it, since every possible has in some way something of Non-Being, but Being is the highest actuality. You will understand that it has no defect, for it is most perfect. Finally, you will understand that it has no diversity, for it is One in the highest degree.

Being, therefore, which is pure Being and most simply Being and absolutely Being, is Being primary, eternal, most simple, most actual, most perfect, and one to the highest degree.

And these things are so certain that Being itself cannot be thought of by an intellect as opposed to these, and one of these traits implies the others. For since it is simply Being, therefore it is simply primary; because it is simply primary, therefore it is not made from another nor from itself, and therefore it is eternal. Likewise, since it is primary and eternal, and therefore not from others, it is therefore most simple.

Furthermore, since it is primary, eternal, and most simple, therefore it contains no potentiality mixed with actuality, and therefore it is most actual. Likewise, since it is primary, eternal, most simple, most actual, it is most perfect. To such a Being nothing is lacking, nor can anything be added. Since it is primary, eternal, most simple, most actual, most perfect, it is therefore one to the highest degree. For what is predicated because of its utter superabundance is applicable to all things. For what is simply predicated because of superabundance cannot possibly be applied to anything but the one. Wherefore, if God is the name of the primary, eternal, most simple, most actual, most perfect Being, it is impossible that He be thought of as not being nor as anything save One alone. "Hear, O Israel, the Lord our God is one God." If you see this in the pure simplicity of your mind, you will somehow be infused with the illumination of eternal light.

But you have ground for rising in wonder. For Being itself is first and last, is eternal and yet most present, is simplest and greatest, is most actual and immutable, is perfect and immense, is most highly one and yet all-inclusive. If you wonder over these things with a pure mind, while you look further, you will be infused with a greater light, until you finally see that Being is last because it is first. For since it is first, it produces all things for its own sake alone; and therefore it must be the very end, the beginning and the consumation, the alpha and the omega. Therefore it is most present because it is eternal. For since it is eternal, it does not come from another; nor does it cease to be nor pass from one thing to another, and therefore has no past nor future but only present being. Therefore it is greatest because most simple. For since it is most simple in essence, therefore it is greatest in power; because power, the more greatly it is unified, the closer it is to the infinite. Therefore it is most immutable, because most actual. For that which is most actual is therefore pure act. And as such it acquires nothing new nor does it lose what it had, and therefore cannot be changed. Therefore it is most immense, because most perfect. For since it is most perfect, nothing can be thought of which is better, nobler, or more worthy. And on this account there is nothing greater. And every such thing is immense. Therefore it is all-inclusive (omnimodal), because it is one to the highest degree. For that which is one to the highest degree is the universal source of all multiplicity. And for this reason it is the universal efficient cause of all things, the exemplary and the final cause, as the cause of Being, the principle of intelligibility, the order of living. And therefore it is all-inclusive, not as the essence of all things, but as the superexcellent and most universal and most sufficient cause of all essences, whose power, because most highly unified in essence, is therefore most highly infinite and most fertile in efficacy.

Recapitulating, let us say: Because, then, Being is most pure and absolute, that which is Being simply is first and last and, therefore, the origin and the final cause of all. Because eternal and most present, therefore it encompasses and penetrates all duration, existing at once as their center and circumference. Because most simple and greatest, therefore it is entirely within and entirely without all things and, therefore, is an intelligible sphere whose center is everywhere and whose circumference nowhere. Because most actual and most immutable, then "remaining stable it causes the universe to move" [Boethius, Cons. III, met. 9]. Because most perfect and immense, therefore within all, though not included in them; beyond all, but not excluded from them; above all, but not transported beyond them; below all, and yet not cast down beneath them. Because most highly one and all-inclusive, therefore all in all, although all things are many and it is only one. And this is so since through most simple unity, clearest truth, and most sincere goodness there is in it all power, all exemplary causality, and all communicability. And therefore from it and by it and in it are all things. And this is so since it is omnipotent, omniscient, and all-good. And to see this perfectly is to be blessed. As was said to Moses, "I will show thee all good" [Exod. 33, 19].

Mechthild of Magdeburg

(1210–1297)

The highly charged and often emotional atmosphere of Medieval piety is reflected in the literary outpourings of many of the mystics. This is especially true of Mechthild of Magdeburg, an ardent and romantic writer whose intensely personal version of the mystic experience has come down to us as a collection of visions, thoughts, and letters in prose and verse entitled *The Flowing Light of the Godhead*.

Mechthild can be numbered among the group of mystics in the Christian tradition—whose interior reception of God manifested itself in images, in highly dramatic and meaningful visions that communicated profound truths about the human soul, the love relationship between the soul and God, or the very nature of God Himself. Mechthild's visions are marked by their romanticism. She was a poetess of no mean talent, and her descriptions of the mystic process owe less to theology or the influence of other writers on the spiritual life than to the literary conventions of her day: the language of courtly love and the style of the minnesingers. In her hands the love song chanted by the soul and its God, so much a part of the fabric of Christian mysticism, might become a dramatized encounter between the soul-bride and the beautiful youth Christ. The events of the inner person assume the shapes and forms of theater pieces or take on the sensuous language of love letters.

Yet none of this should give one the impression that Mechthild was merely a woman of high imagination whose creative fantasies found a suitable subject in religious themes. This is far from the truth. She was a mystic to be taken seriously, and the spiritual insights communicated in *The Flowing Light of the Godhead* commend her as such. Obviously, at the core of her message is the fact of love: love of God for his creation and the love of the yearning soul for its God. Like so many love-mystics, she dwells constantly on the anguish the lover feels when deprived of the object of its love. No less passionately (though less systematically and with perhaps less psychological perceptiveness) than St. John of the Cross, this thirteenth-century religious writes of the "dark night" of the soul. Crying out for the fulfillment of its desire, the longing soul searches for union, passing through painful periods of purification that, if endured and trusted, can lead it nearer to its goal.

Despite the eroticism of her inner life, Mechthild emerges as something of a world-denying mystic. Her soul was, in her own perception, enchained by the fact of her own body, and her writings reveal that she conceived of a deep cleavage between the spiritual life and the life of the world. The intensity of her love for her bridegroom Christ held her, as it were, "imprisoned" and she felt herself unable to dwell anywhere but where that love dwelt. For her this dwelling place was essentially a spiritual realm. This bridegroom who held her captive she painted in colors evoking the immediacy of his humanity and the vividness of his sufferings. In doing this she was expressing the contemporary trend in spirituality, that of the mendicant orders—the Franciscans and the Dominicans—who were responsible for bringing a heightened sense of the humanity and passion of Christ into the popular devotion of the Church.

We do not know a great deal about the events of Mechthild's life.

What we do know we owe to the evidence found in her own book. Apparently born into the nobility of Saxony, and well educated, she had her first spiritual experience at the age of twelve. At twenty-three she renounced the world and began life anew as a Beguine, the lay sisterhood that lived a semireligious communal life without vows and whose aims were mainly philanthropic but included some practice of religious contemplation. Sometime later she changed her affiliation and became a Dominican tertiary. Mechthild was deeply drawn to the image of Christian perfection and so undertook a rigorous regimen of austerities, subjecting her body to mortification and striving for inner detachment.

At the same time she felt compelled to speak out against the religious laxity and materialism of the contemporary Church. Like several other of the greatest of mystics (Catherine of Siena, Hildegarde of Bingen, and Teresa of Avila), Mechthild took up the banner of reform. However, her outcries met with only persecution and mistrust. Part of this reaction can certainly be attributed to the fact that reforms are rarely met with open arms by those whom they most roundly criticize. Yet another part of Mechthild's difficulties stemmed not from her stance as reformer but from her role as author. Feeling deeply that her book had divine origins, she resisted the censure of those who found it suspect. It came under fire particularly because of some of the unorthodox doctrinal assumptions that lay just below the poetic surface of her words. Theology was not one her strong points, and she was criticized for this. Indeed at one point she was even threatened with excommunication. Seeking refuge in the Cistercian convent at Helfta in Thuringia in 1270, she continued work on what she felt to be her divinely inspired book. The remarkable community of women at Helfta was at the time a center of mystical activity under the influence of two visionaries, Mechthild of Helfta and Gertrude the Great, who did much to popularize devotion to the Sacred Heart of Jesus. There Mechthild found the frankly feminine atmosphere of loving and often sentimental adoration of God in keeping with her own temperament. She resided at Helfta for the remaining seventeen years of her life.

The Flowing Light of the Godhead

**How the Bride who is united with God refuses all creaturely
comfort and accepts it of God alone; how she sinks under suffering.**

Thus speaks the Bride of God who has dwelt in the enclosed sanctuary
of the Holy Trinity—"Away from me all ye creatures! Ye pain me and
cannot comfort me!" And the creatures ask, "Why?" The Bride says,
"My Love has left me while I rested beside him and slept." But the
creatures ask, "Can this beautiful world and all your blessings not
comfort you?" "Nay," says the Bride, "I see the serpent of falsehood
and false wisdom creeping in to all the joy of this world. I see also the
hook of covetousness in the bait of ignoble sweetness by which it
ensnares many."

"Can even the Kingdom of Heaven not comfort you?" ask the
creatures. "Nay! it were dead in itself were the living God not there!"
"Now, O Bride, can the saints not comfort thee?"

"Nay! for were they separated from the living Godhead which flows
through them, they would weep more bitterly than I for they have risen
higher than I and live more deeply in God."

"Can the Son of God not comfort thee?"
Yea! I ask Him when we shall go
Into the flowery meadows of heavenly knowledge
And pray Him fervently,
That He unlock for me
The swirling flood which plays about the Holy Trinity,
For the soul lives on that alone.
   If I am to be comforted
According to the merit to which God has raised me,
Then His breath must draw me effortlessly into Himself.
For the sun which plays upon the living Godhead
Irradiates the clear waters of a joyful humanity;
And the sweet desire of the Holy Spirit
Comes to us from both. . . .
Nothing can satisfy me save God alone,
Without Him I am as dead.
Yet would I gladly sacrifice the Joy of His presence

The Revelations of Mechthild of Magdeburg, or *The Flowing Light of the
Godhead,* trans. Lucy Menzies (London: Longmans, Green, and Company, 1953).
pp. 104-108, 192-93, 28-31. Reprinted by permission of Lucy Menzies' Executors.
Footnotes have been omitted.

Could He be greatly honoured thereby.
For if I, unworthy, cannot praise God with all my might,
Then I send all creatures to the Court of Heaven
And bid them praise God for me,
With all their wisdom, their love,
Their beauty; all their desires,
As they were created, sinless by God,
To sing with all the sweetness of their voices
As they now sing.
Could I but witness this praise
I would sorrow no more.

Neither can I bear that a single consolation be given me save by Love alone. I love my earthly friends in a heavenly fellowship and I love my enemies with a holy longing for their salvation. God has enough of all good things save of intercourse with the soul; of that He can never have enough.

When this wonder and this consolation had continued for eight years God wished to comfort me more mightily, far above my deserts. "Nay, dear Lord! do not raise me up too high!" cried this unworthy soul. "It is even now too much for me here in the lowest place. Gladly will I stay here to Thy honour." Then the soul fell down below the ill-fated souls who had forfeited their reward, and it seemed good to her so. There our Lord followed her as some others also did, who, so far as they could bear it, had gone to the state of least joy. For God appeared to them all beautiful and glorious, according as they had here been sanctified in love and ennobled in virtue. St. John says, "We shall see God as He is." (1 St. John, iii. 2.) That is true, but the sun shines after the storm and there are many kinds of storms in this world, just as there are many mansions in Heaven. According as I can bear it and see it, so is it with me.

Then our Lord said: "How long wouldst thou stay here?" The Bride answered: "Ah! leave me dear Lord and let me sink further down, to Thy Glory!" Then soul and body came into such gross darkness that I lost light and consciousness and knew no more of God's intimacy; ever-blessed Love also went its way. Then the soul spoke: "Constancy! where art thou? I entrust to thee the mission of love; thou shalt uphold the glory of God in me!" Then this servitor Constancy strengthened her mistress with such holy patience and joyful forbearance that she lived without care. But Unbelief came and surrounded me with such dark-ness and roared at me in such fury that his voice frightened me and I said to myself, "If thy former grace had been from God He would not so utterly have forsaken thee!"

Then my soul cried: "Where art thou now, O Constancy? Bid true Faith to come to me!" And the heavenly Father spoke to the soul: "Remember what thou didst see and experience when there was nothing between Me and thee!" Then spoke the Son: "Remember what thy body has suffered for My pain." And the Holy Spirit said: "Remember what thou hast written!" Then both soul and body answered with the true faith of Constancy: "As I have praised and loved, enjoyed and known, thus will I go unchanged from here!"

After this came the state of Forsaken-ness of God and so surrounded the soul that it cried: "Welcome blessed Forsaken-ness! Well for me that I was born and that thou, Constancy, shalt now be my waiting-maid, for thou bringest me unaccustomed joy and inconceivable wonders and sweetness beyond what I can bear. But, Lord, Thou must take this sweetness from me and leave me only Forsaken-ness. Well for me, O faithful Lord, that after the transformation of love I can yet bear it in the palate of my soul."

And here I asked all creatures to praise our Lord in the *Te Deum Laudamus*. But they would not and turned their backs on me. Then my soul was glad and said: "Well for me that ye despise me and turn your backs on me, for that praises our Lord immeasurably!"

Now is God marvellous to me and his Forsaken-ness better even than Himself. That the soul knew full well. For as God was about to comfort her she said: "Remember, O Lord, how lowly I am and withhold Thyself from me!" Then our Lord spoke to me: "Grant me that I may cool the glow of My Godhead, the desire of My humanity and the delight of My Holy Spirit in thee." The soul answered: "Yea, Lord, but only if that is well for Thee alone—and not for me!"

After that the Bride came into such great darkess that sweat and cramp racked her body. She was asked by some if she would be a messenger from them to God. She said: "Pain! I command thee that thou now release me, seeing that thou hast reached thy highest power in me." Then Pain rose from soul and body like a dark cloud and went to God and cried with a loud voice: "Lord! Thou knowest well what I desire!" Our Lord met Pain before the gate of the Kingdom and said: "Welcome, Pain! Thou art the garment I wore on my body upon earth: the contempt of the whole world was My most glorious cloak. But however much I prized thee there, thou canst not enter here. But to the maid who will do two things I will give two things. She must be modest and wise and it would help her if thou wouldst be her messenger; then will I embrace her and take her to my heart in union." Pain spoke thus: "Lord! I make many holy, though I myself am not holy and I nourish many holy bodies though I myself am evil, and I bring many to Heaven, though I may never enter in myself." To this our Lord answered: "Pain! thou wast not born in Heaven, therefore canst thou not enter therein. Moreover, thou wast born out of Lucifer's heart, there thou must return and live for evermore."

Ah! blessed Forsaken-ness of God, how lovingly I am bound to thee! Thou strengthenest my will in suffering and makest dear to me the long difficult waiting in this poor body. The nearer I come to thee, the greater and more wonderful God appears to me. Ah! Lord! even in the depths of unmixed humility, I cannot sink utterly away from Thee—

In pride I so easily lost Thee—
But now the more deeply I sink
The more sweetly I drink
Of Thee!

* * *

Of ten characteristics of the Divine Fire and of the nobility of God.

An unworthy creature thought simply about the nobility of God. Then God showed him in his senses and the eyes of his soul, a Fire which burned ceaselessly in the heights above all things. It had burned without beginning and would burn without end. This Fire is the everlasting God Who has retained in Himself Eternal Life from which all things proceed. The sparks which have blown away from the Fire are the holy angels. The beams of the Fire are the saints of God for their lives cast many lovely lights on Christianity. The coals of the Fire still glow; they are the just who here burn in heavenly love and enlighten by their good example: as they were chilled by sin they now warm themselves at the glowing coals. The crackling sparks which are reduced to ashes and come to nothing are the bodies of the blessed, who in the grave will await their heavenly reward. The Lord of the Fire is still to come, Jesus Christ to whom the Father entrusted the first Redemption and the last Judgment. On the Last Day He shall make a glorious chalice for the heavenly Father out of the sparks of the Fire; from this chalice the Father will on the day of His Eternal Marriage drink all the holiness which, with His Beloved Son, He has poured into our souls and our human senses.

Yea! I shall drink from thee
And Thou shalt drink from me
All the good God has preserved in us.
Blessed is he who is so firmly established here

That he may never spill out
What God has poured into him.

The smoke of the Fire is made of all earthly things which man uses
with wrongful delight. However beautiful to our eyes, however pleasant to our hearts, they yet carry in them much hidden bitterness. For
they disappear as smoke and blind the eyes of the highest, till the tears
run.

The comfort of the Fire is the joy our souls receive inwardly from
God, with such holy warmth from the Divine Fire, that we too burn
with it and are so sustained by virtues that we are not extinguished. The
bitterness of the Fire is the word God shall speak on the Last Day,
Depart from Me ye cursed into everlasting fire! (St. Matthew, xxv. 41).
The radiance of the Fire is the glowing aspect of the Divine countenance of the Holy Trinity, which shall so illumine our souls and bodies
that we may then see and recognize the marvellous blessedness we
cannot even name here.

These things have come out of the Fire and flow into it again
according to God's ordinance in everlasting praise.

Wouldst thou know my meaning?
Lie down in the Fire
See and taste the Flowing
Godhead through thy being;
Feel the Holy Spirit
Moving and compelling
Thee within the Flowing
Fire and Light of God.

Angela of Foligno

(1248–1309)

One of the outgrowths of the Franciscan movement was the development of a "third order." The first order consisted of the male followers
of Francis, who were vowed to a life of rigorous poverty, chastity, and
obedience; and the second order, of his female followers, vowed to an
equally rigorous but cloistered life. The third order, or tertiaries, was

instituted for lay persons and was originally intended to offer religiously minded individuals a simple devotional routine that could be carried out in their own homes. It was also to afford them the opportunity of associating with like-minded persons under the inspiration of Francis and the auspices of the Franciscan order. Typically tertiaries lived either in the world or in a community and observed a modified set of rules in accordance with the Spirit of their patron order. They were not bound by vow but made a solemn promise to strive for Christian perfection. The third order attracted a great wealth of religious talent and produced a number of important figures in the history of the Western contemplative tradition. Among these was Angela of Foligno, a woman little known today yet recognized as one of the Church's foremost spiritual writers not only in her own time but of the seventeenth and eighteenth centuries.

An intriguing personality, Angela was one of those contemplatives destined to struggle against great inner obstacles before attaining a deep and abiding union with God. Born into a prosperous Umbrian family, she married young and had a number of children. According to her own account, she lived not only a worldly but an immoral life until the time of her conversion, which appears to have occurred around her thirtieth year. This conversion did not signal an abrupt change in her life. Rather it marked the beginning of a long period of self-discovery and deepening awareness of the nature of God. She refers to this as the period of her penitence and temptations, her orderly account of which stands as one of the classic statements in contemplative literature of the inward flowering of mystical awareness. During this period both her husband and children died and she found herself free to devote herself to the pursuit of God. Having already become a member of the third order of Francis, she seems to have joined with several other tertiaries in a life of complete poverty and dedication to prayer. By the year 1284 she had become known and respected as a spiritual teacher, attracting to herself such young aspirants as Ubertino da Casale, who was later to become one of the luminaries of the "spiritual" wing of the Franciscan movement.

Between her conversion and her emergence as a spiritual figure of repute, Angela underwent severe trials. Her strong will, self-indulgence, and prideful nature appear to have been a constant source of suffering for her. Like so many other writers of the tradition, she recognized that the gravest obstacles to spiritual growth were not to be found outside the self, but within. She saw that the emergence of a rich interior poverty and deep humility was not realizable until the limited nature of the individual personality was viewed in the light of the infinite goodness and greatness of God. Once this recognition was made, a truer evaluation of the self's relationship both to God and to other individuals was possible.

So deep was her conviction that only through knowledge of self and God could one make spiritual progress, and so fully explored was this conviction in her own life, that Angela found herself encircled by a group of tertiaries of both sexes and regarded as a source of counsel. Sometime after 1290 she seems to have formed a sisterhood in her native town of Foligno. For these, her "spiritual children," who took the three vows of religion but pursued uncloistered lives of service to the sick and needy, she was example and guide until her death.

The teachings that aroused so much admiration among her contemporaries can be found in the book *The Divine Consolations of the Blessed Angela of Foligno*. They are teachings that, while not unfamiliar in the annals of contemplative literature, nonetheless have a particularly "Franciscan" tone. Franciscan spirituality lays great stress on the human person of Jesus, seeing in the Gospel narratives of His life and passion the supreme exemplar of the realization of divinity in human life. Rather than emphasizing the majesty of Christ, His kingship or role as judge of mankind, Franciscan devotion turns toward the Christ-child in the manger, the teaching Jesus who walked in poverty along the roads of Galilee, and the man of sorrows who was crucified. This is evident in Angela of Foligno. She, like Francis, focuses on the image of the Passion as the primary model for inner development. In the selection reprinted here she dwells on that symbol and explores its potential as a mediator of spiritual truth.

Closely linked to the image of the Crucified is the image of the poor Christ. Poverty, both in terms of material possessions and of an interior disposition, is at the heart of Franciscan spirituality. The radical stripping-away required of the contemplative is envisioned in terms of poverty and informed by the example of the impoverished Christ who walked among the poorest of the poor and who died naked and seemingly abandoned upon a cross. Angela had deep insight into the spiritual significance of poverty. She sought inner freedom through relinquishing both interior and exterior possessions. Only in imitation of the impoverished Christ, she believed, could one come close to the experience of God as it had been manifested on earth.

This emphasis on the value of poverty in Franciscan spirituality is neither morbid nor world-negating. Instead, the religious genius of Francis is manifested in the fact that, for him, suffering and self-denial were paradoxically linked to the experience of intense joy. Deeply sensitive to the natural world that he was a part of, Francis lived a life that was a hymn to the intrinsic worth and magnificence of creation. In the mystery of poverty he discovered this worth. For only in recognizing the truth that humankind does not own and does not possess can the gift of life be appreciated. Humankind's total dependence on the grace of God is heightened in the vision of Francis, heightened and fulfilled by the realization that His grace is present and that the astounding fact of creation can become the occasion for exquisite gratitude and joy.

The Divine Consolations of the Blessed Angela of Foligno

Of the book of life, which is Christ, wherein man learneth to know God and man, himself, and all things needful for man's welfare.

Ye must know, therefore, that this Book of Life is naught else save Jesus Christ, the Son of God, who is the Incarnate Word and the Wisdom of the Father, and He appeared amongst us in order that we might be instructed by means of His life, His death, and His teaching. For which reason it behoveth us to see what was the manner of life and conversation which He did practise whiles He did dwell within this mortal body.

His life is an ensample and a pattern for every mortal who desireth to be saved. But His life was naught save a most bitter penance, which did ever accompany Him throughout His mortal life, so that from the hour wherein the soul of Christ was created and placed in His most holy body within the womb of the Virgin undefiled, until that last most holy hour wherein His soul departed from His body by cruel death upon the Cross, He was never without this companionship of penance. But it was not thus with the other saints, nor with the apostles nor the Blessed Virgin.

The companions which God the Father in the Highest did in His most wise dispensation give unto His Beloved Son in this world were these. Firstly, the most perfect, complete, and continual poverty; secondly, the most perfect, complete, and continual contempt; thirdly, the utmost suffering. These were the companions who did accompany

The Book of Divine Consolation of the Blessed Angela of Foligno, trans. Mary G. Steegmann (New York: Cooper Square Publication, 1966), pp. 31–63.

Christ during the whole of His life in order to furnish an ensample unto us, that we may choose, love and endure these same companions until we die. For this is the way whereby the soul must reach unto God, and other direct road is there none. Needful is it, therefore, and seemly that the members of the body should follow the same road which had been taken by the head, and that the same companions which had accompanied the head should likewise accompany the members.

*   *   *

Of the great poverty of Christ.

The first companion of Jesus Christ, the Book of Life and our salvation, was therefore, constant, supreme, and perfect poverty. This poverty was of three degrees: one was great, the second was yet greater and was joined with the first, but the third kind, joined with the first and the second, made up the most perfect poverty.

The first degree of this perfect poverty of Christ, who is the Book, the Way, and the Leader of the soul, was that He deigned to be poor in all temporal things of this world. Thus did He own neither land, nor vineyard, nor garden, nor other possessions; He had neither gold nor silver, nor money whatsoever, nor any other thing of His own, neither would He consent to accept of the things of this world aught save what did suffice to succour Him in the depths of His great poverty and supply the needs of His body, that is to say, hunger, thirst, and want, cold and heat, great weariness, austerity and hardship. Yet of bodily necessaries would He accept naught that was delicate or pleasant to the taste, but only coarse and common food such as was found in those places and provinces wherein Christ did live as liveth a beggar, without house or habitation.

The second degree of Christ's poverty was greater than the first, seeing that He did desire to be poor in friends and kindred and in all familiarity with the great and powerful, and finally in all worldly friendship. Wherefore did He not possess, nor desire to possess, any friend whatsoever of His own, nor yet of His mother or His putative father Joseph, or His disciples. For this reason did none hesitate to kick Him, strike Him, and scourge Him, and to speak hurtful words unto Him. And He deigned to be born of a poor and humble mother and to be brought up subject unto a poor carpenter, His putative father. He did likewise deprive Himself of the love and familiar intercourse of kings and rulers, of priests and scribes, and of the love of friends and kindred—so that neither for His mother's sake, nor for any other person, would He leave undone aught the which could be pleasing unto His Almighty Father or according unto His will. Amen.

How Christ revealed Himself poor in power.

The third and supreme degree of poverty was that He did put away from Him His own nature. Firstly, because He made Himself poor and needy, laying aside His own power, He, the Omnipotent, unto whom naught was impossible, desired to appear and to live in the world as a man, weak, infirm, and impotent, in order that beside the human miseries, the helpless childhood and other burdens which He did take upon Himself for our sake, He who was without blame or sin might appear as but a feeble man. Verily He endured much weariness in His journeyings, visitations, and disgrace.

How Christ laid aside His wisdom and His own nature.

. . . . He did lay aside His own nature, making Himself poor in wisdom because He desired to appear as a simple man, one senseless and vain in the sight of men. He appeared not as a philosopher or a doctor of many words, or as one who disputeth noisily, nor yet as a scribe renowned for wisdom and learning; but in the utmost simplicity did He talk with men, showing unto them the way of truth in His life, His virtues, and His miracles. Seeing how that He is the Wisdom of the Father, the Creator and Inspirer of all learning, He might have used all the subtilty of knowledge and of argument, and, had He desired, He might have shown forth His wit and obtained glory; but with such simplicity did He declare the truth that He was esteemed of almost all people to be not only simple and foolish, but even ignorant and vain. Herein did He show unto us the way of truth, that is to say, that neither in learning nor in wisdom should we take glory unto ourselves, for being puffed up with this pride we seek to obtain the name of master before men and to cover ourselves with vain glory. . . .

And He, the King of kings, did say before Pilate that His kingdom was not of this world. He sought not after the kingdom of this world or the temporal lordship over men, but was ever willing to be in subjection; not to be lord or king or prince, but the most humble servant, casting Himself entirely aside. Moreover, He was subject unto His most poor and humble Mother and His putative father, obedient unto them and humbly serving them until His thirtieth year. He was obedient in the midst of His disciples, who were few in number, ignorant, and poor, and albeit He did choose to be as a king or ruler over them, He said that He was not to come to be ministered unto, but to minister unto them, even unto the rendering up of His spirit for them and for the other sinners who were to be redeemed. Yea, He, the Head and Master of those disciples, did suffer hunger and thirst and tribulation; for He was not their Master in order that He might be set above them, but that He might be the first amongst them to suffer affliction and be cast down; and so humble was His intercourse with them that He did minister unto them as they sat at meat, even washing their hands and their feet.

Alas, how great is our folly! The mighty Lord and King of kings was despised and rejected of men, but we do ever seek to be exalted and preferred, and to live in liberty, free from all yoke whatsoever. Neither doth His love constrain us to be the subject and obedient unto any person, but we do always desire to be set above the others. Not thus, not thus, oh Christ, didst Thou act, for Thou knewest that the judgment would be hard exceedingly, for those in authority and power will suffer great torments, and of their lives, their deeds, their sins, and of those in subjection unto them will they be required to render the most strict account.

Thus will our pride be confounded by the Book of Life, who is Himself an ensample. And we do desire to subject ourselves unto those set in authority over us (as He hath ever done), not doing aught according unto our own will, but submitting for love of Him who submitted unto all things for our sake. And for our safety will we not only endure the state of subjection, but, fleeing from all preferment, we will seek with whole hearts and fervent desire to be in subjection and an humble state.

Such, then, was the supreme, constant, and perfect poverty of Jesus Christ our Saviour, who, albeit He was Lord of all riches, did nevertheless choose to be poor amongst us, that He might teach us the love of poverty. And verily He was poor in possessions, in will and in spirit, beyond man's comprehension, and all for the deep love wherewith He loved us. He was poor in riches and needy of all worldly things; He was poor in friends and power, poor in worldy wisdom, in the fame of holiness and in all dignities. And finally, being poor in all things, He preached poverty and said that the poor were blessed and should judge the world. Upon the other hand He did condemn the wealthy and their riches and abundance, saying that they deserve condemnation. He did preach this in deed and by word of mouth and by example, with all His might.

4. The Mystic Flowering
of Fourteenth Century England

Richard Rolle

(1300–1349)

Richard Rolle is recognized as the founder of the English mystical tradition, a tradition that includes such contemplative writers as Walter Hilton, Julian of Norwich, and the author of *The Cloud of Unknowing*. Rolle entered upon the comtemplative life in a rather extraordinary manner. After studying at Oxford University for seven years and conducting his studies in a competent way, he decided, at the age of nineteen, to leave. Declaring his disappointment with the "disputatiousness" of the academic milieu, he exerted his independence and returned to his home in Yorkshire. There, after making the announcement and explaining his decision to his family, he ran away from home to become a hermit. Making a hermit's habit out of two frocks his sister had provided for him, together with his father's raincoat, he entered upon the solitary life in a makeshift manner. His decision was accompanied by the manifestation of certain unusual psychic abilities including an ability to speak and write in different sentences at the same time.

Throughout his hermit life, he traveled from place to place, wandering here and there, finding shelter where he could. He seems to have been in touch with a number of religious communities, and for awhile was spiritual adviser to a community of nuns at Hampole in south Yorkshire.

His temperament was marked by a clear, definite, and resolute ascetic bent, the intrinsic austerity of which was mitigated by some apparent English common sense. He believed in fasting and took abstinence seriously; yet he could also relax the rules when he wanted to. Not attached by vows to any religious order or community, entirely independent as a hermit, he seems at times to be unclear about what was expected of him. As a hermit, he was a distinctly free spirit.

He depicted the presence of God within in terms of interior heat, warmth, or fire. The same presence was experienced as love, a love that is depicted as silent fire. For example, on one occasion Richard said, "I could feel in my heart the warmth of eternal love." He referred to God as "the Beloved," and in expressing how it happens that "the soul rises up with intense delight to her Beloved, he wrote: "The purer the love of the lover, the closer is God's presence to him, the purer his rejoicing."

Rolle was also fascinated with the subject of angels, which he recognized not simply because they belong to a higher or transcendent place but because of their association with music. He referred on occasion to being caught up to "the heights of contemplation and to the source of angels' praise. The angels contemplate divine things, reflect the splendor of God, and shine from the light from the face of God." In mystical experience, he attested, one sometimes experiences the divine music within. Such music is a symbol of cosmic harmony. It illustrates that the several layers or dimensions of the cosmos are integrated. Rolle avowed that the interior singing is in the same key as the music of the spheres.

The Fire of Love

I cannot tell you how surprised I was the first time I felt my heart begin to warm. It was real warmth too, not imaginary, and it felt as if it were actually on fire. I was astonished at the way the heat surged up and how this new sensation brought great and unexpected comfort. I had to keep feeling my breast to make sure there was no physical reason for it! But once I realized that it came entirely from within, that this fire of love had no cause, material or sinful, but was the gift of my Maker, I

Richard Rolle, *The Fire of Love*, trans. Clifton Wolters (London: Penguin Books, 1972), pp. 45, 53–54, 76–7, 88–90, 97–8, 101.

was absolutely delighted and wanted my love to be even greater. And this longing was all the more urgent because of the delightful effect and the interior sweetness that this spiritual flame fed into my soul. Before the infusion of this comfort I had never thought that we exiles could possibly have known such warmth, so sweet was the devotion it kindled. It set my soul aglow as if a real fire were burning there.

Yet as some may well remind us, there are people on fire with love for Christ, for we can see how utterly they despise the world and how wholly they are given over to the service of God. If we put our finger near a fire, we feel the heat; in much the same way a soul on fire with love feels . . . a genuine warmth. Sometimes it is more, sometimes less; it depends on our particular capacity.

What mortal man could survive that heat at its peak—as we can know it, even here—if it persisted? He must inevitably wilt before the vastness and sweetness of love so ardent and heat so indescribable. Yet at the same time he is bound to long eagerly for just this to happen: to breathe his soul out, with all its superb endowment of mind, in this honeyed flame, and, quit of this world, be held in thrall with those who sing their Maker's praise.

*   *   *

Those contemplatives who are most on fire with the love of eternity are like those higher beings whose eagerness for eternal love is most enjoyable and outstanding. They never, or scarcely ever, engage in outside activity or accept the dignity of ecclesiastical preferment or rank. They tend to keep themselves to themselves, ever ready to reach up to Christ with joyful song. In this respect the Church is following the angelic hierarchy, for the supernal angels are not sent out on errands, but attend closely to God. Similarly the masters of contemplative love give themselves to the things of God, and not to lording it over people. Such matters are reserved for those more concerned for that kind of activity, but less interested in spiritual delight. . . . Each of God's chosen has his foreappointed place.

*   *   *

Since the human soul is capable of receiving God alone, nothing less than God can fill it; which explains why lovers of earthly things are never satisfied. The peace known by lovers of Christ comes from their heart being fixed, in longing and in thought, in the love of God; it is a peace that sings and loves and burns and contemplates. Very sweet indeed is the quiet that the spirit experiences. Music, divine and delectable, comes to rejoice it; the mind is rapt in sublime and gay melody and sings the delights of everlasting love. Now from human lips sounds forth again the praise of God; the praise, too, of the Blessed Virgin in whom he glories beyond measure. This need occasion no surprise, for the heart of the singer is altogether ablaze with heavenly fire. And he is transformed into the likeness of Him in Whom is all melody and song and is transported by loving desire for the taste of heaven. A man overflows with inner joy, and his very thought sings as he rejoices in the warmth of his love. . . . Moreover, when he has once had experience of that great thing . . . he knows that when it is missing he is never at ease, but is always pining for love. So he remains vigilant, and sings and thinks of his love and his Beloved—and if he is on his own, sings all the more blithely!

Once a person has known some such experience, he is never thereafter wholly without it, for there always remains a sort of glow, some song or sweetness, even if these are not all present together in equal strength. Yet all are present, unless illness catches him or he is gripped by intolerable hunger or thirst or held up by cold, heat, or travel. It behooves him then who would sing his love for God and rejoice fervently in such singing, to pass his days in solitude. Yet the abstinence in which he lives should not be excessive, nor on the other hand should he display too much extravagance. Better for him slightly to exceed the limit if it is done in ignorance and with the sound intention of sustaining the body than that he should falter by overstrict fasting and through physical weakness be unable to sing. . . .

*   *   *

All the while he is indifferent to worldly power, love dwells in the heart of the solitary. Herein is the foundation of his fervor and his longing for light, because he is tasting the things of heaven and singing his honeyed (not heavy!) song. He offers his praise to his noble Lover, like the seraphim, and since his loving mind is in tune with theirs, he says, "See how I burn in my love; how hungrily I long!" So is the lover's soul consumed with indescribable fire, shot through with that flame which gladdens and glitters with heavenly light. There is no end that I can discover to this fervor and happiness; and as I am always pressing on toward the object of my love, it means that death becomes sweet to me as well as sure.

Because for the sake of the Saviour the holy hermit has made solitude his home, in heaven he will receive a dwelling, golden and glistening, and in the midst of the angelic orders. Because for love of his Creator he dressed in filthy rags, his Maker will clothe him in eternal splendor. Because once he was prepared to live here with features wan and drawn, so now his countenance shines with wonderful glory. In exchange for his revolting garments, he will wear raiment glorious and resplendent with precious stones, forever in the midst of those who dwell in Paradise. Because he has purged himself from vices and avoided all ostentation and has done with all appearance of filth, his warm love for Almighty God has gained for him a song that is sweet and heavenly. The harmonies of those who praise divine charity have filled his mind, and rightly so. And thus it is with courage and not dread that he quits his exile here; and at the end of all, he hears angelic song and rises up, he who has loved so ardently; he is called up to that eternal hall, and honored in the most splendid fashion, to sit on high with the seraphim.

As far as my study of the Scriptures goes, I have found that to love Christ above all else will involve three things: warmth and song and sweetness. And these three, as I know from personal experience, cannot exist for long without there being great quiet. . . .

In these three things (which are the sign of love in its most perfect form) the utmost perfection of the Christian religion is undoubtedly found. I, by the grace of Jesus and to the limit of my meager capacity, have accepted them, yet I dare not equate myself with the saints who displayed them, because they understood such things so much more perfectly. However, let me press forward with all my strength so that my love becomes more fervent, my song more fluent, and my experience of love's sweetness all the fuller. For, my brothers, you are wrong if you suppose that people today cannot be as holy as the prophets and apostles were.

I call it *fervor* when the mind is truly ablaze with eternal love and the heart similarly feels itself burning with a love that is not imaginary but real. For a heart set on fire produces a feeling of fiery love.

I call it *song* when there is in the soul, overflowing and ardent, a sweet feeling of heavenly praise; when thought turns into song; when the mind is in thrall to sweetest harmony.

This twofold awareness is not achieved by doing nothing, but through the utmost devotion; and from these two there springs the third, for unspeakable *sweetness* is present too. Fervor and song bring marvelous delight to a soul, just as they themselves can be the product of very great sweetness.

*   *   *

In a truly loving mind there is always a song of glory and an inner flame of love. They surge up out of a clear conscience, out of an abundant spiritual joy, out of inward gladness. Small wonder if a love like this wins through to a perfect love. Love of this sort is immense in its fervor, its whole direction Godwards, totally unrestrained in its love for him.... There is no tension in the fervor, but there is vigor in this love; there is sweetness in this song, and a warmth about this radiance; his delight in God is irresistible; his contemplation rises with unimpeded ascent. Everything he conquers; everything he overcomes; nothing seems impossible to him. For while a man is striving to love Christ with all his might, he knows it to be true that within him is eternal life, abundant and sweet....

The nature of love is that it is diffusive, unifying, and transforming. It is diffusive when it flows out and sheds the rays of its goodness not merely on friends and neighbors, but on enemies and strangers as well. It unites because it makes lovers one in deed and will and draws into one Christ and every holy soul. He who holds onto God is one in spirit with him, not by nature, but by grace and identity of will. Love has also the power of transforming, for it transforms the lover into his Beloved and makes him dwell in him. Thus it happens that when the fire of the holy Spirit really gets hold of the heart, it sets it wholly on fire and, so to speak, turns it into flame, leading it into that state in which it is most like God. Otherwise it would not have been said, "I have said, 'You are gods; all of you are children of the Most High.'"

Julian of Norwich

(c. 1342–after 1413)

Of the life of Julian of Norwich we know little beyond what can be deduced from the hints contained in the two versions of her book *Revelations of Divine Love*. We know that at the time she composed the second version, she was a recluse whose anchorage was attached to a church in Norwich, England, under the auspices of a Benedictine community. But we do not know if she had yet embraced the solitary life at the time of the first version, when she was granted the vivid series of revelations that form the subject of her book. She writes that the revelations were given in 1373, when she had an illness thought to be fatal. Some years earlier she had apparently petitioned for the realization of three desires: to experience more deeply the passion of Christ, to suffer an intense illness while still relatively young, and to receive the three "wounds" of contrition, compassion, and ardent longing for God. The visions then, long after consciousness of them had faded in her memory, came as the realization of her prayer.

Whether or not she was a recluse at the time of the revelations still does not tell us whether Julian was ever even a professed member of the Benedictine community to which she was attached; for it was usual, though not necessary, for such persons to belong to a religious community. Further, there is nothing specifically Benedictine about her writing to indicate her exact status. Whatever the specifics, she was a recluse.

A few characteristics of the life style of such a person, not an uncommon phenomenon in Medieval England, are worth noting. While the impulse toward solitary enclosure has a long and venerable history within the Christian contemplative tradition, the usual imagery conjured up by the term "recluse" is of a lean, fiercely world-denying desert dweller whose ascetic feats or wrapt contemplation separate him or her body and soul not only from the sphere of ordinary men and women but from the ranks of the many monks and nuns whose lives are spent living out their commitments in the context of a community. Certainly the English recluses of Julian's time received their patrimony from these desert solitaries. Certainly, they venerated the virtues and utter commitment to the interior life that these men and women enshrined. But the actual shape that the life of withdrawal assumed on the English countryside differed as much from the lives of the desert fathers as the northern winter winds differ from the fiery summer skies of Egypt.

The solitary life in the Middle Ages could take various forms. One could be a hermit, a wandering solitary whose good works and vocation might change with the cirmcumstances and the surroundings. The one constant in the hermit's life was dedication to the life of prayer and surrender to the activity of God within the soul. Richard Rolle is an example of such a solitary. One could also be a recluse, a person shut away from normal social life by the act of enclosure. The term can be used as a synonym for an anchorite or anchoress, a person like Julian who was enclosed in his or her own "cell," which usually adjoined or was nearby a church or monastic community. Since an anchorite was generally enclosed for life, a commitment not lightly undertaken or regarded. The individual was vowed to a life of self-denial and prayer.

While reclusiveness was serious business and the emotional and spiritual austerity of such an undertaking is obvious, the physical demands on the solitary were neither extreme nor inhumane. The "cells" of such as Julian were often several rooms, might house more than one solitary, and could include room for a servant or two to take care of daily necessities and to attend to the inevitable contacts with the outside world. Some cells had a window opening into the church so that the individual could particpate in the liturgy. Other cells had a window through which the recluse might receive visitors who came for spiritual direction and advice. The only knowldedge we have of Julian besides her own writings is from the account of Margery Kempe, herself a woman subject to deep if somewhat hysterical interior activity, who wrote of visiting the aging anchoress to receive confirmation of her own visionary experiences. Julian's advice was wise and sane: she counseled her visitor to evaluate the veracity of her experiences by the fruit which they produced. If they moved one to charity, to chasteness, and to strengthened faith, they could be trusted to be from God.

Julian's own visionary revelations led her more deeply into the depths of her own interior life and into the mysteries of God. At the time of her grave illness fourteen visions were impressed upon her soul. Central to these is the unfolding meaning of the passion of Christ. Through this the love of God, which reaches down into the darkest recesses of human suffering and frailty, is shown. It is this infinite love that redeems the apparently unredeemable, that extends hope and strength not only to humankind as a whole but to the individual person. Julian was acutely aware of the greatness of the love that envelops the world, so aware that it can be claimed there is but one theme in her book: God's awesome love. The central theme is played over and over in different keys and variations. In the performance of this theme and variations the abbess' religious optimism is evident. The loving Godhead was revealed to her in distinctive images and phrases that expressed the divine intimacy and friendship that she felt. Most unusual of these images is that of God and/or Christ as a mother. The sweetness of maternal love flows from the Trinity, nurturing and protecting the creation that it has conceived and brought into being. Indeed, Julian was so filled with this sense of the maternal care issuing from the divine that she found it difficult to be reconciled to the very real facts of human sin and corruption. Nevertheless, she was a woman of rich and remarkable faith whose articulation of the overwhelming love of God for the world is one of the most vibrant and explicit in all mystical literature.

Revelations of Divine Love

When I was half way through my thirty-first year God sent me an ilness which prostrated me for three days and nights. On the fourth night I received the last rites of Holy Church as it was thought I could not survive till day. After this I lingered two more days and nights, and on the third night I was quite convinced that I was passing away—as indeed were those about me.

Since I was still young I thought it a great pity to die—not that there was anything on earth I wanted to live for, or on the other hand any pain that I was afraid of, for I trusted God and his mercy. But were I to live I might come to love God more and better, and so ultimately to know and love him more in the bliss of heaven. Yet compared with that eternal bliss the length of my earthly life was so insignificant and short that it seemed to me to be nothing. And so I thought, 'Good Lord, let my ceasing to live be to your glory!' Reason and suffering alike told me I was going to die, so I surrendered my will wholeheartedly to the will of God.

Thus I endured till day. By then my body was dead from the waist downwards, so far as I could tell. I asked if I might be helped and supported to sit up, so that my heart could be more freely at God's disposal, and that I might think of him while my life lasted.

My parish priest was sent for to be at my end, and by the time he came my eyes were fixed, and I could no longer speak. He set the cross before my face and said, 'I have brought you the image of your Maker and Saviour. Look at it, and be strengthened.'

I thought indeed that what I was doing was good enough, for my eyes were fixed heavenwards where by the mercy of God I trusted to go. But I agreed none the less to fix my eyes on the face of the crucifix if I could. And this I was able to do. I thought that perhaps I could look straight ahead longer than I could look up.

Then my sight began to fail, and the room became dark about me, as if it were night, except for the image of the cross which somehow was lighted up; but how was beyond my comprehension. Apart from the cross everything else seemed horrible as if it were occupied by fiends.

Then the rest of my body began to die, and I could hardly feel a

Julian of Norwich. Revelations of Divine Love, trans. Clifton Wolters (London: Penguin Books, 1961), pp. 63–66, 169–71. Footnotes have been omitted.

thing. As my breathing became shorter and shorter I knew for certain that I was passing away.

Suddenly all my pain was taken away, and I was as fit and well as I had ever been; and this was especially true of the lower part of my body. I was amazed at this sudden change, for I thought it must have been a special miracle of God, and not something natural. And though I felt so much more comfortable I still did not think I was going to survive. Not that this experience was any real comfort to me, for I was thinking I would much rather have been delivered from this world!

Then it came suddenly to mind that I should ask for the second wound of our Lord's gracious gift, that I might in my own body fully experience and understand his blessed passion. I wanted his pain to be my pain: a true compassion producing a longing for God. I was not wanting a physical vision or revelation of God, but such compassion as a soul would naturally have for our Lord Jesus, who for love became a mortal man. Therefore I desired to suffer with him.

*   *   *

And at once I saw the red blood trickling down from under the garland, hot, fresh, and plentiful, just as it did at the time of his passion when the crown of thorns was pressed on to the blessed head of God-and-Man, who suffered for me. And I had a strong, deep, conviction that it was he himself and none other that showed me this vision.

At the same moment the Trinity filled me full of heartfelt joy, and I knew that all eternity was like this for those who attain heaven. For the Trinity is God, and God the Trinity; the Trinity is our Maker and keeper, our eternal lover, joy and bliss—all through our Lord Jesus Christ. This was shown me in this first revelation, and, indeed, in them all; for where Jesus is spoken of, the blessed Trinity is always to be understood as I see it.

'*Benedicite Domine!*' I said, and I meant it in all reverence even though I said it at the top of my voice. I was overwhelmed with wonder that he, so holy and aweful, could be so friendly to a creature at once sinful and carnal. I took it that all this was to prepare me for a time of temptation, for I thought that by God's leave I was bound to be tempted by fiends before I died. With this sight of the blessed passion, and with my mental vision of the Godhead, I knew that there was strength enough for me and, indeed, for every living creature against every fiend of hell, and all temptation.

And then he brought our blessed Lady to mind. In my spirit I saw her as though she were physically present, a simple humble girl, still in her youth, and little more than a child. God showed me something of her

spiritual wisdom and honesty, and I understood her profound reverence when she saw her God and Maker; how reverently she marvelled
that he should be born of his own creature, and of one so simple. This
wisdom and honesty, which recognized the greatness of her Creator
and the smallness of her created self, moved her to say to Gabriel in
her utter humility, 'Behold the handmaid of the Lord!' By this I knew
for certain that in worth and grace she is above all that God made, save
the blessed humanity of Christ.

It was at this time that our Lord showed me spiritually how intimately
he loves us. I saw that he is everything that we know to be good and
helpful. In his love he clothes us, enfolds and embraces us; that tender
love completely surrounds us, never to leave us. As I saw it he is
everything that is good.

And he showed me more, a little thing, the size of a hazelnut, on the
palm of my hand, round like a ball. I looked at it thoughtfully and
wondered, 'What is this?' And the answer came, 'It is all that is made.' I
marvelled that it continued to exist and did not suddenly disintegrate; it
was so small. And again my mind supplied the answer, 'It exists, both
now and for ever, because God loves it.' In short, everything owes its
existence to the love of God.

In this 'little thing' I saw three truths. The first is that God made it;
the second is that God loves it; and the third is that God sustains it. But
what he is who is in truth Maker, Keeper, and Lover I cannot tell, for
until I am essentially united with him I can never have full rest or real
happiness; in other words, until I am so joined to him that there is
absolutely nothing between my God and me. We have got to realize the
littleness of creation and to see it for the nothing that it is before we can
love and possess God who is uncreated. This is the reason why we have
no ease of heart or soul, for we are seeking our rest in trivial things
which cannot satisfy, and not seeking to know God, almighty, all-wise,
all-good. He is true rest. It is his will that we should know him, and his
pleasure that we should rest in him. Nothing less will satisfy us. No soul
can rest until it is detached from all creation. When it is deliberately so
detached for love of him who is all then only can it experience spiritual
rest.

God showed me too the pleasure it gives him when a simple soul
comes to him, openly, sincerely and genuinely. It seems to me as I
ponder this revelation that when the Holy Spirit touches the soul it
longs for God rather like this; 'God, of your goodness give me yourself,
for you are sufficient for me. I cannot properly ask anything less, to be
worthy of you. If I were to ask less, I should always be in want. In you
alone do I have all.'

Such words are dear indeed to the soul, and very close to the will and goodness of God. For his goodness enfolds every one of his creatures and all his blessed works, eternally and surpassingly. For he himself is eternity, and has made us for himself alone, has restored us by his blessed passion, and keeps us in his blessed love. And all because he is goodness.

*   *   *

But now I must say a little more about this 'overflowing' as I understand its meaning: how we have been brought back again by the motherhood of mercy and grace to that natural condition which was ours originally when we were made through the motherhood of natural love—which love, indeed, has never left us.

Our Mother by nature and grace—for he would become our Mother in everything—laid the foundation of his work in the Virgin's womb with great and gentle condescension. (This was shown in the first revelation when I received a mental picture of the Virgin's genuine simplicity at the time she conceived.) In other words, it was in this lowly place that God most high, the supreme wisdom of all, adorned and arrayed himself with our poor flesh, ready to function and serve as Mother in all things.

A mother's is the most intimate, willing, and dependable of all services, because it is the truest of all. None has been able to fulfil it properly but Christ, and he alone can. We know that our own mother's bearing of us was a bearing to pain and death, but what does Jesus, our true Mother, do? Why, he, All-love, bears us to joy and eternal life! Blessings on him! Thus he carries us within himself in love. And he is in labour until the time has fully come for him to suffer the sharpest pangs and most appalling pain possible—and in the end he dies. And not even when this is over, and we ourselves have been born to eternal bliss, is his marvellous love completely satisfied. This he shows in that overwhelming word of love,

'If I could possibly have suffered more, indeed I would have done so.'

He might die no more, but that does not stop him working, for he needs to feed us . . . it is an obligation of his dear, motherly, love. The human mother will suckle her child with her own milk, but our beloved Mother, Jesus, feeds us with himself, and, with the most tender courtesy, does it by means of the Blessed Sacrament, the precious food of all true life. And he keeps us going through his mercy and grace by all the sacraments. This is what he meant when he said, 'It is I whom Holy Church preaches and teaches.' In other words, 'All the health and life of sacraments, all the virtue and grace of my word, all the goodness laid up for you in Holy Church—it is I.' The human mother may put her child tenderly to her breast, but our tender Mother Jesus simply leads us into his blessed breast through his open side, and there gives us a glimpse of the Godhead and heavenly joy—the inner certainty of eternal bliss. The tenth revelation showed this, and said as much with that word, 'See how I love you', as looking into his side he rejoiced.

This fine and lovely word Mother is so sweet and so much its own that it cannot properly be used of any but him, and of her who is his own true Mother—and ours. In essence *motherhood* means love and kindness, wisdom, knowledge, goodness. Though in comparison with our spiritual birth our physical birth is a small, unimportant, straightforward sort of thing, it still remains that it is only through his working that it can be done at all by his creatures. A kind, loving mother who understands and knows the needs of her child will look after it tenderly just because it is the nature of a mother to do so. As the child grows older she changes her methods—but not her love. Older still, she allows the child to be punished so that its faults are corrected and its virtues and graces developed. This way of doing things, with much else that is right and good, is our Lord at work in those who are doing them. Thus he is our Mother in nature, working by his grace in our lower part, for the sake of the higher. It is his will that we should know this, for he wants all our love to be fastened on himself. Like this I could see that our indebtedness, under God, to fatherhood and motherhood—whether it be human or divine—is fully met in truly loving God. And this blessed love Christ himself produces in us. This was shown in all the revelations, and especially in those splendid words that he uttered. 'It is I whom you love.'

Anonymous

(late 14th century),

The Cloud of Unknowing

This treatise by an anonymous English mystic of the late fourteenth century has come down to us as one of the classic pieces of literature on the practice of contemplative prayer. An eminently practical document,

The Cloud is expressly not addressed to those unfamiliar with interior prayer nor to the merely curious. Rather its message is for "those who feel the mysterious action of the Spirit in their inmost being stirring them to love. . . ." Not that these "continually feel this stirring, as experienced contemplatives do, but now and again they taste something of contemplative love in the very core of their being."

The Cloud is not an easy book to interpret, despite its readability, and its author, aware that the words might be misinterpreted, warns the reader to take the time to read it thoroughly. For this reason we have chosen to reproduce from the early part of the book several consecutive passages that are not easily misunderstood in the hope that you will feel moved to read further in this remarkable document.

We have no clear picture of the author of The Cloud either from the book itself or from contemporary sources. That the author springs from the fertile mystic soil of the fourteenth-century England, the century that produced so many gems of contemplative literature, we do know. But whether or not a member of a religious order, we do not know which one. There are virtually no autobiographical details tucked away in the pages of this book. Despite this we do know what was deepest and most central to his or her life. We do know the teachings on the art of contemplative prayer and the advice to the young aspirant to the interior life.

That advice is of a supremely practical nature and is supported by the wisdom of a tradition that is as old as Christianity itself. Much of what The Cloud teaches is also found in John of the Cross, Jan van Ruysbroeck, and John Tauler and is reminiscent of such luminaries of Christian prayer as Augustine and Richard of St. Victor. Most distinctively it recalls the tone of that master of the path of darkness to the divine, Pseudo-Dionysius. Yet, while firmly entrenched in this broader tradition, The Cloud is much more than a mere repetition or compilation of other sources. It is a distinctive, masterfully wrought whole that reflects the wisdom and sensitivity of a profound personal experience and that is fairly unusual among books on mysticism, being neither a recounting of that experience nor a poetic outpouring resulting from that experience. Rather it is a guide to the seeker at a particular point on the journey through the shadows of the inner world.

That particular point is the "passageway" into contemplative prayer. The author assumes that the reader is well practiced in both vocal and mental prayer, has acquired a fairly high degree of detachment from the bonds of the world, is living a life governed by the teachings and sacraments of the established Church, and is serious about giving the self up fully to the life of God within. The confused stirrings of love and the experience of silence and spiritual isolation that may confront such a person at this time are bewildering, and the English mystic is there to serve as guide. The author surveys the landscape ahead and points to the path of negation, to the path that deliberately eschews any conceptualization in prayer. All one's thoughts and images must be abandoned, and one must stand as a naked act of love before God. Thus one is, as it were, suspended between two clouds: the cloud of forgetting that separates the individual from all other creatures, and the cloud of unknowing that stands between man and an unknowable God. One is suspended in the "mystic silence" of which Pseudo-Dionysius speaks. This is the essence of contemplative prayer.

The goal of this supension? As with all Christian mystics, it is an encounter with the transcendent in a more essential way than is available through the ordinary operations of the human faculties. It is a knowledge whose predominant element is the experience of love. It is a recapitulation of a mystery central to the Christian faith, the mystery of death and resurrection embodied in the person of Christ. For only in the death of one's limited experiences of self, in the death of an existence that is identified only with what is available to our limited perceptions and is isolated from what surpasses them, can one be resurrected to an experience of one's true self, a true self discovered in the image of God. The agony of death must be real for the resurrection to occur. But on the other side of the abyss is a union, a union that does not obliterate individuality but, paradoxically, fulfills it. In union with God, one's true self is revealed.

The Cloud of Unknowing

What I am describing here is the contemplative work of the spirit. It is this which gives God the greatest delight. For when you fix your love on him, forgetting all else, the saints and angels rejoice and hasten to assist you in every way—though the devils will rage and ceaselessly conspire to thwart you. Your fellow men are marvelously enriched by this work of yours, even if you may not fully understand how; the souls in purgatory are touched, for their suffering is eased by the effects of this

The Cloud of Unknowing and The Book of Privy Counseling, edited by William Johnston (New York: Doubleday, 1973), pp. 48-56 passim. Footnotes have been omitted.

work; and, of course, your own spirit is purified and strengthened by this contemplative work more than by all others put together. Yet for all this, when God's grace arouses you to enthusiasm, it becomes the lightest sort of work there is and one most willingly done. Without his grace, however, it is very difficult and almost, I should say, quite beyond you.

And so diligently persevere until you feel joy in it. For in the beginning it is usual to feel nothing but a kind of darkness about your mind, or as it were, a *cloud of unknowing*. You will seem to know nothing and to feel nothing except a naked intent toward God in the depths of your being. Try as you might, this darkness and this cloud will remain between you and your God. You will feel frustrated, for your mind will be unable to grasp him, and your heart will not relish the delight of his love. But learn to be at home in this darkness. Return to it as often as you can, letting your spirit cry out to him whom you love. For if, in this life, you hope to feel and see God as he is in himself it must be within this darkness and this cloud. But if you strive to fix your love on him forgetting all else, which is the work of contemplation I have urged you to begin, I am confident that God in his goodness will bring you to a deeper experience of himself. . . .

He who with the help of God's grace becomes aware of the will's constant movements and learns to direct them toward God will never fail to taste something of heaven's joy even in this life and, certainly in the next, he will savor it fully. Now do you see why I rouse you to this spiritual work? You would have taken to it naturally had man not sinned, for man was created to love and everything else was created to make love possible. Nevertheless, by the work of contemplative love man will be healed. Failing in this work he sinks deeper into sin further and further from God, but by persevering in it he gradually rises from sin and grows in divine intimacy.

Therefore, be attentive to time and the way you spend it. Nothing is more precious. This is evident when you recall that in one tiny moment heaven may be gained or lost. God, the master of time, never gives the future. We gives only the present, moment by moment, for this is the law of the created order, and God will not contradict himself in his creation. Time is for man, not man for time. God, the Lord of nature, will never anticipate man's choices which follow one after another in time. Man will not be able to excuse himself at the last judgment, saying to God: "You overwhelmed me with the future when I was only capable of living in the present."

But now I see that you are discouraged and are saying to yourself: "What am I to do? If all he says is true, how shall I justify my past? I am twenty-four years old and until this moment I have scarcely noticed time at all. What is worse, I could not repair the past even if I wanted to, for according to his teaching such a task is impossible to me by nature even with the help of ordinary grace. Besides I know very well that in the future, either through frailty or laziness, I will probably not be any more attentive to the present moment than I have been in the past. I am completely discouraged. Please help me for the love of Jesus."

Well have you said "for the love of Jesus." For it is in his love that you will find help. In love all things are shared and so if you love Jesus, everything of his is yours. As God he is the creator and dispenser of time; as man he is consciously mastered time; as God and man he is the rightful judge of men and their use of time. Bind yourself to Jesus, therefore, in faith and love, so that belonging to him you may share all he has and enter the fellowship of those who love him. This is the communion of the blessed and these will be your friends: our Lady, St. Mary, who was full of grace at every moment; the angels, who are unable to waste time; and all the blessed in heaven and on earth, who through the grace of Jesus employ every moment in love. See, here is your strength. Understand what I am saying and be heartened. But remember, I warn you of one thing above all. No one can claim true fellowship with Jesus, his Mother, the angels, and the saints, unless he does all in his power with the help of grace to be mindful of time. For he must do his share however slight to strengthen the fellowship as it strengthens him.

And so do not neglect this contemplative work. Try also to appreciate its wonderful effects in your own spirit. When it is genuine it is simply a spontaneous desire springing suddenly toward God like sparks from fire. It is amazing how many loving desires arise from the spirit of a person who is accustomed to this work. And yet, perhaps only one of these will be completely free from attachment to some created thing. Or again, no sooner has a man turned toward God in love when through human frailty he finds himself distracted by the remembrance of some created thing or some daily care. But no matter. No harm is done; for such a person quickly returns to deep recollection.

And now we come to the difference between the contemplative work and its counterfeits such as daydreaming, fantasizing, or subtle reasoning. These originate in a conceited, curious, or romantic mind whereas the blind stirring of love springs from a sincere and humble heart. Pride, curiosity, and daydreaming must be sternly checked if the contemplative work is to be authentically conceived in singleness of heart. Some will probably hear about this work and suppose that by their own ingenious efforts they can achieve it. They are likely to strain their mind and imagination unnaturally only to produce a false work which is neither human nor divine. Truly, such a person is dangerously deceived. And I fear that unless God intervenes with a miracle inspiring him to abandon these practices and humbly seek reliable counsel he will most certainly fall into mental aberrations or some great spritual evil of the devil's devising. Then he risks losing both body and soul eternally. For the love of God, therefore, be careful in this work and never strain your mind or imagination, for truly you will not succeed this way. Leave these faculties at peace.

Do not suppose that because I have spoken of darkness and of a cloud I have in mind the clouds you see in an overcast sky or the darkness of your house when your candle fails. If I had, you could with a little imagination picture the summer skies breaking through the clouds or a clear light brightening the dark winter. But this isn't what I mean at all so forget this sort of nonsense. When I speak of darkness, I mean the absence of knowledge. If you are unable to understand something or if you have forgotten it, are you not in the dark as regards this thing? You cannot see it with your mind's eye. Well, in the same way, I have not said "cloud," but *cloud of unknowing*. For it is a darkness of unknowing that lies between you and your God.

*　　*　　*

If you wish to enter into this cloud, to be at home in it, and to take up the contemplative work of love as I urge you to, there is something else you must do. Just as the *cloud of unknowing* lies above you, between you and your God, so you must fashion a *cloud of forgetting* beneath you, between you and every created thing. The *cloud of unknowing* will perhaps leave you with the feeling that you are far from God. But no, if it is authentic, only the absence of a *cloud of forgetting* keeps you from him now. Every time I say "all creatures," I refer not only to every created thing but also to all their circumstances and activities. I make no exception. You are to concern yourself with no creature whether material or spiritual nor with their situation and doings whether good or ill. To put it briefly, during this work you must abandon them all beneath the *cloud of forgetting*.

For although at certain times and in certain circumstances it is necessary and useful to dwell on the particular situation and activity of people and things, during this work it is almost useless. Thinking and remembering are forms of spiritual understanding in which the eye of the spirit is opened and closed upon things as the eye of a marksman is on his target. But I tell you that everything you dwell upon during this work becomes an obstacle to union with God. For if your mind is cluttered with these concerns there is no room for him.

Yes, and with all due reverence, I go so far as to say that it is equally useless to think you can nourish your contemplative work by considering God's attributes, his kindness or his dignity; or by thinking about our Lady, the angels, or the saints; or about the joys of heaven, wonderful as these will be. I believe that this kind of activity is no longer of any use to you. Of course, it is laudable to reflect upon God's kindness and to love and praise him for it; yet it is far better to let your mind rest in the awareness of him in his naked existence and to love and praise him for what he is in himself. . . .

If they ask, "Who is this God?", tell them that he is the God who created you, redeemed you, and brought you to this work. Say to your thoughts, "You are powerless to grasp him. Be still." Dispel them by turning to Jesus with loving desire. Don't be surprised if your thoughts seem holy and valuable for prayer. Probably you will find yourself thinking about the wonderful qualities of Jesus, his sweetness, his love, his graciousness, his mercy. But if you pay attention to these ideas they will have gained what they wanted of you, and will go on chattering until they divert you even more to the thought of his passion. Then will come ideas about his great kindness, and if you keep listening they will be delighted. Soon you will be thinking about your sinful life and perhaps in this connection you will recall some place where you have lived in the past, until suddenly, before you know it, your mind is completely scattered.

And yet, they were not bad thoughts. Actually, they were good and holy thoughts, so valuable, in fact, that anyone who expects to advance without having meditated often on his own sinfulness, the Passion of Christ, and the kindness, goodness, and dignity of God, will most certainly go astray and fail in his purpose. But a person who has long pondered these things must eventually leave them behind beneath a *cloud of forgetting* if he hopes to pierce the *cloud of unknowing* that lies between him and his God. So whenever you feel drawn by grace to the contemplative work and are determined to do it, simply raise your heart to God with a gentle stirring of love. Think only of God, the God who created you, redeemed you, and guided you to this work. Allow no other ideas about God to enter your mind. Yet even this is too much. A naked intent toward God, the desire for him alone, is enough.

If you want to gather all your desire into one simple word that the mind can easily retain, choose a short word rather than a long one. A one-syllable word such as "God" or "love" is best. But choose one that is meaningful to you. Then fix it in your mind so that it will remain there come what may. This word will be your defense in conflict and in peace. Use it to beat upon the cloud of darkness above you and to subdue all distractions, consigning them to the *cloud of forgetting* beneath you. Should some thought go on annoying you demanding to know what you are doing, answer with this one word alone. If your mind begins to intellectualize over the meaning and connotations of this little word, remind yourself that its value lies in its simplicity. Do this and I assure you these thoughts will vanish. Why? Because you have refused to develop them with arguing.

5. The Rhineland and the Netherlands: Beyond God to the Godhead

---

Meister Eckhart

(1260–1327)

With large justification, Meister Eckhart is frequently referred to as one of the greatest mystics within the Christian world. Founder of the "Rhineland mystics," Eckhart developed a distinctive approach to the contemplative life, providing some twists that had not been conceived before and requiring the cultivation of fresh terminology.

The biographical details are scanty. Born Johannes Eckhart in 1260, he is better known as Meister after receiving his master's degree in theology from the University of Paris. He entered the Dominican order at the age of fifteen and studied in Cologne, possibly under the great teacher Albertus Magnus, who had instructed Thomas Aquinas. Continuing his education in Paris, Meister Eckhart earned the reputation of being an excellent scholar. He left Paris to take on administrative responsibilities within the Dominican order in Germany, where he demonstrated his capabilities and was appointed to positions of increasing responsibility. Eventually he was elected provincial minister of the order for all of Germany, although the election was not confirmed. Gradually he made his way back to Paris, then went from place to place, as lecturer, homilist, and "trouble shooter" for the Dominicans. He traveled throughout Germany and France, visiting convents, monasteries, and cathedrals.

As he became better known, his lectures raised suspicions because of the idiosyncratic nature of his thought. Some accused him of having associations with heretics; others believed him to be so obtuse regarding matters essential to the faith that they couldn't be sure they understood what his speculations meant. He made statements such as: "The beginning, in which God created heaven and earth, is the first simple Now of eternity, the very now in which God has been from all eternity." And: "God is neither good, nor better, nor the best. If anyone were to say that God is good, it would be as incorrect as to say that white is black." Another: "The Father begets his son in me and I am there the same Son and not another." Such affirmations were perilously close to heretical statements, although the ambiguities and subtleties within them were so great that it was difficult to base charges on literal interpretations. Eventually, however, Eckhart was brought to trial, and twenty-eight of his propositions were condemned as being heretical. Shortly after his death, Pope John XXII issued a Bull which held that Eckhart had retracted twenty-six of the condemned propositions before he died.

The significance of Eckhart's thought derives in part from its originality, but in greater measure to the way it resonated with the religious and intellectual circumstances of the time. Earlier, much of mystical religion was conceived in correspondence with the dominant patterns of theological reflection. The theology, in turn, was sanctioned by Neoplatonic tendencies as well as by a more comprehensive worldview that was both congenial and supportive. Indeed, before Eckhart's time, mystical reflection could be sustained by deeply inscribed contemplative tendencies within the most prevalent patterns of theological reflection. But, by Eckhart's time, the situation was changing. Serious questions had been raised about the intentions of theological reflection. The force of the dominant Medieval worldview had diminished. And in the process mysticism offered itself as an alternative to all that had come under criticism. In some respects, it had become a religious necessity, a posture designed to fill a large vacuum, a response to fundamental interest in the world's intelligibility and order. Some turned to mystical religion in reaction to the more dominant earlier tendency to find similar satisfaction in self-consistent theological reasoning. Some wanted to recapture mystically what had been lost metaphysically. In this context, Eckhart assisted the reconstructive effort. He helped develop the language and construct the schema. He worked to place mystical religion on its own intrinsic base. Understandable, in this fluid situation, his reflections invited criticism. But it was also difficult to know from what basis they should be tested.

The views he set forth, in one way or another, depend upon his insights regarding the matter of *Seelenfünklein* ("spark of the soul"). *Fünklein* (from *funk*, connoting an emission of sparks or rays of light) identifies that part of the soul in which mystical apprehension, or union with God, occurs. Eckhart understood, with orthodox Christians everywhere, that God is eternal. But he added that "the begetting of the Son by the Father and the procession of the Holy Spirit from the Father and the Son take place eternally." Thus the generation of the Son also occurs within the soul. Christ is born there, "in us," and, Eckhart adds, it is there that he is also "crucified, dead, buried, and rises from the dead."

The generation of the Son describes an event that occurs within interior consciousness. Eckhart writes that "had the Virgin not first borne God spiritually he would never have been born from her in bodily fashion." Similarly, "Mary conceived in her heart before she conceived in her body." And, "it is more worthy of God that he should be born spiritually of every virgin, or of every good soul, than that he should have been born physically of Mary."

In such statements, Eckhart affirmed that the soul carries the capacity to receive "the fullness of God." This implies that God is he whom the soul conceives, the one whom the soul bears, he whom the soul brings forth to consciousness. Or, turned the other way around, God comes to birth in the soul as the soul is in process of "God-becoming." In sum, the vision holds that God is father of the soul so that the soul can become, in a mystical sense, the mother of God.

There is much more in Eckhart. The Trinitarian imagery with which he worked encouraged him to make some distinguished statements regarding the nature of the deity Christians worship. In this regard he is famous for adding detail to the *via negativa* approach that had been practiced in the Medieval era, from the time of Pseudo-Dionysius forward. Eckhart held firmly that behind and beyond the self-expression of God lies a hidden, unexpressed, mysterious, essential reality. God, as he is in and of himself, is ineffable. The God about whom we know something is God, but beyond God is the Godhead, defined as "the origin of all things beyond God." The differences between the two are extreme: Eckhart says that God and the Godhead are as distinct as heaven and earth. The Godhead can be likened to an unfathomable abyss: "when the soul reaches the essence of the Godhead itself, it sinks ever deeper into the abyss of the Godhead so that it never comes to the bottom."

The *via negativa*, therefore is more than a technique to approach the nature of God by stipulating what God is not. It is also a "way of inner stillness that brings illumination." It is "the higher way," a way of "lifting the soul above its finite nature." This is how Eckhart perceived it: "What God is in himself no man can tell except he be ravished into the light that God is himself."

Thus, mystical experience reaches it culmination in a "break-through" beyond God to the Godhead; and in that place "where absolute stillness, utter silence and unity reign," there is union with "the unkown one." Because the depths of the Godhead are forever unfathomable, there is no limit to the distance the soul can travel.

For Eckhart, the birth of God within the soul is the decisive early event within interior consciousness. From that event, the soul is compelled to a journey for which there is no ultimate termination: the depths of the Godhead are infinitely penetrable. In this, the soul finds its satisfaction, that is, in sinking ever deeper into that "unbounded freedom."

The Kingdom of God is at hand.

When I think about the Kingdom of God, I am struck dumb by its grandeur; for the Kingdom of God is God himself with all his fullness. The Kingdom of God is no small thing: all the worlds one could imagine God creating would still not be as the Kingdom of God. When the Kingdom appears to the soul and it is recognized, there is no further need for preaching or instruction: it is learnéd enough and has at once secured eternal life. To know and see how near God's Kingdom is, is to say with Jacob: "God is in this place and I did not know it."

God is equally near to every creature. The wise man says: "God has spread his nets and lines out over all things, so that he may be found in any one of them and recognized by whoever chooses to verify this." One authority says: "To see God aright is to know him alike in everything. To serve God with fear is good; to serve him out of love is better; but to love him while fearing is best of all." It is good to have a peaceful life in rest with God; it is better to bear a life of suffering with patience; but to find rest in a life of suffering is best of all. To walk through the fields and say your prayers, and see God, or to sit in church and recognize him, and to know God better because the place is

Raymond Bernard Blakney, Meister Eckhart. A Modern Translation (New York: Harper and Brothers, 1941), pp. 129-132, 165-66, 186-87. Footnotes have been omitted.

peaceful: this is due to man's defective nature and not to God. For God is equally near to everything and every place and is equally ready to give himself, so far as in him lies, and therefore a person shall know him aright who knows how to see him the same, under all circumstances.

St. Bernard asks: "Why do my eyes behold the sky and not my feet? It is because my eyes are more like the sky than my feet." If then my soul is to see God, it must be heavenly. How shall the soul be prepared so that it may see God and know him in itself—how near he is? Now listen! Heaven may not receive any alien impress; neither pain nor want, brought from without, may be stamped upon it. Even so, the soul that is to know God must be so firm and steady in God that nothing can penetrate it, neither hope nor fear, neither joy nor sorrow, neither love nor suffering, nor any other thing that can come in it from without.

So, too, heaven is equidistant from earth at all places. Likewise, the soul ought to be equidistant from every earthly thing, so that it is not nearer to one than to the other and behaves the same in love, or suffering, or having, or forbearance; toward whatever it may be, the soul should be as dead, or dispassionate, or superior to it. Heaven is pure and clear and without spot, touching neither time nor space. Corporeal things have no place in it. It is not inside of time; its orbit is compassed with speed beyond belief. The course of heaven is outside time—and yet time comes from its movements. Nothing hinders the soul's knowledge of God as much as time and space, for time and space are fragments, whereas God is one! And therefore, if the soul is to know God, it must know him above time and outside of space; for God is neither this nor that, as are these manifold things. God is One!

If the soul is to see God, it must not look again on any temporal thing, for as long as the soul dwells on time or space or any image of them it may never know God. If the eye is to distinguish colors, it must first be purged of them all. If the soul is to see God, it must have nothing in common with things that are nothings. For to see God is to know that all creatures are as nothing. Compare one creature to another, and it appears to be beautiful and is something; but compare it with God and it is nothing!

Further, I say that if the soul is to know God, it must forget itself and lose [consciousness of] itself, for as long as it is self-aware and self-conscious, it will not see or be conscious of God. But when, for God's sake, it becomes unself-conscious and lets go of everything, it finds itself again in God, for knowing God, it therefore knows itself and everything else from which it has been cut asunder, in the divine perfection. If I am to know the highest good or the eternal goodness, then surely I must know it where it is good in itself and not where its goodness is separate. If I am to know true being, I must know it where it is being itself, and that is in God and not where it is divided among creatures.

The whole divine being is in God alone. The whole of humanity is not in one man, for one man is not the whole of humanity. But in God all humanity is known to the soul, and all things else, in their highest [reality], for in him they are known as beings.

If a person lived in a beautifully decorated home, he would know much more about it than one who never entered it, but who enjoys talking about it. Thus I am as sure as I am that I live and God lives, that if the soul is to know God it must know him above space and time. And such a soul [thus acquainted with God] knows him, and is aware of how near his kingdom is, that is, God with all his fullness. The authorities in the schools ask often how it is possible for the soul to know God. It is not from God's strictness that he requires so much of man, but rather from his kindness that he expects the soul to progress to that point where it may receive much, as he gives so much to it.

No one ought to think that is is hard to attain this, however hard it sounds and however hard it may be at first to cut one's self asunder and be dead to everything. But once you have come in, no life is easier, nor pleasanter, nor lovelier, for God is very anxious at all times to be near to people, and to teach them how to come to him, if they are only willing to follow him. Nobody ever wanted anything as much as God wants to bring people to know him. God is always ready but we are not ready. God is near to us but we are far from him. God is within; we are without. God is at home; we are abroad.

The prophet says: "God leads the righteous through a narrow way out onto a broad street, so that they may come into his wide and open spaces"—which is to say, into the true freedom of the spirit which has become one spirit with God. May God help us all to follow as he leads us to himself. Amen.

Into the Godhead

*   *   *

I have quoted a Latin text from the Gospel of St. John assigned for reading on this Sunday. It is something our Lord said to his disciples: "A little, and ye see me no more." However small it may be, if anything adheres to the soul, you cannot see me. St. Augustine was asked what eternal life might be and, replying, he said: "You ask me what eternal life is? You had better ask eternal life itself and hear it!" No one knows better what heat is like than something hot. No one knows better what wisdom is than one who has it. No one knows better what eternal life is than eternal life itself. Our Lord Jesus Christ says: "This is life eternal that they should know thee, the only true God!"

You should understand that if the soul beheld God even at a distance, as if through some medium, such as the clouds, for example, and saw him only for a moment, it would never turn back again to this world. How then do you think it would be if a man saw God himself, as he is, without any intervening medium, in his naked essence? All the creatures God ever created, or could create if he chose to, would amount to very little when compared to God himself.

You would not believe me if I told you how great and wide the sky is. If the sky were pricked with the point of a needle, the area of the prick would be less in comparison to the sky and the world put together, than the world is compared to God. Therefore, it is well said: "A little, and ye see me no more." As long as the least of creatures absorbs your attention, you will see nothing of God, however little that creature may be. Thus, in the Book of Love, the soul says: "I have run around looking for him my soul loves and found him not." She found angels and many other things but not him her soul loved, but she goes on to say: "After that, I went a little further and found him my soul loved." It was as if she had said: "It was when I stepped beyond creatures [which are the trifles] that I found my soul's lover." The soul must step beyond or jump past creatures if it is to know God.

Now, you must know that God loves the soul so strenuously that to take this privilege of loving from God would be to take his life and being. It would be to kill God, if one may use such an expression. For out of God's love for the soul, the Holy Spirit blooms and the Holy Spirit is that love. Since, then, the soul is so strenuously loved by God, it must be of great importance....

*   *   *

God Must Give Himself

When God made creatures, they were so small and tight that he could not operate in any of them. Then he made the soul, so like himself, so convenient to himself, that he could give himself to it. Whatever he gives otherwise is nothing to the soul. God must give himself to me to be my own, just as he is his own, or I shall get nothing from him worth while or to my [soul's] taste. Always to receive him like this, one must always deny himself and be detached from self. So disposed, one will always get all God has straight from him and it will be his own as much as it was God's own, just as our Lady does, and all who are in the Kingdom of Heaven.

The word "Father" implies a Son and the phrase "Father of lights" implies an immaculate birth and a universal principle. The Father begets the Son in the eternal mind and also begets the Son in the soul as if in his own nature. He begets the Son in the soul, to be its own and his Being depends on his doing so, for better or for worse.

Once I was asked what the Father is doing in heaven. I replied that he begets his Son and that this activity is so pleasant to him and suits him so well that he never does anything else and that from the two there blossoms forth the Holy Spirit. When the Father begets his Son in me, I am that Son and no other. "If we are sons, then we are true heirs." He who knows the truth knows very well that the word "Father" implies the immaculate birth and the having of sons. Thus we all are in the Son and are the Son.

Notice the phrase "cometh down from above." I said to you before that to receive gifts from above one must be beneath—that is, have true humility. This is the truth to know: not to be humble always is to receive nothing at all, however little it may be. If your eye is on yourself or anything or anybody, you are not humble and you receive nothing, but if your humility is constant, then constantly you receive, and in all fullness. It is God's nature to give and his existence depends on his giving when we are subject to him. If we are not and thus receive nothing from him, we do him violence and even kill him, or if not him, we do violence to ourselves and as much as is possible to us. If you would really give your all to God, see that you are humbly subject to him and exalt him in your mind and heart. "God hath sent our Lord into the world."

I said once on this point that, in the fullness of time, God sent his Son into the soul—that is, when the soul had finished with time. When the soul is freed from time and place, the Father sends his Son into it, and this is what the words mean: "Every good and perfect gift is from above and cometh down from the Father of lights." That we may be prepared to receive the best gifts, may the Father of lights help us. Amen.

Henry Suso
(1300–1366)

Because his theological stature, speculative ability, and historical influence are not as great as Eckhart's, with whom he is associated within the Rhineland school, Henry Suso is not as well known. Or, when he is cited, it is chiefly because of the link with Eckhart. Closer scrutiny confirms, however, that Suso is an important and intriguing figure in his own right, one who symbolizes much more than the perpetuation of Eckhart's orientation.

Suso's biographical details can be sketched as follows. He was born about 1300, became a Dominican at the age of thirteen, lived most of his life in the Lake Constance area, was a teacher for a time in a Dominican priory, eventually became prior, and, at the age of forty, gave up teaching and writing and lived an itinerant life as a preacher and a ready source of pastoral care. Along the way he wrote good poetry, engaged in autobiographical reflections, lent considerable imagination to the contemplative spirit (taking note of the place of color, for example, in interior experience), associated with women throughout his life, and wrote some of the most intriguing paragraphs in the annals of Western contemplative literature.

In matters reflective, he probed the interests advanced by Eckhart, though with considerably less critical rigor. He believed in a Godhead beyond God, but this reality became less abstract, less depersonalized, and, in an affective sense, less remote. Suso characterizes the search for the hidden ground of things in terms of a "love for eternal Wisdom" and construes Wisdom (or the Godhead) in a dominantly feminine way even when utilizing masculine terminology. The highest principle is not as extreme, radical, or awesome for him. But this element of personalization is indication that Suso's approach to matters contemplative is more psychological than speculative or intellectual in tone. It is concerned with practical application and the needs of the individual. Frequently the form in which it is presented is autobiographical. His sermons are meant to be clearly understood by the ordinary individual. Suso recognized that the mystic vision belongs to the world of pastoral care.

His life was not without turmoil. He was under constant criticism because he defended Eckhart's position. In addition, he had a reputation for encouraging women to enter monasteries. On several occasions he was accused of having less than commendable relationships with women. Eventually, his difficulties became sufficiently compounded that he was exiled.

Little Book of Eternal Wisdom

THE SERVANT: Gentle Lord, thou canst offer thyself with such love and tenderness that all hearts should desire thee, and have an ardent longing for thy love. The words of love flow so full of life from thy sweet mouth that they have wounded many hearts in the flower of their youth so deeply that all transient love was completely extinguished in them. And, gentle Lord, my heart longs, my mind yearns; I should gladly hear thee speak of it. Speak, then, my only chosen comfort, one little word to my soul, thy poor handmaid, for under thy shadow I have sweetly fallen asleep, but my heart is wakeful.

ETERNAL WISDOM: Hearken, my daughter, and see; incline thine ear; withdraw wholeheartedly within thyself, forgetting thyself and all things.

I am in myself the incomprehensible Good, who has forever been and always will be, who has never been expressed in words, nor ever will be. I can indeed make myself felt within the heart, but no tongue can properly express me. And yet, since I give myself, the supernatural, immutable Good, to every creature according to its power, in the manner in which it is receptive of me, I will wind the sun's radiance in a cloth and give thee the spiritual meaning in human words concerning myself and my sweet love, thus:

I present myself tenderly before the eyes of thy heart; now embellish me and clothe me spiritually and array me to thy heart's desire. Adorn me with everything that can move thy heart to special love and abundant delight. Behold, everything that thou and all men could conceive of form, beauty, or grace is still more lovely in me than one could express. It is through words of this nature that I make myself known.

Now hear me: I am of noble birth, of high lineage. I am the lovable Word of the Father's heart, whose eyes take blissful pleasure in the

Henry Suso, Little Book of Eternal Wisdom and Little Book of Truth, trans. James M. Clark (New York: Harper and Row, 1953), pp. 71–76.

profound, loving fellowship of my natural sonship and his pure fatherhood and the sweet, ardent ascending love of the Holy Spirit. I am the
throne of heavenly bliss, the crown of joy and happiness. My eyes are
so clear, my mouth so gentle, my cheeks so bright and rosy, and all my
person so fair and lovely and altogether perfect that if, until the last
day, a man were to remain in a fiery furnace for the sake of a mere
glimpse of me, he would still not have deserved it.

See, I am so charmingly adorned in bright raiment, so beautifully
surrounded with the variegated hues of living flowers, of red roses,
white lilies, fair violets, and flowers of every kind that all the lovely
blossoms of the month of May, the green foliage of all bright meadows,
the gentle flowerlets of all fair pastures are like a rough thistle as
compared with my adornment.

In the Godhead I play a game of joy; it gives the angel host of
happiness the most. A thousand years do seem to them a fleeting
dream. All the heavenly hosts fix their eyes on me with a new wonder
and gaze upon me. Their eyes are fastened on mine; their hearts are
inclined toward me; and their soul is bowed down to me without
intermission. Blessed be he who dances the dance of joy and heavenly
bliss by my side, who in complete security will pace, holding my fair
hand, for all eternity! One little word, that sounds so clear from my
sweet mouth, surpasses all the songs of angels, the melody of all harps,
and of all sweet instruments. Ah, look, I am so dear to love, so lovely to
embrace, and so tender for the loving soul to kiss that all hearts should
be fit to break with longing for me. I am gentle and companionable and
present at all times to the pure soul. I am secretly present at table, in
bed, in the path, and on the road. I turn hither and thither. There is
nothing in me that could displease; in me there is everything that is
well pleasing, the heart's desire and the soul's wish. See, I am completely the pure Good. If anyone in this life obtains one tiny drop of me,
all the joys and pleasures of this world become bitterness to him, all
riches and honor become dung and an object of contempt. The dear
ones are surrounded by my sweet love and are swept into the only one,
in a love without images or spoken words; they are swept away into the
Good, from whom they emanated.

My love can also relieve the hearts of beginners of the heavy burden
of sin and give them a free, clean heart and create in them a pure and
blameless conscience. Tell me, what is there in this world which could
outweigh this alone? The whole world could not outweigh such a heart,
for the person who gives his heart to me alone lives happily and dies
safely; he has heaven here and hereafter forever.

Now look, I have said many words to thee, and stand in my lovely beauty unaffected by all of them as is the firmament by thy little finger, for eye never beheld it and ear never heard it and it could never come into any heart. But let this rough sketch serve thee as a distinction between my sweet love and false, transient love.

THE SERVANT: Ah, thou gentle, lovely flower of the field, thou dearly beloved of my heart, in the embrace of the arms of the loving soul, how well known is this to him who has ever experienced thee truly and how strange it is to the man to whom thou art unknown, whose heart and soul are still earthly.

Ah, beloved, incomprehensible Good, this is a beautiful hour, this is a sweet moment, in which I must disclose to thee a hidden wound that my heart still bears from thy sweet love. Lord, sharing in love is like water in fire; beloved Lord, thou knowest that real, fervent love cannot endure any duality. Ah, gentle, only Lord of my heart and soul, this is why my heart so fondly desires that thou shouldst have particular love and affection for me and that thy divine eyes should take particular pleasure in me. Alas, Lord, thou hast so many loving hearts, which love thee dearly and have much influence with thee, alas, gentle, dear Lord, where am I in this regard?

ETERNAL WISDOM: I am a lover of such a nature that I am not compressed by unity nor scattered by a number. I am at all times fully concerned and occupied with thee and endear myself to thee alone and accomplish all that affects thee, as if I were free of all other ties.

THE SERVANT: Ah, whither have I been led away? How completely have I been captivated! How completely has my soul been melted away by thy friendly, sweet words of the beloved One! Ah, turn thy bright eyes away from me, for they have altogether overcome me.

Where was there ever a heart so hard, a soul so cold and lukewarm, that it would not be softened and warmed by thy sweet love on hearing thy sweet, living, loving words, which are so extremely ardent? Alas, wonder of wonders, that he who could look at thee with the eyes of his heart should not wholly melt away with love! Ah, how blessed is the lover who is called thy lover and is so in reality. What sweet consolation and hidden love he may receive from thee!

And, sweet gentle maiden, St. Agnes, the lover of eternal Wisdom, how well thou couldst praise thy dear love, when thou didst say: "His blood has adorned my cheeks with the color of roses."* Ah, gentle Lord, if I were but worthy, if my soul could but be called thy lover! See, if it were possible that all the pleasure, all the joy and love that this

*From the second antiphon from the Office of the Feast of St. Agnes.

world can give, were combined in one person, I would freely give him up for this. . . .

And, but thou, thou beauty with boundless lovingkindness, grace with perfection of form, words, and melody, nobility with virtue, riches with power, freedom within and clarity without, and a quality that I never found in the world, namely, a true recompense and satisfaction in knowledge and power for the longing desires of a truly loving heart. The better one knows thee, the more one loves thee, the more intimate one is with thee, and the more lovely one finds thee. Indeed, what an inexhaustible, complete, pure Good thou art! Look, all ye hearts, how deluded are those who place their love in anything else! Ah, ye false lovers, flee far from me, never again approach me, for I have chosen the only love of my heart, in whom alone heart, soul, desire, and all my powers are satisfied with spiritual love that never dies away! Alas, Lord, if I could but write thee upon my heart, if I could but engrave thee in the very depths of my heart and soul in golden letters, so that thou wouldst never be erased in me! Alas, to my sorrow and misfortune, I have not always occupied my heart with him! What have I gained from all my lovers but lost time, wasted words, an empty hand, few good works, and a conscience burdened with sin!

Reply of ETERNAL WISDOM: I anticipate those that seek me and receive with lovely joy those that desire my love. All of my sweet love that thou canst experience in this world is only a drop in the ocean as compared with the love of eternity.

John Tauler

(c. 1300–1361)

He has been called the "Illuminated Doctor." The richness and depth of his sermons attest to the fact that he well deserves his appellation.

John Tauler was born around the year 1300 in the city of Strassburg into a family of comfortable circumstance. In 1315 he entered the Order of Preachers, the Dominicans, and received under their auspices the best possible education, becoming well versed not only in the Scholastic philosophy of Thomas Aquinas but steeped in the wisdom of the Fathers of the Church, especially Augustine. During this period he also came under the influence of two of his fellow Dominicans, Meister Eckhart and Henry Suso, whose mystical speculations were to touch him deeply.

An intensely active person, Tauler spent most of his adult life as a preacher and spiritual director. He was one of many great preachers in the Rhineland who labored to turn men's minds from their undue preoccupation with external affairs to the mystery of the interior life of God in their own souls. Speaking only occasionally to educated audiences, more often to all classes of people in the rough German dialect of the day, Tauler emerged as one of the most popular and powerful spiritual figures in an era and a locale noted for the vitality of its spirituality. Among the many individuals and groups dedicated to the practice of the interior life with whom he came into contact were the Friends of God, an informal association of persons active in the Rhineland and in Switzerland. Like many mystically oriented persons of the day, Tauler himself among them, the Friends of God sought to counterbalance the extreme external nature of ecclesiastical practice by stressing the transforming personal union of God within their own religious lives.

This intense looking inward characterizes Tauler's mysticism. At the same time it can be said that his words are among the most practical in all of contemplative literature. Like his fellow Dominican, Meister Eckhart, Tauler accepted the concept of the ground of the soul, what he calls the "inner man," which exists in the individual alongside the "outer man" and which is the highest of human faculties exalting man above himself and allowing him to dwell in God. This inner man must guide and direct its outer counterpart, leading it by its superior knowledge. For this to happen, the individual must acquire a deep and abiding humility. Thus where Eckhart lays emphasis on the soaring union with God in the ground of the soul, almost assuming the turning inward that this requires, Tauler is primarily a preacher of penance.

The necessary humility that such a turning requires has as its pivot point the passion of Christ. The five wounds of the crucified, in the Illuminated Doctor's view, can teach humans how to abandon themselves and how to suffer. By following the master down this narrow path, the disciples escape from the five "prisons" that enslave them and keep them from union with God. The prisons are love of creatures, love of self, undue reliance on the powers of reason (which hinders one's progress in faith), attachment to devotional feelings and visionary experiences, and lastly self-will. Breaking through these bonds, one enters into the mystic way, a way strewn with joy but also darkened by painful interior purgings through which the sufferer must pass in faith, hope, and humility in order to arrive at last at the innermost part of the soul, where God dwells. Here in this hidden darkness, this wild desert, one encounters the modeless Unity in which all multiplicity is lost. One is in the realm that Eckhart describes as the Godhead, a realm beyond the powers of reason, of imagination, and of all powers of the spirit. Paradoxically, Tauler perceives this Unity not only as a self-contained experiential phenomenon but also as the source of clear distinctions. An encounter with Unity for him teaches the truths of a Trinitarian faith.

Tauler's personal brand of faith can be seen in his *First Sermon for the Feast of Christmas*, in which he uses beautiful imagery to describe the eternal generation of the Son from the Father within the essence of the Godhead. The sermon gives us a glimpse into the power and eloquence of his preaching. In it he elaborates on the three births of Christ: within the Godhead, in the course of human history, and in the human soul. His words must be read and reread; no synopsis or commentary can touch the depths that are stirred by his direct and luminous prose. What one especially notices—and what is not always true of the writings of so many contemplatives—is the extent to which the Christian liturgy is the firm base upon which the structure of Christian mysticism is erected. Tauler is not alone in charting the interior dimensions of his soul by the symbolic map of the Bible. He is not alone in allowing the traditional images of devotion, such as the Virgin Mary, to carry him deeper into the meaning of the God experience. His understanding of the festivals and observances of the Church, such as Christmas, is not limited to a historical memorial nor reduced to a moral lesson. For him, the unfolding depths of the mystic life are plumbed in the liturgy; through its celebration, the eternal ground of being is entered by the narrow gateway of the human soul, made conscious, given form and expression, realized. The individual is transformed by membership in that mystical body—the Church—that is the very life of Christ in the world. Such an understanding of the role of liturgy and traditional imagery informs much of the contemplative tradition.

In the *Sermon for the First Sunday after the Epiphany*, Tauler takes as his starting point the Lucan passage that recounts the story of the young Christ child straying from his parents to return to the temple of Jerusalem. Speaking of how God is gained by detachment from crea-tures, he touches on one of the central themes of Western mysticism: self-emptying. Whether this relinquishing of self assumes the form of a deep faith that transcends the bounds of reason, takes on the aspect of interior silence, causes anguish through unendurable spiritual deprivation, or finds an outlet in ascetic zeal, it is necessary to foster the inner life. Through its cleansing power, the soul is prepared to be a receptive vessel for the influx of the divine.

The Three Births of Christ

Today the church celebrates three births, each of which is such a source of joy and delight that we should break forth into jubilation, love and thanksgiving, and whoever does not feel such sentiments should mistrust himself. The first birth and the most sublime, is that whereby the Heavenly Father begets His only Son in the Divine essence, and in the distinction of the Divine persons. The second birth is that which made Mary a mother in virginity most pure and inviolate. The third is that by which every day and every hour God is truly and spiritually begotten in our souls by grace and love. These three births are shown forth by the three masses of Christmas Day. The first is sung at midnight, commencing with the words: "Thou art My Son; this day have I begotten Thee" (PS. ii, 7), that is to say, in eternity.

This brings home to us the hidden birth accomplished in the darksome mystery of the inaccessible Divinity. The second mass begins with these words: "Today light has shined upon us" (Isaias ix, 2). It figures the glory of human nature Divinely influenced by its union with the Word. That mass is celebrated partly in the night and partly in the day, because the birth it represents is partly known to us and partly unknown. The third mass is sung in the daytime, and begins with the words: "A Child is born to us, and a Son is given to us." It figures that mysterious birth which should happen, and does happen, every day and every instant in holy souls, when they dispose themselves for it by deep attention and sincere love; for one can never experience that birth except by the recollection of all one's powers. In that nativity God belongs to us and gives Himself to us so completely, that nothing whatever is more our own than He is. And that is what those words say to us: "A Child is born to us, and a Son is given to us." He is, therefore,

The Sermons and Conferences of John Tauler, trans. Walter Elliott (Washington: Apostolic Mission House, 1910), pp. 66–71 and 117–19, 121–23.

our own; He is ours totally and everywhere, for He is always being begotten within us.

Let us speak first of the ineffable birth represented by the third mass of Christmas, and let us explain how it may be brought about in us in a manner the most perfect and efficacious. To that end let us consider the qualities of that first generation, by which the Father begets the Son in eternity. The ineffable riches of the Divine good are so overflowing that God cannot contain Himself, and by His very nature He is forced to expend and communicate Himself. "It is God's nature to expend Himself," says St. Augustine. The Father has thus poured Himself out into the other two Divine persons; after that He communicated Himself to creatures. The same saint says further: "It is because God is good that we are good, and all the good that the creature has is good with the essential goodness of God." What, then, is the peculiar character of the Divine generation? The Father, inasmuch as He is Father, turns inward to Himself and His Divine intelligence; He sees Himself and penetrates Himself with a gaze which wholly embraces His Divine essence, and then, just as He sees and knows Himself, so does He utter Himself completely; and the act whereby He knows Himself and the Word whereby He utters Himself is also the act whereby He begets His Son in eternity.

Thus the Father Himself remains within Himself in the unity of His essence, and goes out of Himself in the distinction of persons. Again He returns into Himself, and therein He rests in unspeakable self-delight, and that self-delight goes forth and overflows in effable love which is the Holy Spirit. Thus does God dwell within Himself and go forth out of Himself to return again into Himself. Therefore, is all outgoing for the sake of ingoing again. And hence in the material universe is the movement of the heavenly spheres most noble and most perfect, because it unceasingly returns again to the origin and beginning from which it first set forth. And so also is the course of man ever noblest and most perfect when it returns again upon its source and origin.

The quality which the Heavenly Father has in this His incoming and outgoing, the same should every man have who will become the spiritual mother in this divine bringing forth. He must enter wholly into himself, and again go out of himself; as the soul has three noble powers, wherein it is the true image of the blessed Trinity—memory, understanding and free will. Through these powers is the soul capable of receiving and clinging to God, and all that God is, has and can bestow, and in this way it can gaze upon Him in eternity. For the soul is created between time and eternity; with its superior part it belongs to eternity, and with the inferior—the sensitive, animal powers—it belongs to time.

But both the higher and lower powers of the soul wander away into time and into the fleeting things of time, and this is because of the kinship between its higher and lower powers. Very easy is it in this straying thus to go astray from eternity. If we would be born again with the Divine birth, then we need to start back again, earnestly struggle inwardly and there gather up all our powers, lower and higher, if we would restore all dissipation of mind to unity, since united forces are ever the strongest, and they become united when drawn back from multiplicity. When a hunter would hit the mark he shuts one eye in order that with the other he may look straighter; when one would think deeply about anything, he closes all his senses and unites all his powers in his inmost soul, out of which, as branches from a tree, all the senses go forth into activity. When all our powers of sense and motion are thus by an inward movement assembled together in the highest power, which is the force and foundation of them all, then happens an outward, yea, an overflowing movement beyond and above self, by which we renounce all ownership of will, of appetite and of activity. There remains for thee then only a pure and clear intention to be of God and of God's purposes, to be nothing whatever of self, or ever to become anything of self, to be for Him alone, to give room to Him alone, whether in things high or low, so that He may work His will in thee and bring about His birth in thee, and therein remain unhindered by thee to the end.

If two are to be made one, then must one stand passive and the other active. If my eye is to receive an image, it must be free from all other images; for if it already has so much as one, it cannot see another, nor can the ear hear a sound if it be occupied with one already. Any power of receiving must first be empty before it can receive anything. Hence St. Augustine says: "Empty thyself if thou wouldst be filled. Go forth, if thou wouldst enter in." And elsewhere he says: "O noble soul, O noble creature of God, wherefore goest thou outside theyself in search of Him who is always and most certainly within thee, and through Whom thou art made a partaker of the divine nature? What hast thou to do or why dost thou concern thyself with creatures?"

When a man thus clears the ground and makes his soul ready, without doubt God must fill up the void. The very heavens would fall down to fill up empty space, and much rather will God not allow thee to remain empty, for that would be against His nature, His attributes; yea, and against His justice. If, therefore, thou wilt be silent, the Word of this Divine birth shall speak in thee and shall be heard; but, if thou speakest, be sure He will be silent. Thou canst not serve the Word better than by being silent and by listening. If thou goest out of self, He without doubt goeth in, and so it will be much or little of His entering in, according to much or little of thy going out.

An illustration of this going out of self is given in the book of Moses, how God made Abraham go forth from his country and his kinsfolk, so that He might show him all good things. The Divine birth in the soul of man—that means certainly all good things, and that alone is its meaning. The country or region out of which the soul must go—that means the body, with its lusts and concupiscences of whatever kind. The friends he must have—these are his inclinations and the sensitive or sensible powers with their images, which draw him on and fasten him down. These set love and pain in motion, joy and sorrow, longing and dread, care and frivolity. These friends are very near akin to us; against them we must be strictly on our guard if we would wholly elude them, and if we would have born in us the all-good that this Divine birth really is for us. A proverb says: A boy kept too much at home behaves like a calf when away from home, which means that men who have not gone beyond their natural life, nor raised themselves above what the senses furnish to be seen, heard, tasted, moving about—men who have thus never gone forth from this the native home of all sensible life, are veritable animals when there is question of understanding the high things of God. Their interior being is like a mountain of iron, in which no gleam of light ever shines. When outward things and images and forms are gone, they no longer know and feel anything. They are indeed, at home; but for that very reason they do not experience this wonderful resignation. Therefore did Christ say: "If any man come to Me and hate not his father, and mother, and wife, and children, and brethren, and sisters, yea, and his own life also, he cannot be My disciple" (Luke xiv, 26).

We have so far spoken of the first and last births, and how by the last we learn a lesson about the first. And now we shall instruct you about the second birth, in which this night the Son of God is born of His mother and becomes our Brother. In eternity He was born a Son without a mother, and in time He was born a Son without a father. Now Saint Augustine tells us: "Mary is much more blessed because God was born spiritually in her soul than because He was born her fleshly Son." Now, whosoever would experience this spiritual and blessed birth in his soul, as Mary did in her soul, should consider the qualities of Mary, that mother of God both fleshly and spiritual. She was a virgin, all chaste and pure, and yet she was retired and separated from all things, and so the angel found her. It is thus that one must be who would bring forth God in his soul. That soul must be chaste and pure. If it has strayed away from purity, then must it come back and be made pure again; for the meaning of virginity in this teaching, is to be outwardly unfruitful and inwardly very fruitful. And this virgin soul must close its outward senses, having little external occupation, for from such it can have little fruit. Mary thought of nothing else but of Divine things. Inwardly the soul must have much fruit; the beauty of the King's daughter is all within. Hence must this virgin soul live in detachment in all its habits, senses, behavior, in all its speech. Thus will it bear many and great fruits, namely, God's Son, God's Word, Who is all in all and contains all things in Himself.

Mary was a wedded virgin, and so must the soul be wedded, as St. Paul teaches. Thou must sink thy fickle will deep into the Divine will, which is immovably steadfast, so that thy feebleness may be strengthened. Mary lived retired, and so must the soul espoused to God be in retirement, if it will experience the interior regeneration. But not alone from those wanderings after temporal things which appear to be faulty, but even from the sensible devotion attached to the practice of virtue, must the soul refrain. It must establish rest and stillness as an enclosure in which to dwell, hiding from and cutting off nature and the senses, guarding quiet and interior peace, rest and repose. It is of this state of the soul that we shall sing next Sunday in the introit of the mass: "While all things were in quiet silence, and the night was in the midst of her course, Thine Almighty Word, O Lord, came down from Heaven, out of Thy royal throne" (Wisdom xviii, 14-15). That was the Eternal Word going forth from the Father's heart. It is amid this silence, when all things are hushed in even eternal silence, that in very truth we hear this word; for when God would speak thou must be silent. When God would enter in, all things must go out. When our Lord entered Egypt, all the idols in the land fell down. However good or holy anything may seem, if it hinders the actual and immediate Divine generation in thee it is an idol. Our Lord tells us that He has come bringing a sword, cutting off all that clings to men, even mother, brother, sister; for whatever is intimately joined to thee without God is thy enemy, forming, as it does, a multitude of imaginations covering and hiding the Divine Word.

Although this tranquility may not as yet wholly possess thee, nor last all the time within thee, yet thou shouldst so constantly cultivate interior silence as a means of experiencing the Divine birth, that it shall finally become a spiritual habit. What is easy to a well-practiced man may seem impossible to an unpracticed one, for practice makes perfect. May God grant us all the grace of inner stillness, and thereby the birth of His Divine Word in our souls. *Amen.*

God Is Gained by Detachment from Creatures

We read in the Holy Gospel that when our Lord was twelve years old He went with His parents to the temple, and that when they started homeward He remained there and they knew it not. Then when they missed Him on the journey and could not find Him among their kinsfolk and acquaintance, they must go back to the temple seeking Him. And so they found Him.

We may use this event to show thee, that if thou wouldst find the Divine generation thou must quit all men, and go back to the source from which thou hast sprung. All the powers of the soul, intelligence and understanding, memory and will, lead thee into multiplicity. Therefore, thou must give them all up in so far as they lead thee into the life of the senses and of images in which thou seekest and findest thyself; then and not otherwise shalt thou find the Divine generation. It is not to be found among kinsfolk and acquaintance, but, on the contrary, the search for it among them only leads thee astray.

And now it may be asked: Shall a man find this birth in certain works which are in themselves Divine, but which give us representations of God contributed by our senses, showing God's goodness, wisdom and mercy—framed by our own reason and yet Godlike in very truth? I answer no. Although these are good and Godlike, yet they come from our outward life of the human senses, and the Divine generation must come from within us and direct from God. When this Divine illumination shines within thee in actual reality, then thy activity must all cease and thy soul's powers must minister to God's and not to thy own activity; or, rather, God must alone be active and thou must rest passive. When thou hast given up thy own willing and knowing, then does God enter in, and He then lights up thy soul brilliantly with His presence. Wherever God would know Himself, there must thy power of knowing thyself cease to act. Do not imagine that thy reason may ever be so highly developed as to be able to know God by its native power in this Divine generation. If this light shines within thee, it borrows no rays from thy natural knowledge, but rather both thy reason and thyself must be brought to nothing before God, and His light shall possess thee. And when He thus comes to thee, He will bring with Him everything that thou hast renounced for His sake increased a thousandfold, to be known and enjoyed by thee in a new and all-embracing form. An example of this is given us in the Gospel, where our Lord conversed with the Samaritan woman at the well, and she left her pitcher and ran into the city and announced to the people that the Messias had come, and they believed her. But when they hastened out to the well and saw our Lord Himself, then they said to her: "We now believe, not for thy saying, for we ourselves have heard Him and know that this, indeed, is the Saviour of the World" (John iv, 42). And so in very truth, all created things and all sciences, added to thy own wisdom, cannot give thee the knowledge of God as God is divinely known. Wilt thou gain this knowledge? Then thou must give up all knowledge and become oblivious to all created things, even to thyself.

Alas, then, thou mayst complain, what will become of my poor mind, standing thus vacant and inert? Can such a way be right, since it directs my thoughts to an unknown knowledge? And how can this really be, for I cannot know at all without knowing something? If I know anything I am not, according to thy teaching, rightly prepared for God. Must I actually be in utter darkness? Yes, I answer, undoubtedly; thou art never better off than when thou art sunk in the darkness of unknowing. And if thou askest: Is this to be my final state, from which I shall never return? I answer: Yes; certainly yes. Again, if thou wouldst know what this darkness is, what name it has, I answer that it is thy soul reduced to a state of pure and simple receptivity, which alone can fit thee to attain to perfection. Out of this thou art not to come forth, except it be by a way that is not the way of truth. Thou mayst, indeed, do so, but it must be by the way either of the senses, the world or the devil. And that path will lead thee necessarily into transgressions; perhaps it may lead thee so far from God as to cause thy eternal downfall. Let there be no going backwards, therefore; thou art to press ever forward with thy longing for God, until all thy capacity for Him has been filled by His blessed presence; thy soul's longing will never cease until it is entirely filled with God. Unformed matter never rests till its form is granted it to the extent of its capacity; nor does the soul of man every find repose till it possesses God according to the fulness of its capacity. . . .

And now thou mayst ask an explanation about the Divine generation of the Son of God, of which we have been treating. May I, thou wilt ask, have a sign given by which I shall know it has happened? Yes, certainly; and the sign is threefold. Men often ask me, if one may ever attain to such a spiritual state that nothing hinders his perfection— neither the lapse of time, nor the oppressive weight of material existence, nor the distractions of the multitudes about him. And in very truth a man has reached that freedom, when this Divine generation has come to him; all created things after that are instinctively referred to

God, and to His birth within the soul. Take an example from a stroke of lightning. Whatever object is struck it is instantly turned toward the lightning. A man may turn his back away from it, but when struck he is quickly swung around again; the tree's leaves are all drawn toward the lightning that strikes it. So when this Divine birth strikes the soul it is instantly turned toward it, carrying with it all the conditions and circumstances of its existence, even the most unfavorable ones being transformed into benefits, by the soul's new relationship to God. No matter what thou seest or hearest, it all comes to thee sanctified by the Divine generation in thy soul. Everything becomes, as it were, God to thee, for thou knowest and lovest naught but God. It is like a man who has been gazing straight at the sun in the sky; when he turns to look at other objects he sees the sun's disc shining in them. And if thou shouldst fail in this, and dost not seek and love God alone in everything, even the least, then instantly know that this Divine birth hath failed within thee.

Thou mightest ask: Ought not a man to continue to practice penance? Is he not to blame if, on account of this Divine state, he ceases his penitential exercises? I answer that all such practices, including vigils, fasts, tears, sorrowful prayer, disciplines and hair shirts, are good, because the flesh lusteth against the spirit and the body is grown too strong for the soul, producing an unceasing conflict. Here in this life the flesh is bold and strong, for this earth is its native home, and the world around us is allied with this fleshly uprising. Food and drink and all the comforts of life are injurious to the spirit, which is in exile in this mortal existence. But in Heaven everything favors the spirit. There is its fatherland and its home, and Heaven's freedom from fleshly hindrance is granted the soul, if it would but direct its thoughts and its love to Heaven's inhabitants, who are its real friends and kindred. Here below in our exile we must weaken the fleshly instincts and appetites, lest they overpower the spirit. This we succeed in doing by painful penances, putting a curb on the body's ease and comfort. Thereby the soul holds its own against the uprising of fleshly passions, and finally reduces them to captivity. Only lay on the appetites the curb and the fetter of heavenly love, and thou shalt most quickly and most overwhelmingly subjugate them. Hence about nothing does God complain so severely as about our want of love. Love is like the hook on a fisherman's line; the fish must take the hook or the fisherman can never catch him. After the hook is once in his mouth, the fish may swim about and even swim away from the shore, but the fisherman is sure to finally land him. And this I compare with love. Whoever is caught by love is held perfectly fast, and yet in a sweet captivity. Whoever has received the gift of Divine love, obtains from it more freedom from base natural tendencies than by practicing all possible penances and austerities. He it is that can most sweetly endure all misfortunes that happen to him or threaten to overwhelm him; he is the one who most readily forgives all the injuries that can be inflicted on him. Nothing brings thee nearer to God; nothing makes God so much thy own, as the sweet bond of love. Whosoever has found this way never seeks any other. Whosoever is caught by this hook is so entirely captive, that feet, hands, mouth, eyes and heart—everything that is himself—becomes God's own. Therefore, if thou wouldst conquer these enemies, namely, corrupt natural tendencies, and render them harmless, love is thy best weapon. Therefore, it is written: "Love is strong as death, [its] jealousy hard as hell" (Cant. viii, 6). Death cuts the soul from the body, but love cuts all things from the soul. When the soul loves, then whatsoever is not God or Godlike, it suffers not to rest with it for an instant. Whosoever is enlisted in this warfare and treads this path, what he does or what he does not in active good works, or what he is not able to do, makes no difference—whether something or nothing, all is for love. The work of perfect love is more fruitful to a man's own soul and to the souls of all other men with whom he deals, and it brings more glory to God, than all other works, even if these be free from mortal sin, but are done in a state of weaker love. The mere quiet repose of a soul with perfect love, is of more worth to God and man than the active labors of another soul. Therefore, do thou but cleave fast and firm to this hook of Divine love and thou shalt be God's happy captive, and the more entirely captive, the more perfectly free shalt thou be. That this captivity and liberty may be vouchsafed us, we pray God the Father, and God the Son, and God the Holy Ghost. *Amen.*

Jan van Ruysbroeck

(1293–1381)

The soaring beauty of his prose and the profoundity of his insights into the depths of the interior life place Jan van Ruysbroeck among the greatest writers in the contemplative tradition. Born in the small

Flemish village of Ruysbroeck, from which he takes his name, Jan left home at an early age to take up residence with his uncle, a canon of a cathedral in Brussels, and his companion, a devout priest. The two ecclesiastics brought the boy up in an atmosphere of prayer and saw to it that he had a religious education. Gifted with a fine intellect, Jan entered the priesthood and was given the position of cathedral chaplain, a post he held for twenty-six years.

During this time he apparently came into contact with certain members of a flourishing sect known as the Brethren of the Free Spirit who espoused a pantheistic doctrine and proclaimed their freedom from any system of sacraments or code of law. Committed to an orthodox faith, Ruysbroeck opposed the teachings of this sect. He was especially concerned about the way their practices could affect one's inner world, and so advocated those orthodox tenets of the mystical life that the Brethren of the Free Spirit neglected: the activity of divine grace, a free turning of the will to God, and the necessity for a conscience free from mortal sin.

At the age of fifty, drawn by the necessities of his developing life of prayer and finding the bustle and distractions of the city no longer endurable, Ruysbroeck and his two older companions retired to the forest of Soignes outside Brussels to devote themselves to lives of contemplation. Soon joined by disciples, they formed a small community that was eventually placed under the rule of the Augustinian canons. For the remaining thirty-eight years of his life the Flemish mystic remained in the forest, his life of interiority giving support to his activities as prior of the community and giving birth to his writings on the "God-seeing" life.

The Adornment of the Spiritual Marriage is one of the works he produced at this time. Its lucid descriptions of the progress of the interior life are some of the most moving in all literature on spirituality. It is neatly structured and corresponds to the traditional three phases of the mystic process: the purgative, the illuminative, and the unitive. In *The Adornment* the idea of progress, implicit in all Christian mysticism, is given great stress. Emphasis is also placed on the need for an ever deepening interior life, a life Ruysbroeck perceives in images of growth and change.

To the first of these unfolding stages Ruysbroeck applies the term the "Active Life." The entire first segment of *The Adornment* is given over to a description of this life. It is primarily concerned with the development of the Christian character, assumed as the only solid foundation on which to erect the structure of the mystic life. The individual's natural life, Ruysbroeck writes, may be "adorned with virtues," thus preparing it for the coming of the spirit of Christ. These virtues are not merely of an outward nature, involving the elimination of mortal sin, but extend into the very heart of the person. It is especially important for the individual at this stage, the purgative phase, to order personal intentions, extending a loving will in the direction of God and having Him in mind in all things.

The second segment of the book, which corresponds to the traditional illuminative phase, is entitled the "Spiritual Life." It deals essentially with the interior progress of the soul that, responding to the invitation of God, deliberately seeks its reconstruction in the image of its true archetype, the spirit of Christ. The transfiguration begins with the "lower powers" or sense life and extends to the "higher powers" of memory, understanding, and will. Inundated by the divine radiance that illuminates them, the soul's powers proceed to that unity of spirit where they have their origins and where, outside time, the Eternal Birth of Christ takes place. In this ground in the depths of one's being, true union with God occurs, producing a profound yet simple communion that enables the soul to consider itself a "secret friend of God."

Beyond this state is yet another life, the "Superessential Life," which forms the topic for the third segment of *The Adornment* and which corresponds to the unitive phase. In this life there is a genuine transcendence, a passing beyond the spirit into the deep quiet of the Godhead that, unutterable and inconceivable, lies beyond time and the grasp of human reason. Here Divine Love imparts itself as movement: as grace it unites one to itself through one's virtues and good works and as an indrawing tide it draws one without means back toward itself where one is sunk in the darkness and stillness of the divine rest. Thus at the height of the mystic life the individual participates in God's dual life of rest and work, remaining in peaceful union yet constantly sent out into the world to embody His love.

The selections reprinted here are from all three segments of *The Adornment* to illustrate the different themes and intents of each of the three "Lives" of the mystic path. "Of the Second Coming of Christ" is from the first section, on the "Active Life." In it the beauty of Ruysbroeck's metaphorical language is clearly shown. "Of the Pain and Restlessness of Love," "A Parable of the Ant," and "Of a Loving Strife Between the Spirit of God and Our Spirit" are from the second part of the book, on the "Spiritual Life." In the last selection, "Showing the Three Ways by Which One Enters into the God-Seeing Life," the Flemish mystic plumbs the depths of the inner world to reveal the outlines of the "Superessential Life."

The Adornment of the
Spiritual Marriage

Of the second coming of Christ.

The second coming of Christ our Bridegroom takes place every day within good men; often and many times, with new graces and gifts, in all those who make themselves ready for it, each according to his power. We would not speak here of a man's first conversion, nor of the first grace which was given to him when he turned from sin to the virtues. But we would speak of an increase of new gifts and new virtues from day to day, and of the present coming of Christ our Bridegroom which takes place daily within our souls.

Now we must consider the why and the wherefore, the way and the working of this coming. Its wherefore is fourfold: God's mercy and our destitution, God's generosity and our desire. These four things cause the growth of virtue and of nobleness.

Now understand this: when the sun sends its beams and its radiance into a deep valley between two high mountains, and, standing in the zenith, can yet shine upon the bottom and ground of the valley, then three things happen: the valley becomes full of light by reflection from the mountains, and it receives more heat, and becomes more fruitful, than the plain and level country. And so likewise, when a good man takes his stand upon his own littleness, in the most lowly part of himself, and confesses and knows that he has nothing, and is nothing, and can nothing, of himself, neither stand still nor go on, and when he sees how often he fails in virtues and good works: then he confesses his poverty and his helplessness, then he makes a valley of humility. And when he is thus humble, and needy, and knows his own need; he lays his distress, and complains of it, before the bounty and the mercy of God. And so he marks the sublimity of God and his own lowliness; and thus he becomes a deep valley. And Christ is a Sun of righteousness and also of mercy, Who stands in the highest part of the firmament, that is, on the right hand of the Father, and from thence He shines into the

John of Ruysbroeck, The *Adornment of the Spiritual Marriage, Etc.* trans. C. A. Wynschenk (New York: E. P. Dutton, 1916). pp. 17–19, 74–76, 80–81, 122–23, 167–170.

bottom of the humble heart; for Christ is always moved by helplessness, whenever a man complains of it and lays it before Him with humility. Then there arise two mountains, that is, two desires; one to serve God and praise Him with reverence, the other to attain noble virtues. Those two mountains are higher than the heavens, for these longings touch God without intermediary, and crave His ungrudging generosity. And then that generosity cannot withhold itself, it must flow forth; for then the soul is made ready to receive, and to hold, more gifts.

These are the wherefore, and the way of the new coming with new virtues. Then, this valley, the humble heart, receives three things: it becomes more radiant and enlightened by grace, it becomes more ardent in charity, and it becomes more fruitful in perfect virtues and in good works. And thus you have the why, the way, and the work of this coming.

*   *   *

Of the pain and restlessness of love.

Of this inward demand and this invitation, and also because the creature lifts itself up and offers itself, and all that it can do, and yet can neither attain nor acquire the unity—of these things spring a ghostly pain. When the inmost part of the heart and the source of life have been wounded by love, and one cannot obtain that which one desires above all things, but must ever abide where one does not wish to be: from these two things pain comes forth. Here Christ is risen to the zenith of the conscience, and He sends His Divine rays into the hungry desires and into the longings of the heart; and this splendour burns and dries up and consumes all the moisture, that is, the strength and the powers of nature. The desire of the open heart, and the shining of the Divine rays, cause a perpetual pain.

If, then, one cannot achieve God and yet cannot and will not do without Him, from these two things there arise in such men tumult and restlessness, both without and within. And so long as a man is thus agitated, no creature, neither in heaven nor on earth, can give him rest or help him. In this state there are sometimes spoken from within sublime and salutary words, and singular teachings and wisdom are given. In this inward tumult one is ready to suffer all that can be suffered, that one may obtain that which one loves. This fury of love is an inward impatience which will hardly use reason or follow it, if it cannot obtain that which it loves. This inward fury eats a man's heart and drinks his blood. Here the sensible heat of love is fiercer than at any other stage in man's whole life; and his bodily nature is secretly wounded and consumed without any outward work, and the fruits of the virtues ripen more quickly than in all the degrees which have been shown heretofore.

In the like season of the year, the visible sun enters the sign of Leo, that is, the Lion, who is fierce by nature, for he is the lord over all beasts. So likewise, when a man comes to this way, Christ, the bright Sun, stands in the sign of the Lion, for the rays of His heat are so fierce that the blood in the heart of the impatient man must boil. And when this fierce way prevails, it masters and subdues all other ways and works; for it wills to be wayless, that is, without manner. And in this tumult a man sometimes falls into a desire and restless longing to be freed from the prison of his body, so that he may at once be united with Him Whom he loves. And he opens his inward eyes and beholds the heavenly house full of glory and joy, and his Beloved crowned in the midst of it, flowing forth towards His saints in abounding bliss; whilst he must lack all this. And therefrom there often spring in such a man outward tears and great longings. He looks down and considers the place of exile in which he has been imprisoned, and from which he cannot escape; then tears of sadness and misery gush forth. These natural tears soothe and refresh the man's heart, and they are wholesome to the bodily nature, preserving its strength and powers and sustaining him through this state of tumult. All the manifold considerations and exercises according to ways or manner are helpful to the impatient man; that his strength may be preserved and that he may long endure in virtue.

*   *   *

A parable of the ant.

A brief parable I will give to those who dwell in the tumult of love, that they may endure this state nobly and becomingly, and may attain to higher virtues. There is a small insect called the ant. It is strong and sagacious, and very loth to die. It lives by choice amongst the congregation of its fellows, in hot and dry soil. The ant works during summer, and gathers grain for food for the winter. And it splits the grain in two lest it should sprout and be spoiled, and be of no use when nothing can be gathered anymore. And it seeks no strange ways, but always goes forth by the same way. And if it abides its time, it shall be able to fly.

Thus should these men do. They should be strong in abiding the coming of Christ, sagacious against the communications and inspirations of the devil. They should not desire death; but God's glory alone, and for themselves new virtues. They should dwell in the congregation of their heart and of their powers, and should follow the drawing and the inviting of the Divine Unity. They should dwell in warm and dry soil, that is, in the fierce tumult of love and in a great restlessness. And they should labour during the summer of this life, and gather the fruits of virtue for eternity; and they should split these fruits in two. The one part is, that they should ever desire the most high fruition of Eternity; and the other part is that, by means of the reason, they should always restrain themselves as much as they can, and abide the time which God has ordained to them, and thus the fruit of virtue is preserved unto eternity. And they should not follow strange paths or singular ways; but they should follow the track of love through all storms to that place whither love shall lead them. And if they abide the time, and persevere in all virtues, they shall behold the Mystery of God and take flight towards It.

*   *   *

Of a loving strife between the spirit of God and our spirit.

In this storm of love two spirits strive together: the spirit of God and our own spirit. God, through the Holy Ghost, inclines Himself towards us; and, thereby, we are touched in love. And our spirit, by God's working and by the power of love, presses and inclines itself into God: and, thereby, God is touched. From these two contacts there arises the strife of love, at the very deeps of this meeting; and in that most inward and ardent encounter, each spirit is deeply wounded by love. These two spirits, that is, our own spirit and the Spirit of God, sparkle and shine one into the other, and each shows to the other its face. This makes each of the spirits yearn for the other in love. Each demands of the other all that it is; and each offers to the other all that it is and invites it to all that it is. This makes the lovers melt into each other. God's touch and His gifts, our loving craving and our giving back: these fulfil love. This flux and reflux causes the fountain of love to brim over: and thus the touch of God and our loving craving become one simple love. Here man is possessed by love, so that he must forget himself and God, and knows and can do nothing but love. Thereby the spirit is burned up in the fire of love, and enters so deeply into the touch of God, that it is overcome in all its cravings, and turned to nought in all its works, and empties itself; above all surrender becoming very love. And it possesses, above all virtues, the inmost part of its created being, where every creaturely work begins and ends. Such is love in itself, foundation and origin of all virtues.

Showing the three ways by which one enters into the God-seeing life.

The inward lover of God, who possesses God in fruitive love, and himself in adhering and active love, and his whole life in virtues according to righteousness; through these three things, and by the mysterious revelation of God, such an inward man enters into the God-seeing life. Yea, the lover who is inward and righteous, him will it please God in His freedom to choose and to lift up into a superessential contemplation, in the Divine Light and according to the Divine Way. This contemplation sets us in purity and clearness above all our understanding, for it is a singular adornment and a heavenly crown, and besides the eternal reward of all virtues and of our whole life. And to it none can attain through knowledge and subtlety, neither through any exercise whatsoever. Only he with whom it pleases God to be united in His Spirit, and whom it pleases Him to enlighten by Himself, can see God, and no one else. The mysterious Divine Nature is eternally and actively beholding and loving according to the Persons, and has everlasting fruition in a mutual embrace of the Persons in the unity of the Essence. In this embrace, in the essential Unity of God, all inward spirits are one with God in the immersion of love; and are that same one which the Essence is in Itself, according to the mode of Eternal Bliss. And in this most high unity of the Divine Nature, the heavenly Father is origin and beginning of every work which is worked in heaven and on earth. And He says in the deep-sunken hiddenness of the spirit: BEHOLD, THE BRIDEGROOM COMETH; GO YE OUT TO MEET HIM.

These words we will now explain and set forth in their relation to that superessential contemplation which is the source of all holiness, and of all perfection of life to which one may attain. Few men can attain to this Divine seeing, because of their own incapacity and the mysteriousness of the light in which one sees. And therefore no one will thoroughly understand the meaning of it by any learning or subtle consideration of his own; for all words, and all that may be learnt and understood in a creaturely way, are foreign to, and far below, the truth which I mean. But he who is united with God, and is enlightened in this truth, he is able to understand the truth by itself. For to comprehend and to understand God above all similitudes, such as He is in Himself, is to be God with God, without intermediary, and without any otherness that can become a hindrance or an intermediary. And therefore I beg every one who cannot understand this, or feel it in the fruitive unity of his spirit, that he be not offended at it, and leave it for that which it is: for that which I am going to say is true, and Christ, the Eternal Truth, has said it Himself in His teaching in many places, if we could but show and explain it rightly. And therefore, whosoever wishes to understand this must have died to himself, and must live in God, and must turn his gaze to the eternal light in the ground of his spirit, where the Hidden Truth reveals Itself without means. For our Heavenly Father wills that we should see; for He is the Father of Light, and this is why He utters eternally, without intermediary and without interruption, in the hiddenness of our spirit, one unique and abysmal word, and no other. And in this word, He utters Himself and all things. And this word is none other than: BEHOLD. And this is the coming forth and the birth of the Son of Eternal Light, in Whom all blessedness is known and seen.

*   *   *

Now if the spirit would see God with God in this Divine light without means, there needs must be on the part of man three things.

The first is that he must be perfectly ordered from without in all the virtues, and within must be unencumbered, and as empty of every outward work as if he did not work at all: for if his emptiness is troubled within by some work of virtue, he has an image; and as long as this endures within him, he cannot contemplate.

Secondly, he must inwardly cleave to God, with adhering intention and love, even as a burning and glowing fire which can never more be quenched. As long as he feels himself to be in this state, he is able to contemplate.

Thirdly, he must have lost himself in a Waylessness and in a Darkness, in which all contemplative men wander in fruition and wherein they never again can find themselves in a creaturely way. In the abyss of this darkness, in which the loving spirit has died to itself, there begin the manifestation of God and eternal life. For in this darkness there shines and is born an incomprehensible Light, which is the Son of God, in Whom we behold eternal life. And in this Light one becomes seeing; and this Divine Light is given to the simple sight of the spirit, where the spirit receives the brightness which is God Himself, above all gifts and every creaturely activity, in the idle emptiness in which the spirit has lost itself through fruitive love, and where it receives without means the brightness of God, and is changed without interruption into that brightness which it receives. Behold, this mysterious brightness, in which one sees everything that one can desire according to the emptiness of the spirit: this brightness is so great that the loving contemplative, in his ground wherein he rests, sees and feels nothing but an incomprehensible Light; and through that Simple Nudity which enfolds all things, he finds himself, and feels himself, to be that same Light by which he sees, and nothing else. And this is the first condition by which one becomes seeing in the Divine Light. Blessed are the eyes which are thus seeing, for they possess eternal life.

6. The Italian Mystic Renaissance: The Two Catherines

Catherine of Siena

(1347–1380)

Of the approximately thirty theologians formally granted the title Doctor of the Church by the papacy, only two are women. One of these is Teresa of Avila. The other is Catherine of Siena, Dominican tertiary, ardent reformer, and mystic of the first rank.

Much of Catherine's religious activity was of a public nature. Furthermore, her ecstasies and unusual mode of life evoked much interest during her lifetime. Consequently, we know more about her life and personality than we do about many other figures within the contemplative tradition.

She was born Catherine Benincasa, the youngest of twenty-five children of a prosperous Sienese dyer and his wife. Her early years were full of both the ordinary joys of childhood and a precocious longing toward the ascetic life that manifested itself in the practice of penances and, at age seven, a vow of perpetual virginity. At first her austerities met with sharp opposition within her family, but young Catherine's perseverance and sincerity soon won over her detractors. At sixteen she became a Dominican tertiary, one of a group of devout women who lived under religious vows in their own homes. Following this she lived virtually as a recluse for three years, absorbed in ecstatic prayer and speaking only to her confessor. This period ended in 1367 with her famous mystical marriage to Christ, after which she felt impelled to devote herself to a more active life, attending especially to the needs of the sick and poor. Then the death of her father and a political revolution in Siena put an end to the prosperity of the Benincasa family, which was broken up.

The end of this period in her life signaled the beginning of another. The 1370s saw the emergence of her public ministry as peacemaker in the troubled seas of Italian political life. One outstanding example will serve as a illustration. Several years of unrest erupted openly when a plague and famine in Tuscany sparked Florence, at the head of a league of Italian states, into open rebellion against the forces of the papacy. At the time, the papacy was situated in the foreign city of Avignon. Catherine, becoming known as a powerful agent of reconciliation, was sent to the papal court of Gregory XI on behalf of the Florentines. Her impassioned and stern correspondence with both sides of the feud had already netted some results. But in this instance her firm conviction that Christian rulers must unite in the mutually supportive bonds of their Christianity could not win out against the vicissitudes of political life. She had Gregory virtually convinced of the need for reconciliation. But the Florentine ambassadors, whom she expected daily, delayed their coming to Avignon. When they finally arrived, it was clear that the Florentines had been divided among themselves at home. The ambassadors refused to acknowledge her position as intermediary. Despite this blow to her plans (and affront to her person), Catherine redirected her energy to persuading the Pope to return to Rome. Triumphing over amazing obstacles, she succeeded.

This untiring devotion to the cause of political and intrafamilial peace never left Catherine. The number of scarred and shattered bonds she healed in her short lifetime is astounding. At the root of her zeal was her sorrow over the corruptions of the Church, a Church that had the responsibility of making Christ manifest in the world and that was falling far short of its task. Catherine's efforts were not directed toward finding any one practical solution to a given situation. Rather she looked deep into the roots of problems, noting the pride and corruption of the human heart, then invoked the model of Christ, into whose image all persons must be reformed. The strength of her conviction in this truth is attested to by the fact that she did indeed succeed in moving the hearts of many.

Nonetheless, the weighty burden of the troubled Church was too much even for Catherine's strong shoulders. To her grief, she witnessed one of the most painful fissures ever to rend the fabric of the Church body, the Great Schism. Pope Gregory had returned to the Eternal City, but the discords there proved too much for him. Having become alienated from Catherine and her ideals, he died exhausted and disappointed in 1378. His successor, proclaimed Urban VI, made peace with the beleaguered city of Florence. But his harsh measures toward the clergy aroused antagonism. The College of Cardinals announced that the papal election had been invalid. The cardinal of Geneva, who took the name Clement VII, was appointed to replace Urban. Europe became divided in its allegiance, and war raged between the two camps. Through all this the Sienese dyer's daughter remained faithful to Urban, wrote on his behalf to the ruling monarchs of France, Hungary, and Naples, to the magistrates of the Italian cities, and to the dissenting cardinals. Her already frail health gave way under the unrelenting strain. Dedicating herself as a sacrificial victim in expiation for the sins of the Church and of the Roman people, she died on April 30, 1380.

The mystic vision that sustained this woman in her untiring and selfless activity is one of the most vital in the entire contemplative tradition. Her great work on the interior life, *The Dialogue*, has been referred to as an example of theological spirituality, for it is based firmly on orthodox doctrine and the time-honored ascetic teachings of the Church. *The Dialogue* was dictated to her secretaries while in a state of ecstasy, but, it is arresting to note, emerged as one of the most practical and accessible of all contemplative documents. Rarely has a contemplative writer lavished as much care on descriptions of the essential early stages of the spiritual life, carefully delineating the pitfalls that might cause a young soul to stumble. It is almost as though Catherine cared less for the extraordinary occurrences within her (and so spent less time dwelling on them) than for the health and growth of others. Repeatedly, she extended her hand to others to guide them through the labyrinths of their own inner worlds.

The book reveals the Sienese saint's devotion to Christ crucified, especially as symbolized in His blood, and shows the extent to which she accepted the axiom that suffering can be an instrument of self-knowledge and that self-abandonment can be the road that leads to God. She instructs the reader, in her gentle yet firm manner, to accept the lessons of suffering that lead one to profound humility, an embrace of one's true smallness in the light of the infinite perfection, and to burning love, a recognition of the mercy and goodness of God.

The same precepts that are set out in *The Dialogue* are found in her letters in a more personal and engaging form. The letters illustrate that her mysticism was never divorced from daily life. The letter reprinted here was written to a hermit, Brother William of England, of the Brothers of St. Augustine. In it Catherine gives advice to a man whose withdrawal from society was calculated to teach him more about the God-life than he could learn in the world. Catherine counsels him about the dangers of misplaced asceticism, exhorting him to remember the goal of such practices, namely, the increase of love in the interior life.

To Brother William of England

Dearest son in Christ sweet Jesus: I Catherine, servant and slave of the servants of Jesus Christ, write to you in His precious Blood, with desire to see you in true light. For without light we shall not be able to walk in the way of truth, but shall walk in shadows. Two lights are necessary. First, we must be illumined to know the transitory things of the world, which all pass like the wind. But these are not rightly known if we do not know our own frailty, how inclined it is, from the perverse law which is bound up with our members, to rebel against its Creator. This light is necessary to every rational creature, in whatever state it may be, if it wishes to have divine grace, and to share in the blessing of the Blood of the Spotless Lamb. This is the common light, that everybody in general ought to have, for whoever has it not is in a state of condemnation. This is the reason; that, not having light, he is not in a state of grace; for one who does not know the evil of wrong, nor who is cause of it, cannot avoid it nor hate the cause. So he who does not know good, and virtue the cause of good, cannot love nor desire that good.

The soul must not stay content because it has arrived at gaining the general light; nay, it ought to go on with all zeal to the perfect light. For since men are at first imperfect rather than perfect, they should advance in light to perfection. Two kinds of perfect people walk in this perfect light. There are some who give themselves to castigating their body perfectly, doing very great harsh penance; and that the flesh may not rebel against the reason, they have placed all their desire rather on mortifying their body than on slaying their self-will. These people feed at the table of penitence and are good and perfect; but unless they have a great humility and conform themselves not wholly to judge according to the will of God and not according to that of men, they often wrong

Saint Catherine of Siena as Seen in her Letters, trans. Vida D. Scudder (New York: E. P. Dutton and Company, 1906).

their perfection, making themselves judges of those who do not walk in the same way in which they do.

This happens to them because they have put more thought and desire on mortifying their body than on slaying their self-will. Such men as these always want to choose times and places and mental consolations to suit themselves; also, worldly tribulations, and their battles with the devil; saying, through self-deceit, beguiled by their own will—which is called spiritual self-will—"I should like this consolation, and not these assaults or battles with the devil; not for my own sake, but to please God, and possess Him more fully, because I seem to possess Him better in this way than in that." Many a time, in such a way as this, the soul falls into suffering and weariness, and becomes unendurable to itself through them, and thus wrongs its state of perfection. The odour of pride clings to it, and this it does not perceive. For, were it truly humble and not presumptuous, it would see well that the Sweet Primal Truth gives conditions, time and place, and consolation and tribulation, according as is needful to our perfection, and to fulfil in the soul the perfection to which it is chosen. It would see that everything is given through love, and therefore with love.

All things ought to be received with reverence, as is done by the second class of people, who abide in this sweet and glorious light, who are perfect in whatever condition they are, and, in so far as God permits them, hold everything in due reverence, esteeming themselves worthy of sufferings and scandals in the world, and of missing their consolations. As they hold themselves worthy of sufferings, so they hold themselves unworthy of the reward which follows suffering. These have known and tasted in the light the eternal will of God, which wishes naught but our good, and that we be sanctified in Him, therefore giving His gifts. When the soul has known this will, it is arrayed therein, and cares for nothing save to see in what wise it can grow, and preserve its condition perfect, for glory and praise of the Name of God. Therefore, it opens the eye of the mind upon its object, Christ crucified, who is rule and way and doctrine for perfect and imperfect: and sees the loving Lamb, Who gives it the doctrine of perfection, which seeing it loves.

Perfection is this: that the Word, the Son of God, fed at the table of holy desire for the honour of God and for our salvation; and with this desire ran with great zeal to the shameful death of the Cross, avoiding neither toil nor labour, not drawing back for the ingratitude and ignorance of us men who did not recognize His benefits, nor for the persecution of the Jews, nor for mockery or insults or criticism of the people, but underwent them all, like our captain and true knight, who was come to teach us His way and rule and doctrine, opening the door with the keys of His precious Blood, shed with ardent love and hatred against sin. As says this sweet, loving Word, "Behold, I have made you a way, and opened the door with My blood. Be you then not negligent to follow it, and do not sit yourselves down in self-love, ignorantly failing to know the Way, and presumptuously wishing to choose it after your own fashion, and not after Mine who made it. Rise up then, and follow Me: for no one can go to the Father but by Me. I am the Way and the Door."

Then the soul, enamoured and tormented with love, runs to the table of holy desire, and sees not itself in itself, seeking private consolation, spiritual or temporal, but, as one who has wholly destroyed his own will in this light and knowledge, refuses no toil from whatever side it comes. Nay, in suffering, in pain, in many assaults from the devil and criticisms from men, it seeks upon the table of the Cross the food of the honour of God and the salvation of men. And it seeks no reward, from God or from fellow-creatures; such men serve God, not for their own joy, and the neighbour not for their own will or profit, but from pure love. They lose themselves, divesting them of the old man, their fleshly desires, and array them in the new man, Christ sweet Jesus, following Him manfully. These are they who feed at the table of holy desire, and have more zeal for slaying their self-will than for slaying and mortifying the body. They have mortified the body, to be sure, but not as a chief aim, but as the tool which it is, to help in slaying self-will; for one's chief aim ought to be and is to slay the will; that it may seek and wish naught save to follow Christ crucified, seeking the honour and glory of His Name, and the salvation of souls. Such men abide ever in peace and quiet; there are none who can offend them, because they have cast away the thing that gives offence—that is, self-will. All the persecutions which the world and the devil can inflict run away beneath their feet; they stand in the water, made fast to the twigs of eager desire, and are not submerged. Such a man as this rejoices in everything; he does not make himself a judge of the servants of God, nor of any rational creature; nay, he rejoices in every condition and every type that he sees, saying, "Thanks be to Thee, eternal Father, that Thou hast many mansions in Thy House." And he rejoices more in the different kinds of men that he sees than he would do in seeing them all walk in the same way, for so he sees the greatness of God's goodness more manifest. He joys in everything, and gets from it the fragrance of roses. And even as to a thing which he may expressly see to be sin, he does not pose as a judge, but regards it rather with holy true compassion, saying, "To-day it is thy turn, and to-morrow mine, unless it be for divine grace which preserves me."

Oh, holy minds, who feed at the table of holy desire, who have attained in great light to nourish you with holy food, clothed with the sweet raiment of the Lamb, His love and charity! You do not lose time in accepting false judgments, either of the servants of God or of the servants of the world; you do not take offence at any criticism, either against yourselves or others. Your love toward God and your neighbour is governed well, and not ungoverned. And because it is governed, such men as these, dearest son, never take offence at those whom they love; for appearances are dead to them, and they have submitted themselves not to be guided by men, but only by the Holy Spirit. See then, these enjoy in this life the pledge of life eternal.

I wish you and the other ignorant sons to reach this light, for I see that this perfection is lacking to you and to others. For were it not lacking to you, you would not have fallen into such criticism and offence and false judgment, as to say and believe that another man was guided and mastered by the will of the creature and not of the Creator. My soul and my heart grieve to see you wrong the perfection to which God has called you, under pretence of love and odour of virtue. Nevertheless, these are the tares which the devil has sowed in the field of the Lord; he has done this to choke the seed of holy desire and doctrine sowed in your fields. Will then to do so no more, since God has of grace given you great lights; the first, to despise the world; the second, to mortify the body; the third, to seek the honour of God. Do not wrong this perfection with spiritual self-will, but rise from the table of penance and attain the table of the desire of God, where the soul is wholly dead to its own will, nourishing itself without suffering on the honour of God and the salvation of souls, growing in perfection and not wronging it.

Therefore, considering that this condition cannot be had without light, and seeing that you had it not, I said that I desired and desire to see you in true and perfect light. Thus I pray you, by the love of Christ crucified—you and Brother Antonio and all the others—that you struggle to win it, so that you may be numbered among the perfect and not among the imperfect. I say no more. Remain in the holy and sweet grace of God. I commend me to all of you. Bathe you in the Blood of Christ crucified. Sweet Jesus, Jesus Love.

Catherine of Genoa

(1447–1510)

Ardent, affectionate, and pierced by the fiery wound of divine love, Catherine of Genoa, born the fifth child of the noble Fieschi family, was destined to become one of the most original and influential figures in the history of the Christian contemplative tradition. From an early age this elegant woman felt herself drawn to the religious life and tried to gain admittance to a convent in which her sister was already a nun. Refused on account of her age, she was married by her family to Giulano Adorni, a marriage of political convenience designed to unite the opposing Guelph and Ghibelline factions of the city. It was an unhappy union for Catherine. Abandoned by her husband and disgusted by the round of distractions in which she had immersed herself to compensate for the wretchedness of her married life, she received a sudden illumination that irrevocably changed the course of her life.

She embarked upon a regimen of extreme penance and mortification. Four years later her repentant husband returned to move with her to an impoverished district of Genoa to undertake the care of the sick in a nearby hospital. For the next twenty years or so, she continued this work of charity, went daily to communion, and was guided solely by the spirit of God that moved so forcefully within her. In 1499, because of failing health, she resigned her post at the hospital, and, for the first time in her life, attached herself to a spiritual director and confessor, Don Cattaneo Marabotto, who was to become one of her disciples and the cobiographer of her Life. She soon attracted a small group of devoted disciples for whom she served as inspiration and guide. She died at the age of sixty-three, her already frail health undermined by a prolonged and painful illness that her followers claimed was of supernatural origin.

Like so many of the great mystics, Catherine of Genoa combined an interior life of ecstatic and incessant contemplation with an exterior life of unflagging activity. The events of her life indicate some of the latter; only her own words can convey the former. These words are some of the most penetrating in all Christian literature. Untutored in the subtleties of theology and unhindered by the fetters of literary convention, Catherine spoke passionately of what consumed her: the annihilation of her own self-love in the fires of the perfect love of God. The fact that she was guided almost solely by inner inspiration for the bulk of her adult life is reflected not only in the highly personal style of her sayings, but in her somewhat unorthodox attitude toward religious practices. As an example, the daily reception of communion that she felt compelled to practice was practically unheard of in her day.

What did this mystic say that could so capture the imagination of generations of avid readers? She spoke of her conviction that the total surrender of the will and the rejection of earthly concerns were necessary to achieve union with God. She saw the world and the body as chains that must be broken before one could aspire to the spiritual life. A high degree of outer and inner mortification was thus necessary to begin to purify the soul. This purification prepared the soul to attain the state of "pure love" in which God took complete possession and one no longer acted independently of His will. In this purified state there must be nothing of self, for God alone could accomplish the perfect works He desired of the soul. An austere vision, yes, but Catherine's words do not sound a stern or gloomy note. They are ecstatic, aching with love, singing in the thrall of rapture. They speak of a joy and a desire that transcend all else. They issue from the depths of contemplative heights.

The selections reprinted here are taken from *The Life and Works of St. Catherine of Genoa*, the work of her confessor and confidant, Cattaneo Marabotto, and Ettore Vernazza, a philanthropic Genoese lawyer, both of whom were her devoted disciples. The book contains a faithful record of her utterances plus some comments and interpolations by the two biographers. We have included a narrative account of her conversion experience at the age of twenty-six, which marked her entry into the life of intense interior communication that was to characterize the rest of her adult life as well as a first-person account of the gradual transformation of her soul and an ecstatic description of the state of union with the divine.

The Life and Works of
St. Catherine of Genoa

At the end of these ten years Catherine was called by God and suddenly converted in a remarkable manner. For the three months previous to her conversion she was filled with great sadness and profound disgust with life, which led her to avoid all company and mope in solidute; so deep was her melancholy that she became insufferable to herself, not knowing what it was she really wanted. For five years she had sought distraction in the pleasures and vanities of the world, as a compensation for her wretchedness during the early years of her married life, but this had had the effect of only increasing her distress instead of lessening it.

Finding herself one day in the Church of St. Benedict—it was the eve of that saint's feast—she said to him in the extremity of her grief: 'Pray to God that He may keep me sick in bed for three months.' She spoke these words in desperation, not knowing where to turn to find relief from the torment in her soul.

Two days later she was persuaded by the sister of hers who was a nun to go and see the chaplain of her convent. She had no desire to go to confession, but her sister had said to her: 'At least go and talk to him, for he is a good priest,' and in fact he was a saintly man. She had hardly knelt down before him when her heart suddenly pierced by an immense love of God, with such a clear awareness of her own miseries and sins and of God's goodness, that she was ready to swoon. The feeling produced in her a change of heart that purified her and drew her wholly away from the follies of the world. She was almost beside herself and cried out in her heart with burning love: 'No more world! No more sin!' At that moment she felt that, if she had possessed a thousand worlds, she would have spurned them all.

While she thus knelt, incapable of speech and almost senseless, her confessor did not notice anything amiss. He was called away on some matter, and when he returned shortly afterwards, she recovered herself so far as to be able to murmur: 'Father, if you don't mind, I would like to leave this confession for another time.' Rising to her feet, she left him

The Life and Sayings of Saint Catherine of Genoa, trans. Paul Garvin (Staten Island: Alba House, 1964), pp. 23-25, 113-116, 82-83.

and returned home, all on fire and pierced to the heart by the love that God had inwardly shown her. As if beside herself, she chose the most private room there was, and there gave vent to her burning tears and sighs. The only prayers she could think of to say was: 'O Love, is it possible that you have called me with so much love and have revealed to me in one moment what no tongue can describe?' In the following days the only sounds that came from her were deep sighs, and so keen was the sorrow she felt for the sins she had committed against God's goodness that if she had not been sustained by a superhuman power, her heart would have burst and she would have surely died.

Christ appeared to her in spirit with His Cross on His shoulder, dripping with blood. The whole house seemed to her to be full of streams of His blood, and she saw that it had all been shed for love alone. Horror of sin and disgust at herself made her cry out: 'O Lord, if it is necessary, I am ready to confess my sins in public.'

A few days after this she made a general confession with such contrition and compunction as to pierce her soul. Though God had already pardoned all her sins, consuming them in the fire of His love at the very moment He had struck her heart with it, yet He wished her to satisfy the claims of justice and led her along the path of satisfaction for sin. This period of contrition and illumination lasted some fourteen months, after which the memory of her former life was withdrawn from her mind and she never again saw even a shadow of her past sins, as if they had been cast into the depths of the sea.

*   *   *

Since Love took charge of everything, I have not taken care of anything, and I have never been able to work with my intellect, memory and will, any more than if I had never had them. Indeed every day I feel myself more occupied in Him, and with greater fire.

This came about because Love freed me more and more from all interior and exterior imperfections and kept on consuming them little by little. When He had consumed one of them, He would show it to the soul, and seeing, it, the soul would be fired all the more with love, and would be kept in such a state that it could not see anything in itself that might be an obstacle to love. Love, for the sight would have driven it to despair. It needed always to live with the purity that He sought, and if there was any imperfection to be removed, the soul was not shown or allowed to see it, or given the thought of attending to it or troubling about it, as though it were something that had nothing to do with the soul.

I had given the keys of the house to Love, with ample power to do all that was necessary, without respect for the soul or body, and to see that not a jot should be wanting of all that the law of pure love requires. When I saw that Love accepted the charge and was setting to work, I turned to Him and stood still, watching Him as He worked. He did all with such love and care and in so just a manner as to content me inwardly and outwardly, and I was so rapt at the sight that if he had cast me body and soul into hell, it would have seemed all love and consolation to me.

I saw that Love's eye was so open and pure, His sight so keen and His vision so far-reaching, that I was astounded at all the imperfections He found, and showed me so clearly that I was obliged to acknowledge them. He let me see many things that to me and others would have seemed just and perfect, but which He found unjust and imperfect— there was not a thing in which He found no fault.

If I spoke of the spiritual things that often beset me, at once my Love would reprove me, saying that I ought not to speak but let myself wholly burn, without attempting any word or act to bring relief to soul or body. If I was silent and took no heed of anything, but simply said: 'If the body is dying, let it die. If it can't carry on, let it be. Nothing matters to me,' then Love would still reprove me saying: 'I want you to shut your eyes tight so that you see nothing of the work I am doing in you as if it were in you. I want you to be dead, and every sight however perfect annihilated in you. I do not want you to do anything which may be of your own self.'

When I had locked my mouth and stood like an inert thing from Love's tightening grasp within me, I felt such interior peace and contentment that I was unsupportable to myself. I did nothing but sigh and lament without speaking, and paid no heed to what was happening, so that I seemed dead in my own self. And then Love said: 'You find it insupportable; what is the matter? If you can feel, then you must be still alive. I do not want you to sigh and lament. I want you to be as the dead and dying. Look, I do not want a sign of life in you.'

After this reproof I ceased to perform, as formerly, any interior or exterior act that could be perceived by anyone. But when things were spoken of that were of the kind I felt in my mind, my eyes made ready to understand the meaning according to my purpose. But as I could not act or speak, I waited to see whether from somewhere something was said to me, in hopes of secretly finding some little shelter from the great assault on me.

Likewise with my eyes I sought all the shelter I could, looking now to one side and now to the other, to forget somewhat the great burning I felt. This was not done voluntarily on my part, or sought by me to take shelter from myself, but my natural inclination acted thus without being able to choose. I was not aware of it, and I thought I could not do otherwise.

But Love said: 'I do not like this seeing and hearing. It is all a defense of your natural self, which has got to die.' I did not know what to do or say against the keen sight of Love assailing me so hardily. The human part of me felt little of its wonted desire for food, and I could eat hardly anything.

One day I said to my confessor: 'Do you think I should try and eat, lest it should be the cause of some harm to soul or body through my negligence?' I was answered from within by Love and from without by my confessor: 'Who is this that is troubled, and talks of eating and not eating, as though conscience were pricking? Be silent. I know you, and you cannot deceive me.' When my self found it was discovered and could not deny these imperfections uncovered by Love, it turned to Him and said: 'Since your eye is so sharp and penetrating, I give you welcome. Keep on with what you are doing, though I feel the pain of it. Content your will, strip me of this unsightly covering and clothe me with Love, full, pure and sincere.'

Love annihilated not only the outer malignant part of me, but also the inner spiritual part, the part that enjoyed and understood and seemed to want to be wholly transformed in God and to annihilate the outer part. When the spiritual part had labored so hard that it seemed to have overcome and laid low the outer part by depriving it of all its ways and means of nourishment, and established peace in all it had won from it, then Love, insatiable and raging came and said: 'What are you thinking of doing? I want you all for myself. Do not think I shall spare you the smallest possession of soul or body. I will leave you stark naked. I am so keen-eyed that, when I begin to sift you, every perfection remains a defect in my sight. The higher up you may go, however great a perfection you may have, the higher will I ever stand above you, to ruin all your perfections.'

*   *   *

So great was the feeling I had in that sweet union that it is not to be wondered at if I was out of my sense. I saw nothing but God alone, without myself and outside myself. The sight is so absorbing that nothing else can be seen or enjoyed or desired. The being both of body and soul remains as if dead, unable to act inwardly or outwardly. But how can I describe in words the immeasurable and the indescribable? I am at a loss to speak of its greatness and excellence; it is impossible to

express it in words, or for anyone to understand it who had not
experienced it.

O marvel, that cannot be made known by words or signs or symbols,
by sighs or cries, or in any manner! I seem to be imprisoned and
besieged on all sides. You poor tongue, that can find no words.! You
poor mind, you are defeated! Will, how peaceful you are! You desire
nothing further, for you are drowned in overabundance. Memory, you
are full to the brim, unoccupied and carefree. All my faculties have lost
their natural activity, and are altogether imprisoned and plunged in the
furnace of divine love, with such profound, exceeding joy that they
seem already beatified and brought to the desired haven, where
without taste are tasted the intimate flames of that pure love whose
measureless power would consume hell itself.

*   *   *

I see without eyes, I understand without mind, I feel without feeling,
and I taste without taste. I have no shape nor size, so that without
seeing I see such divine activity and energy that, beside it, all those
words like perfection, fullness and purity and that I once used now
seem to me all falsehoods and fables when compared with that Truth
and Directness. The sun that once seemed so bright now seems dark.
What seemed sweet now now seems bitter, for all beauty and sweetness that has an admixture of the creature is corrupt and spoilt. When
the creature finds himself cleansed and purified and transformed in
God, then he sees what is true and clean. This sight, which is not seen,
cannot be spoken or thought of.

7. The Reformation: New Dimensions of Christian Spirituality

Jacob Boehme

(1575–1624)

The Reformation marked not only the divergence of two main streams of ecclesiastical and doctrinal Christianity but the divergence of two main streams of mysticism as well. The Catholic stream, flowing directly out of the traditional contemplative milieu and preserving its symbols, language, and practices, is represented in the sixteenth century by the Spanish Carmelites and in the seventeenth century by the various schools of French mysticism. The other stream cannot necessarily be associated with the Protestant churches nor even with the various Christian or marginally Christian sects that came into existence during the years of Christendom's great upheavals. Rather, a tradition of personal apprehension of transcendence, highly symbolic, emphasizing ideas of regeneration, and often using the terminology of alchemy or astrology, evolved primarily in Germany and England. Perhaps the earliest and best-known exponent of this trend in mysticism is Jacob Boehme.

An obscure yet intriguing writer, Boehme's vision of the transcendent life is highly personalized. Believing himself called to penetrate the deepest mysteries of God, humankind, and nature, he wrote of what he personally learned from divine illumination. The unique interpretation of Christian symbolism that emerged from this encounter left its mark on the later thinkers of German Romanticism and on seventeenth- and eighteenth-century English religious philosophy. In his perception God the Father is the indefinable matter of the universe that in itself is neither good nor evil but that contains the seeds of both. This impenetratable and unconscious abyss knows itself in the Son and expresses itself in the Holy Ghost. The individual, being part of the created universe that, like God, contains both good and evil, can choose to unite with the Christ principle of light and wisdom, thereby conquering the Satanic principle of darkness and gaining eternal life.

Boehme was interested in describing, often in complex and mythic imagery, the alchemy of this union between Christ and the individual. For him the center of the individual's soul comes out of eternity; there is in the human an essence that remains untouched by corruptible matter and by the terror of the unconscious wrath of the Godhead. What he calls "the innermost birth" is the act of discovering this inward dowry and having Christ come consciously to birth within. The collection of devotional writings entitled *The Way to Christ*, from which our selections are taken, deals with this birthlike process.

Boehme was not an educated man. Son of a farmer and himself a shoemaker in Silesia for most of his life, he lived in a state of religious exaltation from childhood, his writings springing freely and naturally from the immediacy of what he experienced. The publication of his first work in 1612 aroused the fierce opposition of a local Lutheran pastor who forced the municipal authorities to intervene and order Boehme to cease writing. He continued his work privately, however, and the publication of *The Way to Christ* in 1623 renewed the uproar over his controversial productions. Most of his writing was published after his death the following year. Included among his topics are an inquiry into the Divine Essence, an explanation of his cosmological theories, an allegorical interpretation of the Book of Genesis, and a treatise on baptism and the Eucharist.

The selections reprinted here show Boehme at his most accessible. What makes much of his work difficult reading is his highly personal vocabulary. Much of it is derived from alchemy and astrology, obscure biblical passages, the Old Testament Apocrypha, the Kabbalists, Luther, the Swiss theosophist Paracelsus, among other sources. All of it he uses in his own way, weaving a symbolic pattern of thought that creates a vast and mythic view of the cosmos.

As has been mentioned, *The Way to Christ* is a collection of devotional tracts. The first of these, from which the first selection is taken, is entitled "Of True Repentance." In it, the soul seeks a relationship with God's wisdom, the noble Sophia, a relationship expressed in erotic metaphor. In doing this, the soul seeks entry into the mystery of the Godhead. At the same time, the soul observes the distinction between Creator and creature, always honoring the principle of Christian mysticism that the individual essences of both God and human are maintained even during ecstatic union. The purpose of the third tract, "Of the Supersensual Life," from which the second selection is taken, is to set out in dialogue form Boehme's schema of mystic union. His view differs from that of the early Christian and Medieval world, which generally saw the process of union as an ascent, a gradual scaling of a ladder whose base was planted upon finite earth and whose upper rungs were thrust into the infinity beyond earth. The influence of Pseudo-Dionysious, with his emphasis on an unknowable divine principle, can be seen in this schema. Boehme's tack was to deny the necessity of ascent: "Heaven and Hell are everywhere present." The finite need not negate itself to enjoy union, rather it must remove the self-created barriers within itself that prevent it from being fully grasped by the Infinite.

The Way to Christ

Of true repentance.

Dear Soul! You must be uninterruptedly sincere! You shall certainly receive, in the holy name JESUS, a love-kiss from the noble Sophia, for she stands ever knocking before the Soul's door, warning the sinner of wicked ways. But if one wants her Love she is ready to kiss him with a ray of her sweet Love, by which the heart is joyed. But her marriage to the Soul is not immediately consummated nor is that image which was distorted in Paradise immediately restored. Here is dangerous ground for man, since both Lucifer and Adam fell at this point, which might happen again because man is still firmly bound by vanity.

There must be persistency to your decision. Before you can be crowned you must be tried. Sophia removes her ray of Love from you again to see whether you will remain true. She keeps you begging, not answering you by even a single glance of her Love. If she is to crown you, you must already have been judged because you must be made to taste the rancid beer which you, by your abominations, have poured

Jacob Boehme, *The Way to Christ,* trans. John Joseph Stoudt (New York: Harper & Row, 1947) pp. 20-2, 32-3, 115-6, 121-24.

into yourself. You must first come before hell's gates and prove your victory and demonstrate the power of her energizing Love in the face of the Devil's attacks.

Christ was tempted in the wilderness. And, if you would appropriate Him, then you must follow His whole pattern from Incarnation to Ascension. Though you neither can nor dare do as He did, yet you must follow His way completely, and, in imitation of Him, continually die to the soul's vanity. For the Virgin Sophia betroths herself to the soul by no other means than by this property which blossoms forth in the soul out of Christ's Death like a new heavenly growth. In its corruption the body cannot comprehend it because it must first die to vanity; but that heavenly image which faded in Adam—the real Seed of the woman in which God became man and brought His heavenly Essentiality into human nature—does comprehend this, the noble Pearl, in the manner in which it appeared in Mary at the fulfilment of the Covenant.

Therefore be careful what you do. When you give your word, keep it. She wants to crown you more than you want [to be crowned]. But you must be firm when the tempter approaches with the world's pleasure, beauty and glory. These the mind must reject, saying, "I shall be a labourer in Christ's vineyard, not the master. For I am God's keeper over all that I have, to do with as His Word teaches. My heart shall humble itself with the lowliest in the dust."

In whatever position you are, humility must be your primary aim or else you will not achieve marriage with her, since true humility is born out of this marriage. Your soul's free will must be like a knight. Then, if the Devil cannot conquer the soul by vanity, if the soul cannot be baited, then he comes along with unworthiness and with all the sins in the book. Here perseverance counts.

A creature cannot conquer the Devil otherwise than by making Christ's merits primary, for here many [creatures] fare badly, so that it may even seem to external reason that such a person is senseless, possessed by the Devil. When the Devil must leave and forsake the robber's castle which he owns in many a heart, then he fiercely defends himself. Here one must fight, for heaven and hell contend one with the other.

If the soul remains steadfast, defeating all the Devil's assaults, disesteeming all temporalities for the sake of the noble Sophia's Love, then the treasured knightly crown will be given it as a token of victory. Then the Virgin [Sophia], who revealed herself out of the precious name JESUS as Christ the serpent-killer, as the anointed of God, comes into the soul, and kisses it in the innermost essence with her sweet Love, and, as a token of victory, infuses Love into its desires. Then the heavenly Adam is resurrected from the dead in Christ. There is no pen in the world with which I might describe this for this is the marriage of the Lamb when the noble Pearl is planted—and that with great triumph—though first it is but small, like a mustard seed, as Christ says.

When this marriage is over the soul shall see to it that the Pearl-tree grows and increases as it has promised the Virgin. For the Devil will come soon enough with storms, and with atheists, who will scoff at it, mock it, and proclaim it madness. Then must man enter in upon Christ's Way upon the Cross. Then it will be a demonstrated fact that, since he permits himself to be called a Christian, he must permit himself to be called a fool and a godless person. Yet, his best friends, who previously had flattered his fleshly inclinations, now become his enemies and hate him, even though they do not know why. Then Christ hides His bride [the soul] under the Cross so that it may be unknown to the world. The Devil also conceals these children from the world so that not many more such branches may grow in the garden which he thinks he owns. This I set down for the information of the Christian-minded reader, so that he knows what to do if he fares similarly.

Of the supersensual life.

The DISCIPLE SAID TO HIS MASTER: "How may I come to the supersensual life so that I can see God and hear Him speak?" The MASTER said: "When you can leap for a moment into that where no creature dwells then you can hear what God speaks."

DISCIPLE: "Is it near or far?" MASTER: "It is within you. Could you halt volition and thought for but one hour then you could hear God's inexpressible words."

DISCIPLE: "How can I hear when I stop volition and thought? 'MASTER: "When you stop willing and thinking self then the eternal hearing, seeing and speaking will be revealed within you, and God will see and hear through you. Your ego-centric hearing, willing and seeing hinders you from seeing and hearing God."

DISCIPLE: "With what shall I see and hear God, since He is beyond nature and creature? 'MASTER: "When you are silent then you are as God was before nature and creature came to be, just like the essence out of which He created your natural, creaturely existence. Then you will hear and see by the same means with which God 'saw' and 'heard' within you before your ego-centric willing, seeing and hearing began.

DISCIPLE: "But what prevents me from achieving this?" MASTER: "Your ego-centric willing, hearing and seeing hinders you. You are also hindered by your striving against that out of which you came. By your ego-centric will you break yourself off from God's Will, and with your ego-centric seeing you see only into your own will. And by the self-centredness of earthly, material things your ego-centric will plugs up your hearing, leading you into a 'ground,' and overshadowing you with that which you do will so that you cannot come to the supernatural, supersensual life."

DISCIPLE: "Standing as I do within nature, how may I come through nature into the ground of supersensuality without destroying nature?"
MASTER: "For that three things are necessary: the first is that you must give your ego-centric will over to God. The second is that you must hate your ego-centric will so that you do not do that to which your own will drives you. The third is that you prostrate yourself patiently before the Cross of Our Lord Jesus Christ in order to bear the temptations of nature and creature yourself. And when you do this God will speak into you. He will bring your resigned will into Himself, into the supernatural ground, and then you will hear what the Lord speaks within you."

*   *   *

DISCIPLE: "But it is hard to be despised by the world!" MASTER: "That which now seems heavy you will afterwards learn to love the most."

DISCIPLE: "How will it happen that I shall love that which despises me?" MASTER: "Now you have earthly wisdom. But when you have been reclothed in heavenly Wisdom then you will see that all the world's wisdom is foolishness, and that the world hates your enemy—mortality—which you in your will also hate. Then will you love the despairing of the mortal body."

DISCIPLE: "How can man hate and love himself at the same time?"
MASTER: "What you love of yourself you love, not as yours, but as the given Love of God. You love God's ground within you by which you learn God's Wisdom and Miracles, as well as your fellow-men. That aspect of yourself which you hate is your ego-centricity, the foundation of evil. You do this in order to crush I-ness, to become a divine ground. Love hates I-ness because I-ness is dead. Love and I-ness cannot exist together, for Love owns heaven and lives in its own being. In a similar way, I-ness owns the world and its works and also lives to itself. Just as heaven rules earth, just as Eternity rules time, so Love rules the natural life."

DISCIPLE: "Please tell me, dear Master, why must love and suffering, friends and foe, live together? Would it not be better if Love were along?" MASTER: "If Love stood not in suffering then there would be nothing to love or to release from pain. Neither could Love be known if there was nothing to love."

DISCIPLE: "What is Love's energy, virtue, height, and magnitude?" MASTER: "Its virtue is the no-thing, and its energy is in everything. Its height is in God and its magnitude greater than God. He who finds Love finds the no-thing in the all."

DISCIPLE: "Dear Master, tell me how I am to understand this!" MASTER: "When I say, 'Its virtue is the no-thing,' you are to understand that when you leave all creaturehood, when you become a no-thing to all nature and creature, then you are in the Eternal One, in God Himself, and then you will experience the highest of virtues—Love. When I say, 'Its energy is in everthing,' then you are to perceive both physically and in your soul that when this great Love is kindled within you it burns as no fire can burn. You will also see how Love has emanated into all of God's Works and that it is the inmost and outermost ground of all things: inwardly the energy and outwardly the form. When I say further, 'Its height is as God,' you are to perceive how, within yourself, Love bears you as high as God Himself, as can be seen in Our dear Lord Jesus Christ's Humanity, who brought Love to the highest throne of God's Might. But when I also say, 'its magnitude is greater than God,' it is also true for Love enters where God does not dwell. For when Our dear Lord Christ stood in hell, hell was not God, but Love was there and destroyed death. Similarly when you are anxious, God is not that anxiety; but His Love is there to lead you from anxiety to God. When God hides Himself in you, Love is there to reveal Him to you. And when I further say, 'He who finds Love finds the no-thing and the all,' it is also true, for he finds a supernatural, supersensual *Ungrund*, without abiding place to which nothing can be compared. Man therefore compares it with no-thing because Love is deeper than self-consciousness. It is a no-thing to all things because it is incomprehensible. Because it is a no-thing it is free of all things and is that one, inexpressible good. But that I finally say, 'He who finds Love finds the all,' is also true. Love begins all things, Love rules all things. If you find it you will enter in upon the Ground from which all things proceed and in which they subsist: then you are lord of God's Works."

DISCIPLE: "Dear Master! Tell me where Love dwells in man?" MASTER: "Love dwells in that place within man's self where he is not."

DISCIPLE: "Where is that place in man where man does not dwell?" MASTER: "Wherever his soul is resigned to the ground of its being. For where the soul dies to the ego-centric will and can will nothing except what God wills, there Love dwells. In so far as the soul dies to self, so far has it appropriated Love's dwelling-place. Where previously there had been ego-centric will now there is no-thing. And where there is no-thing God's Love operates."

DISCIPLE: "How may I attain Love without dying to my self-will?" MASTER: "If you want to attain it yourself it will shun you. But if you yield yourself fully to it, then you are dead to your own will and then it will become the life of your bestial nature. Love does not kill you. It quickens you according to its will. Then you live, yet not you, but Love's will becomes your will. Then are you dead yet you live to God."

DISCIPLE: "Why do so few people find Love, since many seek it?" MASTER: "They all seek it in selfish desire as an imagined meaning in the something, to which all have an ego-centric, natural inclination. Though Love offers itself to them it can find no place within them to live, for the imaginativeness of selfish inclinations wants to own it. But Love flees, for it lives only in the no-thing, and therefore the ego-centric will cannot find it."

DISCIPLE: "What is Love's duty in the no-thing?" MASTER: "Its duty is to press ceaselessly in upon the something, and when it finds a resigned place within the something it possesses it, rejoicing therein with its fire-flaming more than the Sun of the world. Love's duty is ceaselessly to kindle fire in the something, and glow within itself."

George Fox

(1624-1691)

Not all Reformation mysticism outside the Catholic fold was of such an eclectic variety as Boehme's. The call to the interior life made itself felt in many ways. As we have seen, the longing for a personal encounter with the transcendent is part of the equipment necessary for the mystic journey. Often during the Reformation, this longing went hand in hand with the need to seek beyond the existing forms of religious practice and organization. But the search for alternative forms might not mean, as it did for Boehme, that one drew one's inspiration from such non-Christian sources as alchemy and astrology. Often, the mystic impulse was given shape upon a purely Scriptural base, unfettered by the traditional theological assumptions of any established church. George Fox, the founder of the Society of Friends or Quakers, was one individual whose inner experience of God led him along such a path.

A native of Leicestershire, England, Fox recalled his childhood as one of unusual seriousness and inwardness. He was brought up "in country business" and enjoyed especially the care of sheep, an occupation he took delight in for its "innocency and solitude." As he grew he became increasingly withdrawn from society. At about the age of twenty he felt compelled to give up all ties of family and friendship, and he spent the next years in search of some relief from his internal struggles. Having consulted many a priest and religious person to dispel his encroaching despair, he grew more and more dissatisfied with the comfort they offered him. Then in 1646 he won a victory over his despair. It was "opened" to him that true belief and the effective ministry of Christ could not be taught and was not the perogative of the priesthood but was open to all Christians. Further, he came to the realization that God did not dwell in holy temples "but in people's hearts." What was necessary for a truly Christian life was a reliance on the "Inner Light" of the living Christ who spoke authentically only in the silence of the soul. The word of God enshrined in the Scriptures could activate and teach one of this Inner Light.

He abandoned attendance at church and began to travel and preach his newfound faith. He encountered much opposition and was frequently imprisoned but with apostolic vigor he continued his journeying. His moral earnestness attracted followers and he formed a stable organization, the "Friends of Truth," who held to his tenets that consecrated buildings and ordained ministers were irrelevant to Christian worship. When these fellow friends gathered for worship, they did so without a set liturgy or prearrangement of any kind, believing that God could inspire and use any one of them at any time to act as His minister. The group was often persecuted and imprisoned, especially for their refusal to take oaths or pay tithes and their disavowel of flattery of speech or behavior in respect to social superiors.

The Journal or Historical Account of the Life, Travels, Sufferings, Christian Experiences and Labour of Love in the Work of the Ministry of that Ancient, Eminent and Faithful Servant of Jesus Christ, George Fox is the document from which the following selection is taken. In it, Fox recounts in vivid detail the events of his long ministry, always putting forward his belief in the immediate presence of Christ in the soul that enables man to perform good works and lead a virtuous life.

Fox's perception of the activity of God within is very different from that of most of the other mystics represented in this book. It is less informed by traditional symbolism and theology, and its effects are more visible in the moral sphere than in the affective faculties. He seems less concerned with the precise movements of God within the soul or with the progress toward a transcendent union than with the direct apprehension of the Inner Light that manifests itself in the practices and attitudes of everyday life. Nevertheless, he deserves to be included here as an example of a trend in Christian interiority that has had vitality and consequence for the entire tradition.

The Journal [of] George Fox

After this I went to another ancient priest at Mansetter in Warwickshire, and reasoned with him about the ground of despair and temptations; but he was ignorant of my condition: he bid me take tobacco and sing psalms. Tobacco was a thing I did not love, and psalms I was not in a state to sing; I could not sing. He bid me come agian, and he would tell me many things; but when I came he was angry and pettish, for my former words had displeased him. He told my troubles, sorrows, and griefs to his servants, so that it was got among the milk-lasses. It grieved me that I should open my mind to such a one. I saw they were all miserable comforters, and this increased my troubles upon me. I heard of a priest living about Tamworth, who was accounted an experienced man. I went seven miles to him, but found him like an empty, hollow cask. I heard of one called Dr. Cradock, of Coventry, and went to him; I asked him the ground of temptations and despair, and how troubles came to be wrought in man? He asked me, 'who was Christ's father and mother?' I told him Mary was his mother, and that he Was supposed to be the son of Joseph; but he was the son of God. As we were walking together in his garden, the alley being narrow, I chanced, in turning to set my foot on the side of a bed; at which he raged as if his house had been on fire. Thus all our discourse was lost, and I went away in

George Fox, *A Journal or Historical Account of the Life, Travels, Sufferings, Christian Experiences, and Labour of Love in the Work of the Ministry of the Ancient, Eminent, and Faithful Servant of Jesus Christ* (Philadelphia: Marcus T. C. Gould, 1831), pp. 70-5 sorrow, worse than I was when I came. I thought them miserable comforters, and saw they were all as nothing to me; for they could not reach my condition. After this I went to another, one Macham, a priest, in high account. He would needs give me some physic, and I was to have been let blood; but they could not get one drop of blood from me, either in arms or head, though they endeavoured it, my body being, as it were, dried up with sorrows, griefs, and troubles, which were so great upon me, that I could have wished I had never been born, or that I had been born blind, that I might never have seen wickedness nor vanity; and deaf, that I might never have heard vain and wicked words, or the Lord's name blasphemed. When the time called Christmas came, while others were feasting and sporting themselves, I looked out poor widows from house to house, and gave them some money. When I was invited to marriages I went to none at all; but the next day, or soon after, I would go and visit them; and if they were poor I gave them some money; for I had wherewith both to keep myself from being chargeable to others, and to administer something to the necessities of others.

About the beginning of the year 1646, as I was going into Coventry, a consideration arose in me, how it was said, that 'all christians are believers, both Protestants and Papists;' and the Lord opened to me that if all were believers, then they were all born of God, and passed from death to life; and that none were true believers but such: and though others said they were believers, yet they were not. At another time, as I was walking in a field on a First-day morning, the Lord opened unto me, 'that being bred at Oxford or Cambridge was not enough to fit and qualify men to be ministers of Christ:' and I wondered at it, because it was the common belief of people. But I saw it clearly as the Lord opened it to me, and was satisfied and admired the goodness of the Lord, who had opened this thing unto me that morning. This struck at priest Stevens' ministry, namely, that 'to be bred at Oxford or Cambridge was not enough to make a man fit to be a minister of Christ.' So that which opened in me, I saw struck at the priest's ministry. But my relations were much troubled, that I would not go with them to hear the priest; for I would go into the orchard of the fields, with my bible, by myself. I asked them, did not the apostle say to believers, 'that they needed no man to teach them, but as the anointing teacheth them?' Though they knew this was scripture, and that it was true, yet they were grieved, because I could not be subject in this matter, to go to hear the priest with them. I saw that to be a true believer was another thing than they looked upon it to be; and I saw that being bred at Oxford or Cambridge did not qualify or fit a man to be a minister of Christ; what then should I follow such for? So neither them, nor any of the disssenting people could I join with; but was as a stranger to all, relying wholly upon the Lord Jesus Christ.

At another time it was opened in me, 'that God who made the world did not dwell in temples made with hands.' This at the first seemed strange, because both priests and people used to call their temples or churches, dreadful places, holy ground, and the temples of God. But the Lord showed me clearly, that he did not dwell in these temples which men had commanded and set up, but in people's hearts. Both Stephen and the apostle Paul bore testimony, that he did not dwell in temples made with hands, not even in that which he had once commanded to be built, since he put an end to the typical dispensation; but that his people were his temple, and he dwelt in them. This opened in me, as I walked in the fields to my relation's house. When I came there, they told me Nathaniel Stevens, the priest, had been there, and said, 'he was afraid of me for going after new lights.' I smiled in myself, knowing what the Lord had opened in me concerning him and his brethren; but I told not my relations, who though they saw beyond the priests, yet went to hear them, and were grieved because I would not go also. But I showed them by the scriptures, there was anointing within man to teach him, and that the Lord would teach his people himself. I had great openings concerning the things written in the Revelations; and when I spoke of them, the priests and professors would say, that was a sealed book, and would have kept me out of it. But I told them, Christ could open the seals, and that they were the nearest thing to us; for the epistles were written to the saints that lived in former ages, but the Revelations were written of things to come.

After this I met with a sort of people that held, women have no souls, (adding in a light manner,) no more than a goose. I reproved them, and told them that was not right; for Mary said, 'My soul doth maginify the Lord, and my spirit hath rejoiced in God my saviour.'

Removing to another place I came among a people that relied much on dreams. I told them except they could distinguish between dream and dream they would confound all together; for there were three sorts of dreams: multitude of business sometimes caused dreams; and there were whisperings of satan in man in the night season; and there were speakings of God to man in dreams. But these people came out of these things, and at last became Friends.

Though I had great openings, yet great trouble and temptations came many times upon me, so that when it was day I wished for night, and when it was night I wished for day; and by reason of the openings I had in my troubles, I could say as David said, 'Day unto day uttereth speech, and night unto night showeth knowledge.' When I had openings they answered one another, and answered the scriptures; for I had great openings of the scriptures; and when I was in troubles, one trouble also answered to another.

*   *   *

About the begining of the year 1647 I was moved of the Lord to go into Derbyshire, where I met with some friendly people, and had many discourses with them. Then passing into the Peak country, I met with more friendly people, and with some in empty high notions. And travelling on through some parts of Leicestershire, and into Nottinghamshire, I met with a tender people, and a very tender woman, whose name was Elizabeth Hootton. With these I had some meetings and discourses; but my troubles continued, and I was often under great temptations. I fasted much, walked abroad in solitary places many days, and often took my bible, and sat in hollow trees and lonesome places till night came on; and frequently in the night walked mournfully about by myself: for I was a man of sorrows in the time of the first workings of the Lord in me.

During all this time I was never joined in profession of religion with any, but gave up myself to the Lord, having forsaken all evil company, taken leave of father and mother, and all other relations, and travelled up and down as a stranger in the earth, which way the Lord inclined my heart; taking a chamber to myself in the town where I came, and tarrying sometimes more, sometimes less in a place: for I durst not stay long in a place, being afraid both of professor and profane, lest, being a tender young man, I should be hurt by conversing much with either. For which reason I kept much as a stranger, seeking heavenly wisdom, and getting knowledge from the Lord; and was brought off from outward things, to rely on the Lord alone. Though my exercises and troubles were very great, yet were they not so continual but that I had some intermissions, and was sometimes brought into such an heavenly joy, that I thought I had been in Abraham's bosom. As I cannot declare the misery I was in, it was so great and heavy upon me, so neither can I set forth the mercies of God unto me in all my misery. Oh! the everlasting love of God to my soul, when I was in great distress! when my troubles and torments were great, then was his love exceeding great. Thou, Lord, makest a fruitful field a barren wilderness, and a barren wilderness a fruitful field! thou bringest down and settest up! thou killest and makest alive! all honour and glory be to thee, O Lord of glory! The knowledge of thee in the spirit is life; but that knowledge which is fleshly works death. While there is this knowledge in the flesh, deceit and self will conform to any thing, and will say, yes, yes, to that it doth not know. The knowledge which the world hath, of what the prophets and apostles spake, is a fleshly knowledge; and the apostates from the life, in which the prophets and apostles were, have got their words, the holy scriptures, in a form, but not in the life nor spirit that gave them forth. So they all lie in confusion; and are making provision for the flesh, to fulfil the lusts thereof, but not to fulfil the law and command of Christ in his power and spirit: for that, they say they cannot do; but to fulfil the lusts of the flesh, that they can do with delight.

After I had received that opening from the Lord, that to be bred at Oxford or Cambridge, was not sufficient to fit a man to be a minister of Christ, I regarded the priests less, and looked more after the dissenting people. Among them I saw there was some tenderness; and many of them came afterwards to be convinced, for they had some openings. But as I had forsaken the priests, so I left the separate preachers also, and those called the most experienced people; for I saw there was none among them all that could speak to my condition. And when all my hopes in them and in all men were gone, so that I had nothing outwardly to help me, nor could tell what to do; then, Oh! then I heard a voice which said, 'There is one, even Christ Jesus, that can speak to thy condition.' When I heard it, my heart did leap for joy. Then the Lord let me see why there was none upon the earth that could speak to my condition, namely, that I might give him all the glory. For all are concluded under sin, and shut up in unbelief, as I had been, that Jesus Christ might have pre-eminence, who enlightens, and gives grace, faith, and power. Thus when God doth work, who shall let it? This I knew experimentally. My desires after the Lord grew stronger, and zeal in the pure knowledge of God, and of Christ alone, without the help of any man, book, or writing. For though I read the scriptures that spake of Christ and of God, yet I knew him not but by revelation, as he who hath the key did open, and as the Father of life drew me to his son by his spirit. Then the Lord gently led me along, and let me see his love, which was endless and eternal, surpassing all the knowledge that men have in the natural state, or can get by history or books. That love let me see myself, as I was without him; and I was afraid of all company: for I saw them perfectly, where they were, through the love of God which let me see myself. I had not fellowship with any people, priests, nor professors, nor any sort of separated people, but with Christ who hath the key, and opened the door of light and life unto me. I was afraid of all carnal talk and talkers, for I could see nothing but corruptions, and the life lay under the burden of corruptions. When I was in the deep, under all shut up, I could not believe that I should ever overcome; my troubles, my sorrows, and my temptations were so great, that I often thought I should have despaired, I was so tempted. But when Christ opened to me how he was tempted by the same devil, and had overcome him, and had bruised his head; and that through him and his power, light, grace, and spirit, I should overcome also, I had confidence in him. So he it was that opened to me, when I was shut up, and had neither hope nor faith. Christ, who had enlightened me, gave me his light to believe in, and gave me hope, which is himself, revealed himself in me, and gave me his spirit and grace, which I found sufficient in the deeps and in weakness. Thus in the deepest miseries, and in the greatest sorrows and temptations that beset me, the Lord in his mercy did keep me. I found two thirsts in me; the one after the creatures, to have got help and strength there; and the other after the Lord the creator, and his son Jesus Christ; and I saw all the world could do me no good. If I had had a king's diet, palace, and attendence, all would have been as nothing; for nothing gave me comfort but the Lord by his power. I saw professors, priests, and people, were whole and at ease in that condition which was my misery, and they loved that which I would have been rid of. But the Lord did stay my desires upon himself, from whom my help came, and my care was cast upon him alone. Therefore, all wait paitently upon the Lord, whatsoever condition you be in; wait in the grace and truth that comes by Jesus; for if ye so do, there is a promise to you, and the Lord God will fulfil it in you. And blessed are all they indeed that do indeed hunger and thirst after righteousness, they shall be satisfied with it. I have found it so; praised the Lord who filleth with it, and satisfieth the desires of the hungry soul. Oh! let the house of the spiritual Israel say, his mercy endureth for ever! It is the great love of God, to make a wilderness of that which is pleasant to the outward eye and fleshly mind; and to make a fruitful field of a barren wilderness. This is the great work of God. But while people's minds run in the earthly, after the creatures and changeable things, changeable ways and religions, and changeable uncertain teachers, their minds are in bondage, and they are brittle and changeable, tossed up and down with windy doctrines, thoughts, notions, and things; their minds being out of the unchangeable truth in the inward parts, the light of Jesus Christ, which would keep them to the unchangeable. He is the way to the Father; who, in all my troubles preserved me by his spirit and power: praised be his holy name for ever!

8. Spain in the Sixteenth Century: Anatomies of the Inner Life

---

Ignatius of Loyola

(1491–1556)

Few personalities in the history of the Catholic Church have exerted as profound an influence on the spirituality of their own and succeeding generations as has Ignatius of Loyola. This soldier-priest, whose mature spirituality has been characterized as "contemplation in the midst of activity," was born into the provincial Spanish nobility. From his heritage he acquired the sense of proud loyalty, duty, obedience, and practical realism that characterized his soldier ancestors. At the same time he seems to have been endowed with a carefree, vivacious temperament that he indulged fully in his youth. Sent as a page to the court of a relative, he fully enjoyed the gambling, dueling, and romance he discovered there.

In 1517 Ignatius entered military service in the war being waged between the Holy Roman Emperor, Charles V, who was also King of Spain, and Francis I of France. It was in the course of his duties in this war, at the battle of Pampeluna in 1521, that he received the wound that was to change the course of his life. He was sent to convalesce in the family castle at Loyola, where, desiring some reading material, he was given The Life of Christ and a collection of saints' lives to peruse. The long hours he spent pouring over these volumes were hours that were to determine the shape of his future. He found himself drawn to the values enshrined in these pages, yet was torn between them and the

171

style of life he had previously enjoyed. The result of the inner struggle he experienced was a resolution to reform his "worldly" life.

He undertook a pilgrimage to Jerusalem, going by way of a sanctuary of the Virgin Mary in Catalonia. At the shrine he stripped himself of his wealth, dressed in sackcloth, and kept a vigil in true chivalric fashion before her altar. His next stop was the town of Manresa. There he received an illumination that has come to be considered a decisive event in his spiritual development. For nearly a year he remained at Manresa, praying and doing penance. In that time he gradually evolved a method for communicating and sharing with others the religious insights and inspirations he received. The result was the outline of the famous *Spiritual Exercises*, a portion of which is reproduced here.

The *Exercises* have had a large effect on the spirituality of the church from the sixteenth century to the present, chiefly as a result of the influence of the Society of Jesus — the Jesuits — which Ignatius founded. After his stay at Manresa, he continued on to Rome and Jerusalem. Following this he returned to Spain for a prolonged period of study, a task which he continued in Paris. The fruit of all this self-cultivation was the foundation of the Society in 1534, when he and six companions made vows of poverty and chastity, dedicating themselves to lives of apostolic labor with an intention to embark upon a pilgrimage to the Holy Land. This being prevented, they offered their services to the pope. In 1540, the Society was sanctioned and Ignatius became its first general. Chief among his aims was the reform of the church from within, especially through education, a more frequent use of the sacraments, and the preaching of the gospel in the non-Christian world.

The spread of the Society was rapid. Its influence grew. At the time of Ignatius' death, the Society had over a thousand members, and missions in such far-flung places as India, Malaya, the Congo, Brazil, Ethiopia, Japan, and China. The *Spiritual Exercises* went to all these lands and served as spiritual direction for all members of the Society in their diverse and widespread occupations.

Spiritual Exercises

Purpose of the Exercises.

The purpose of these Exercises is to help the exercitant to conquer himself, and to regulate his life so that he will not be influenced in his decisions by any inordinate attachment.

Presupposition.

In order that the one who gives these Exercises and he who makes them may be of more assistance and profit to each other, they should begin with the presupposition that every good Christian ought to be more willing to give a good interpretation to the statement of another than to condemn it as false. If he cannot give a good interpretation to this statement, he should ask the other how he understands it, and if he is in error, he should correct him with charity. If this is not sufficient, he should seek every suitable means of correcting his understanding so that he may be saved from error.

Principle and Foundation.

Man is created to praise, reverence, and serve God our Lord, and by this means to save his soul. All other things on the face of the earth are created for man to help him fulfill the end for which he is created. From this it follows that man is to use these things to the extent that they will help him to attain his end. Likewise, he must rid himself of them in so far as they prevent him from attaining it.

Therefore we must make ourselves indifferent to all created things, in so far as it is left to the choice of our free will and is not forbidden. Acting accordingly, for our part, we should not prefer health to sickness, riches to poverty, honor to dishonor, a long life to a short one, and so in all things we should desire and choose only those things which will best help us attain the end for which we are created.

The Spiritual Exercises of St. Ignatius, trans. Anthony Mottola (New York: Doubleday, 1964), pp. 47–9, 53–6.

Particular Examination of Conscience to be Made Every Day.

This exercise is performed at three different times, and there are two examinations to be made.

   The *first time:* As soon as he arises in the morning the exercitant should resolve to guard himself carefully against the particular sin or defect which he wishes to correct or amend.

   The *second time:* After the noon meal he should ask God our Lord for what he desires, namely, the grace to remember how many times he has fallen into the particular sin or defect, and to correct himself in the future. Following this he should make the first examination demanding an account of his soul regarding that particular matter which he proposed for himself and which he desires to correct and amend. He should review each hour of the time elapsed from the moment of rising to the moment of this examination, and he should make note on the first line of the following diagram, a mark for each time that he has fallen into the particular sin or defect. He should then renew his resolution to improve himself until the time of the second examination that he will make.

   The *third time:* After the evening meal he will make a second examination, reviewing each hour from the first examination to this second one, and on the second line of the same diagram he will again make a mark for each time that he has fallen into the particular sin or defect.

Four Additional Directions

The following directions will help to remove more quickly the particular sin or defect.

   I. Each time that one falls into the particular sin or defect, he should place his hand on his breast, repenting that he has fallen. This can be done even in the presence of many people without their noticing it.

   II. Since the first line of the diagram represents the first examination, and the second line, the second examination, at night the exercitant should observe whether there is an improvement from the first line to the second, that is, from the first examination to the second.

   III. He should compare the second day with the first, that is to say, the two examinations of the present day with the two examinations of the preceding day, and see if there is a daily improvement.

IV. He should also compare one week with another and see if there is a greater improvement during the present week than in the past week. It may be noted that the first large G denotes Sunday. The second is smaller and stands for Monday, the third, for Tuesday, and so forth.

G ――――――――――――――――――――――

G ――――――――――――――――――――――

G ――――――――――――――――――――――

G ――――――――――――――――――――――

G ――――――――――――――――――――――

G ――――――――――――――――――――――

G ――――――――――――――――――――――

*Method of Making the General Examination
of Conscience*

This examination contains five points:

I. The first point is to render thanks to God for the favors we have received.

II. The second point is to ask the grace to know my sins and to free myself from them.

III. The third point is to demand an account of my soul from the moment of rising until the present examination; either hour by hour or from one period to another. I shall first make an examination of my thoughts, then my words, and then my actions in the same order as that given in the Particular Examination of Conscience.

IV. The fourth point is to ask pardon of God our Lord for my failings.

V. The fifth point is to resolve to amend my life with the help of God's grace. Close with the "Our Father."

General Confession and Holy Communion.

Anyone who of his own accord wishes to make a general Confession during the period of the Spiritual Exercises will find, among many other advantages, these three:

I. Although anyone who confesses once a year is not required to make a general confession, by doing so he will gain much more profit and merit because of the greater sorrow he will have for his sins and for the wickedness of his whole life.

II. Just as during the Spiritual Exercises a person gains a more intimate knowledge of his sins and their malice than at a time when he is not occupied with his interior life, so now because of this greater understanding and sorrow for his sins, he will find greater profit and merit than he would have had before.

III. After making a better confession and being better disposed, he will be more worthy and better prepared to receive the most Holy Sacrament, which will help him not only to avoid sin but also to preserve and increase grace.

It would be best to make this general confession immediately after the Exercises of the first week.

The First Exercise.

This meditation is made with the three powers of the soul, and the subject is the firtst, second, and third sins. It contains, the preparatory prayer, two preludes, three principal points, and a colloquy.

Prayer: The purpose of the preparatory prayer is to ask of God our Lord the grace that all my intentions, actions, and words may be directed purely to the service and praise of His Divine Majesty.

The first prelude is a mental image of the place. It should be noted at this point that when the meditation or contemplation is on a visible object, for example, contemplating Christ our Lord during His life on earth, the image will consist of seeing with the mind's eye the physical place where the object that we wish to contemplate is present. By the physical place I mean, for instance, at temple, or mountain where Jesus or Blessed Virgin is, depending on the subject of the contemplation. In meditations on subject matter that is not visible, as here in meditation on sins, the mental image will consist of imagining, and considering my soul imprisoned in its corruptible body, and my entire being in this vale of tears as an exile among brute beasts. By entire being I mean both body and soul.

The second prelude is to ask God our Lord for what I want and desire. The request must be according to the subject matter. Therefore, if the contemplation is on the Resurrection I shall ask for joy with Christ rejoicing; if it is on the passion, I shall ask for pain, tears, and suffering with Christ suffering. In the present meditation I shall ask for shame and confusion, for I see how many souls have been damned for a single mortal sin, and how often I have deserved to be damned eternally for the many sins I have committed.

Note

The preparatory prayer without change, and the two preludes mentioned above, which may be changed at times if the subject matter requires it, are to be made before all contemplations and meditations.

The first point will be to recall to memory the first sin, which was that of the angels, then to apply the understanding by considering this sin in detail, then the will by seeking to remember and understand all, so that I may be the more ashamed and confounded when I compare the one sin of the angels with the many that I have committed. Since they went to hell for one sin, how many times have I deserved it for my many sins. I will recall to mind the sin of the angels, remembering that they were created in the state of grace, that they refused to make use of their freedom to offer reverence and obedience to their Creator and Lord, and so sinning through pride, they fell from grace into sin and were cast from heaven into hell. In like manner my understanding is to be used to reason more in detail on the subject matter, and thereby move more deeply my affections through the use of the will.

The second point is to employ the three powers of the soul to consider the sin of Adam and Eve. Recall to mind how they did such long penance for their sin and what corruption fell upon the whole human race, causing so many to go to hell. I say to recall to mind the second sin, that of our first parents. Recall that after Adam had been created in the Plain of Damascus and placed in the earthly paradise, and Eve had been formed from his rib, they were forbidden to eat the fruit of the tree of knowledge, and eating it they committed sin. After their sin, clothed in garments of skin and cast out of paradise, without the original justice which they had lost, they lived all their lives in much travail and great penance.

The understanding is likewise to be used in considering the subject matter in greater detail and the will is to be employed as already explained.

The third point is to recall to mind the third sin. This is the particular sin of any person who went to hell for fewer sins than I have committed. I say to consider the third particular sin. Recall to mind the grievousness and malice of sin against our Creator and Lord. Let the understanding consider how in sinning and acting against Infinite Goodness, one has justly been condemned forever. Close with acts of the will, as mentioned above.

Colloquy. Imagine Christ our Lord before you, hanging upon the cross. Speak with Him of how, being the Creator He then became man, and how, possessing eternal life, He submitted to temporal death to die for our sins.

Then I shall meditate upon myself and ask "What have I done for Christ? What am I now doing for Christ? What ought I do for Christ?" As I see Him in this condition, hanging upon the cross, I shall meditate on the thoughts that come to my mind.

The colloquy is made properly by speaking as one friend speaks to another, or as a servant speaks to his master, now asking some favor, now accusing oneself for some wrong deed, or again, making known his affairs to Him and seeking His advice concerning them. Conclude with the "Our Father."

Teresa of Avila

(1515–1582)

Many regard Teresa of Avila as one of the greatest mystics of the Western world. Certainly no one before her time, and perhaps none since, probed the interior life with such care, resoluteness, and emotional intensity. In addition, she is a writer of great beauty and skill who remains one of Spain's most celebrated authors.

The details of her life can be sketched briefly. She was born March 28, 1515, in Avila, in a large family, of religiously sensitive parents. Her mother died in 1529, when Teresa was barely fourteen years of age. Two years later she was sent by her father to a boarding school, where,

after a year or so, her health collapsed. While convalescing in the home
of her half sister, Teresa gave serious thought to her own vocation. In
1539 she suffered an attack of catalepsy, an illness characterized by a
trancelike state of consciousness in which there is some loss of voluntary motor control and some paralysis. While in this condition a year
later, though much improved, she decided to enter a Carmelite convent. Her partial paralysis continued until 1542, at which time it
disappeared—only to recur intermittently until 1554.

In 1555 she understood herself to "be addressed by interior voices
and to see certain visions and experience revelations." This experience
brought her to a place of greater religious clarity; she referred to it as a
"final conversion after nearly twenty years on the stormy sea." The
experience pertained to her deep awareness of a conflict between the
compulsions of "the world and of God." She was brought to a resolution of the conflict, although the struggle was lifelong, through an
abandonment of worldly attachments in favor of a more total worship
of God. Commenting on this sequence of interior realization, she wrote:

> ... more than eighteen of the twenty-eight years which have gone since I began
> prayer have been spent in this battle and conflict which arose from my having
> relations both with God and with the world. . . . During the remaining years, the
> conflict has been light . . . but I believe I have been serving God and have come
> to know the vanity inherent in the world.

It was in these terms—contempt for the world, abandonment of all
possessions, utter and simple devotion to God—that she sought to
restore Carmelite life to its original austerity.

Thus in 1558 she began to correct the relaxed atmosphere of Carmelite monastic life during the fourteenth and fifteenth centuries. And in
1562 the first convent of the new Carmelite reform was opened under
rules of strict and complete austerity. Although this development
created hostility among many of the Carmelites, Teresa was encouraged by the leaders of the order to establish more convents and
monasteries.

In 1567 she met a young Carmelite priest, John of the Cross, and
invited him to initiate the Carmelite reform within monastic houses for
men. Within a year, John had helped establish a monastery of the
"primitive rule," involving a restoration of the original conditions of
austerity.

Conflict ensued. Teresa was asked to establish about sixteen additional convents, but then was forbidden to do so. John of the Cross was
imprisoned in 1577. A settlement was reached in 1579 wherein the
Carmelites of the Primitive Rule were given independent jurisdiction.

Teresa was asked to continue the reform; she began traveling from place to place again, though in a state of frail health. En route to Avila, she was stricken, and died October 4, 1582.

She is noted both for her work within the Carmelite order and for her devotional writings, which have become spiritual classics. These include *The Life of the Mother Teresa of Jesus* (1611), the story of her life to the year 1579; *The Book of the Foundations*, which describes the founding of the convents; *The Way of Perfection; The Interior Castle; Conceptions on the Love of God*, together with many letters and poems.

Several themes are dominant in her writings. First, she understands the goal of human life to be the vision of God, which is consonant with the realization of perfection. She depicts the motion toward perfection in terms of an ascent of a mountain, the ascent of Mount Carmel. In strong language she emphasizes that the road is arduous, that the way requires a perpetual interior cleansing, that the soul exists in a state of conflict and strife, that the enemies are both interior and exterior, and that the obstacles never cease until the goal is reached. With this stress upon the difficulties of the pilgrimage is a certain buoyancy regarding expectations of realization. Teresa talks freely about the powers of grace and love. She commends a humble spirit. She directs those whom she counsels to the unquenchable resources of prayer. And she knows firsthand about union with God, a union that provides a foretaste of the splendor yet to be. Her penchant for counting all other things as naught derives from the compelling attractiveness of that splendor.

The selections reprinted here are taken from *The Interior Castle*, a work of lyric beauty expressive of the full maturity of her religious experience. In it she skillfully fashions an account of the inner journey, using the metaphor of the castle.

I began to think of the soul as if it were a castle made of a single diamond or of a very clear crystal, in which there are many rooms, just as in heaven there are many mansions. . . . At the center and in the midst of them all is the chiefest mansion where the most secret things pass between God and the soul.

Beginning with the first mansions—those of Humility, which lie just inside the walls of the castle and are in close proximity to the venomous creatures, or occasions of sin, outside—Teresa tells of a soul's journey to God. Included here are excerpts from the sixth and seventh mansions. The first excerpt treats of the mystic "Wound of Love" received by the soul that has been betrothed but not yet united to its future spouse. This wound occurs at a period of spiritual maturity when years of prayer and inner development are about to bear fruit. It is part of the final purging that takes place, preparing the soul for union with God. The second excerpt fairly sings of that occurrence, describing in radiant prose the full flowering of the soul's potential: the consummation of the spiritual marriage in a lasting embrace of love.

The Interior Castle

Treats of the desires to enjoy God which He gives the soul and which are so great and impetuous that they endanger its life. Treats also of the profit which comes from the favour granted by the Lord.

Have all these favours which the Spouse has granted the soul been sufficient to satisfy this little dove or butterfly (do not suppose that I have forgotten her) and to make her settle down in the place where she is to die? Certainly not; she is in a much worse state than before; for, although she may have been receiving these favours for many years, she is still sighing and weeping, and each of them causes her fresh pain. The reason for this is that, the more she learns about the greatness of her God, while finding herself so far from Him and unable to enjoy Him, the more her desire increases. For the more is revealed to her of how much this great God and Lord deserves to be loved, the more does her love for Him grow. And gradually, during these years, her desire increases, so that she comes to experience great distress, as I will now explain. I have spoken of years, because I am writing about the experiences of the particular person about whom I have been speaking here. But it must be clearly understood that no limitations can be set to God's acts, and that He can raise a soul to the highest point here mentioned in a single moment. His Majesty has the power to do all that He wishes and He is desirous of doing a great deal for us.

The soul, then, has these yearnings and tears and sighs, together with the strong impulses which have already been described. They all seem to arise from our love, and are accompanied by great emotion, but they are all as nothing by comparison with this other, for they are like a smouldering fire, the heat of which is quite bearable, though it causes pain. While the soul is in this condition, and interiorly burning, it often happens that a mere fleeting thought of some kind (there is no way of telling whence it comes, or how) or some remark which the soul hears

"Interior Castle," in *The Complete Works of Saint Teresa of Jesus*, Vol. II, trans. E. Allison Peers (New York: Sheed and Ward, 1946), pp. 323–6, 326–8, 333–6.

about death's long tarrying, deals it, as it were, a blow, or, as one might say, wounds it with an arrow of fire. I do not mean that there actually is such an arrow; but, whatever it is, it obviously could not have come from our own nature. Nor is it actually a blow, though I have spoken of it as such; but it makes a deep wound, not, I think in any region where physical pain can be felt, but in the soul's most intimate depths. It passes as quickly as a flash of lightning and leaves everything in our nature that is earthly reduced to powder. During the time that it lasts we cannot think of anything that has to do with our own existence: it instantaneously enchains the faculties in such a way that they have no freedom to do anything, except what will increase this pain.

I should not like this to sound exaggerated: in reality I am beginning to see, as I go on, that all I say falls short of the truth, which is indescribable. It is an enrapturing of the senses and faculties, except, as I have said, in ways which enhance this feeling of distress. The understanding is keenly on the alert to discover why this soul feels absent from God, and His Majesty now aids it with so lively a knowledge of Himself that it causes the distress to grow until the sufferer cries out aloud. However patient a sufferer she may be, and however accustomed to enduring great pain, she cannot help doing this, because this pain, as I have said, is not in the body, but deep within the soul. It was in this way that the person I have mentioned discovered how much more sensitive the soul is than the body, and it was revealed to her that this suffereing resembles that of souls in purgatory; despite their being no longer in the body they suffer much more than do those who are still in the body and on earth.

I once saw a person in this state who I really believed was dying; and this was not at all surprising, because it does in fact involve great peril of death. Although it lasts only for a short time, it leaves the limbs quite disjointed, and, for as long as it continues, the pulse is as feeble as though the soul were about to render itself up to God. It really is quite as bad as this. For, while the natural heat of the body fails, the soul burns so fiercely within that, if the flame were only a little stronger, God would have fulfilled its desires. It is not that it feels any bodily pain whatsoever, notwithstanding such a dislocation of the limbs that for two or three days afterwards it is in great pain and has not the strength even to write; in fact the body seems to me never to be as strong as it was previously. The reason it feels no pain must be that it is suffering so keenly within that it takes no notice of the body. It is as when we have a very acute pain in one spot; we may have many other pains but we feel them less; this I have conclusively proved. In the present case, the soul feels nothing at all, and I do not believe it would feel anything if it were cut into little pieces.

You will tell me that this is imperfection and ask why such a person does not resign herself to the will of God, since she has surrendered herself to Him so completely. Down to this time she had been able to do so, and indeed had spent her life doing so; but now she no longer can because her reason is in such a state that she is not her own mistress, and can think of nothing but the cause of her suffering. Since she is absent from her Good, why should she wish to live? She is conscious of a strange solitiude, since there is not a creature on the whole earth who can be a companion to her—in fact, I do not believe she would find any in Heaven, save Him Whom she loves: on the contrary, all earthly companionship is torment to her. She thinks of herself as of a person suspended aloft, unable either to come down and rest anywhere on earth or to ascend into Heaven. She is parched with thirst, yet cannot reach the water; and the thirst is not a tolerable one but of a kind that nothing can quench, nor does she desire it to be quenched, except with that water of which Our Lord spoke to the Samaritan woman, and that is not given to her.

*   *   *

Let us now return to what we were discussing when we left this soul in such affliction. It remains in this state only for a short time (three or four hours at most, I should say); for, if the pain lasted long, it would be impossible, save by a miracle, for natural weakness to suffer it. On one occasion it lasted only for a quarter of an hour and yet produced complete prostration. On that occasion, as a matter of fact, the sufferer entirely lost consciousness. The violent attack came on through her hearing some words about "life not ending." She was engaged in conversation at the time—it was the last day of Eastertide, and all that Easter she had been afflicted with such aridity that she hardly knew it was Easter at all. So just imagine anyone thinking that these attacks can be resisted! It is no more possible to resist them than for a person thrown into a fire to make the flames lose their heat and not burn her. She cannot hide her anguish, so all who are present realize the great peril in which she lies, even though they cannot witness what is going on within her. It is true that they can bear her company, but they only seem to her like shadows—as all other earthly things do too.

And now I want you to see that, if at any time you should find yourselves in this condition, it is possible for your human nature, weak as it is, to be of help to you. So let me tell you this. It sometimes happens that, when a person is in this state that you have been considering, and has such yearnings to die because the pain is more than she can bear, that her soul seems to be on the very point of leaving the body, she is really afraid and would like her distress to be alleviated lest she should in fact die. It is quite evident that this fear comes from natural weakness, and yet, on the other hand, the desire does not leave her, nor can she possibly find any means of dispelling the distress until the Lord Himself dispels it for her. This He does, as a general rule, by granting her a deep rapture or some kind of vision, in which the true Comforter comforts and strengthens her so that she can wish to live for as long as He wills.

This is a distressing thing, but it produces the most wonderful effects and the soul at once loses its fear of any trials which may befall it; for by comparison with the feelings of deep anguish which its spirit has experienced these seem nothing. Having gained so much, the soul would be glad to suffer them all again and again; but it has no means of doing so nor is there any method by which it can reach that state again until the Lord wills, just as there is no way of resisting or escaping it when it comes. The soul has far more contempt for the world than it had previously, for it sees that no worldly thing was of any avail to it in its torment; and it is very much more detached from the creatures, because it sees that it can be comforted and satisfied only by the Creator, and it has the greatest fear and anxiety not to offend Him, because it sees that He can torment as well as comfort.

There are two deadly perils, it seems to me, on this spiritual road. This is one of them—and it is indeed a peril, and no light one. The other is the peril of excessive rejoicing and delight, which can be carried to such an extreme that it really seems as if the soul is swooning, and as if the very slightest thing would be enough to drive it out of the body; this would really bring it no little happiness.

Now, sisters, you will see if I was not right in saying that courage is necessary for us here and that if you ask the Lord for these things He will be justified in answering you as He answered the sons of Zebedee: "Can you drink the chalice?" I believe, sisters, that we should all reply: "We can"; and we should be quite right to do so, for His Majesty gives the strength to those who, He sees, have need of it, and He defends these souls in every way and stands up for them if they are persecuted and spoken ill of, as He did for the Magdalen—by His actions if not in words. And in the end—ah, in the end, before they die, He repays them for everything at once, as you are now going to see. May He be for ever blessed and may all creatures praise Him. Amen.

Describes the difference between spiritual union and spiritual marriage. Explains this by subtle comparison.

Let us now come to treat of the Divine and Spiritual Marriage, although this great favour cannot be fulfilled perfectly in us during our lifetime, for if we were to withdraw ourselves from God this great blessing would be lost. When granting this favour for the first time, His Majesty is pleased to reveal Himself to the soul through an imaginary vision of His most sacred Humanity, so that it may clearly understand what is taking place and not be ignorant of the fact that it is receiving so sovereign a gift. To other people the experience will come in a different way. To the person of whom we have been speaking the Lord revealed Himself one day, when she had just received Communion, in great splendour and beauty and majesty, as He did after His resurrection, and told her that it was time she took upon her His affairs as if they were her own and that He would take her affairs upon Himself; and He added other words which are easier to understand than to repeat.

This, you will think was nothing new, since on other occasions the Lord had revealed Himself to that soul in this way. But it was so different that it left her quite confused and dismayed: for one reason, because this vision came with great force; for another, because of the words which He spoke to her; and also because, in the interior of her soul, where He revealed Himself to her, she had never seen any visions but this. For you must understand that there is the greatest difference between all the other visions we have mentioned and those belonging to this Mansion, and there is the same difference between the Spiritual Betrothal and the Spiritual Marriage as there is between two betrothed persons and two who are united so that they cannot be separated any more.

As I have already said, one makes these comparisons because there are no other appropriate ones, yet it must be realized that the Betrothal has no more to do with the body than if the soul were not in the body, and were nothing but spirit. Between the Spiritual Marriage and the body there is even less connection, for this secret union takes place in the deepest centre of the soul, which must be where God Himself dwells, and I do not think there is any need of a door by which to enter it. I say there is no need of a door because all that has so far been described seems to have come through the medium of the senses and faculties and this appearance of the Humanity of the Lord must do so too. But what passes in the union of the Spiritual Marriage is very different. The Lord appears in the centre of the soul, not through an imaginary, but through an intellectual vision (although this is a subtler one than that already mentioned), just as He appeared to the Apostles, without entering through the door, when He said to them: "Pax vobis". This instanteeoous communication of God to the soul is so great a secret and so sublime a favour, and such a delight is felt by the soul, that I do not know with what to compare it, beyond saying that the Lord is pleased to manifest to the soul at that moment the glory that is in Heaven, in a sublimer manner than is possible through any vision or spiritual consolation. It is impossible to say more than that, as far as one can understand, the soul (I mean the spirit of this soul) is made one with God, Who, being likewise a Spirit, has been pleased to reveal the love that He has for us by showing to certain persons the extent of that love, so that we may praise His greatness. For He has been pleased to unite Himself with His creature in such a way that they have become like two who cannot be separated from one another: even so He will not separate Himself from her.

The Spiritual Betrothal is different: here the two persons are frequently separated, as is the case with union, for, although by union is meant the joining of two things into one, each of the two, as is a matter of common observation, can be separated and remain a thing by itself. This favour of the Lord passes quickly and afterwards the soul is deprived of that companionship—I mean so far as it can understand. In this other favour of the Lord it is not so: the soul remains all the time in that centre with its God. We might say that union is as if the ends of two wax candles were joined so that the light they give is one: the wicks and the wax and the light are all one; yet afterwards the one candle can be perfectly well separated from the other and the candles become two again, or the wick may be withdrawn from the wax. But here it is like rain falling from the heavens into a river or a spring; there is nothing but water there and it is impossible to divide or separate the water belonging to the river from that which fell from the heavens. Or it is as if a tiny streamlet enters the sea, from which it will find no way of separating itself, or as if in a room there were two large windows through which the light streamed in: it enters in different places but it all becomes one.

Perhaps when St. Paul says: "He who is joined to God becomes one spirit with Him," he is referring to this sovereign Marriage, which presupposes the entrance of His Majesty into the soul by union. And he also says: "For me to live is Christ, to die is gain." This, I think, the soul may say here, for it is here that the little butterfly to which we have referred dies, and with the greatest joy, because Christ is now its life.

John of the Cross

(1542–1591)

One of the greatest of the Spanish poets, John, or San Juan de La Cruz (Saint John of the Cross) as he is known in his native country, brought mystical awareness to the heights of lyric beauty and provided an anatomy, or grammar, of the interior life that has been consulted by practitioners of religious sensitivity from the sixteenth century to the modern era.

He was born in Fontiveros, in the modern province of Avila, on June 24, 1542. He became a Carmelite monk at Medina del Campo in 1563, attended the University of Salamanca, and was ordained a priest in 1567. He helped Teresa of Avila restore the life of austerity to her Carmelite convent in 1568, then opened a Discalced (meaning shoeless, barefoot) Carmelite monastery in 1569. Even had he not been author and poet, he would be remembered historically as a cofounder of the Discalced Carmelites.

His life was one of great turmoil. The attempt to bring greater austerity into the life of the Carmelite communities created resistance and friction. John was twice kidnapped by members of the order and imprisoned, in 1576 and again in 1577–1578. While in prison, he wrote some of his finest poetry, including a portion (the first thirty stanzas) of his famous *Spiritual Canticle*, a commentary on biblical Song of Songs. He escaped from prison in 1578, and eventually gained a position of leadership within the order. But dissension plagued the community until John's final days. The record finds him withdrawing into absolute solitude before his death on December 14, 1591.

Though his career was important, it is for his writings and his tracing of the pathways of the interior life that John is best known. The two most famous poems are *The Spiritual Canticle*, a book whose purpose, as he says in the Prologue, is to treat the "sayings of love understood mystically," and *The Dark Night of the Soul*. The latter was originally Part IV of a larger work, *Ascent of Mt. Carmel*. It describes the process by which the soul gives up its attachments to all things, invoking the pattern of the crucifixion of Christ, prior to the bestowal of its glory. *Ascent of Mt. Carmel* reconstructs the entire interior process, following the same schematic pattern that is presented in *The Spiritual Canticle*:

purgation, illumination, and union. The purpose of *Ascent* is to describe the steps of mystical ascent.

The thesis in all his books is that the soul must travel through darkness (without clear vision, in a state of uncertainty) if it is to come to union with God. The key distinction in *The Dark Night* is between "active" and "passive" nights. Both involve a stripping away, a process of purification, a removal of all imperfections and impurities. "Active" refers to the capacity the individual possesses to effect certain steps within this process on his own; he can prepare the senses and the spirit, for example. "Passive" denotes the soul's incapacity to effect union with God. The soul is brought to this awareness through the "active night." In the "passive night," God accomplishes what the soul realizes it is incapable of doing. Both modes are necessary to effective interior purification, and both imply cleansing of both senses and spirit. And as the soul travels through the process of purification, it penetrates ever more deeply through separating screens to the core of reality.

John explains that divine grace acts upon the soul like fire acting upon a piece of wood. First the fire must dry the wood, driving out all moisture (or all entities contrary to its nature). In the process, the wood is charred, made unsightly, and becomes a source of foul odors. Then the fire kindles the wood and transforms it into fire. The wood becomes of the same substance as that which has been acting upon it. So too, he explains, God strips one of everything contrary (faculties, feelings, and affections), "leaving the understanding dark, the will dry, the memory empty, and the affections in deep affliction." The purpose is for the soul to be transformed into God so that God can become the life of the soul. John calls this "assimilation into God, a total assimilation into the divine essence." Love, he adds, is "like fire, which ever rises upward with the desire to be absorbed in the center of its sphere." This is the vision, and the care with which it is worked out prompts us to offer some comments regarding John's achievement.

Readers of this volume are familiar with the tendency of writers on this subject to identify steps and stages in the contemplative life. We have encountered many examples of the conviction that the interior life can be principled, but requires a process with a capacity for growth and development. Appropriately, there have been a number of portrayals of the interior life that liken the transition from the state of dispersed self-awareness to an effective recognition of the divine presence to a passage, journey, or pilgrimage that is marked by periods and seasons, each one possessing distinct obstacles and providing great challenges. One of the clearest examples of this tendency was provided by Bonaventura, who depicted the ascent toward God as following its own step-by-step *itinerarium*. It is appropriate to depict the interior life in this fashion, given the contrasts between corporeal and spiritual natures, and between sensible, intelligible, and transintelligible realities. Indeed, the imagery of the ladder of ascent, supported by the pattern of Platonic thought, translates into a portrayal of the religious life that is progressive and ascendent. In this respect, John of the Cross continued a pattern of interpretation that had become typical. He contributed both data and style to an intellectual enterprise that had won both philosophical and religious respectability in the West many centuries before. As many before him had done, John set out to schematize the stages of ascent. He is recognized within the tradition and, significantly, from the outside as well, to have achieved his goal in exemplary fashion. The schema that he provided has been utilized as a sure guide by more recent explorers of the regions of self-consciousness.

His uniqueness in this respect derives from the manner in which he proceeded. The significant advance he gave to the entire undertaking was due to a shift in genre. To be sure, much of the language John used, as many of his commentators have emphasized, is formal and abstract, influenced by some of the most erudite passages in previous theological literature, particularly by the writings of Thomas Aquinas. But this says only part of it. For while John perpetuated an interest in the contemplative life that had registered before, he did so in a very different form. He was poet, first of all. And some would say that poetic language, indeed, the poetic mentality—the style of The Song of Songs is supporting evidence—is much more in keeping with the nature of contemplative experience than any other means of expression. It is much better able to capture the affective characteristics of that experience. Because John was an extraordinarily gifted and sensitive poet, his portrayals reach literary heights and penetrative depths of unique dimensions.

It is in keeping with these stylistic considerations that John utilized The Song of Songs, as Bernard of Clairvaux, William of St. Thierry, John of Ford, and others did before him, as the chief medium through which his own insights were expressed. Yet, significantly, that same medium is employed as the basis for the most exact description of the variegated motion of the interior life that the Christian world has known. It was never decided by any authoritative ruling body—religious communities, ecclesiastical officers, or anyone else—that John's schematic account should have this veritable paradigmatic quality and status. On the contrary, there had been concerted attempts to keep portions of his writings concealed; not until the twentieth century, nearly four hundred years after they were written, did they become available in unexpurgated editions. But this matters little. The schema has become known, used, consulted, and compared with portrayals of the interior life that derive from other cultures and other religious traditions. Thousands upon thousands of readers have found his works to exhibit a powerful inherent authority. As a result they, more than any other single source, have informed what we refer to in these pages as "the classical paradigm" of spirituality in the Christian world.

Given this fact, it is all the more intriguing that the dominant lines of the pattern were recorded during a time of extreme privation. These are prison writings, fundamentally, set down by a man who felt the ravages of alienation most acutely. Teresa of Avila had talked of rooms within a castle: John envisioned them from within an abnormally small cell located in a prison wall. The awareness of suffering, abandonment, forsakenness, the abyss, and the perils of the dark night gave him the surest clues to the truest nature of the passions of the soul. Ultimately, therefore, it was God who suffered too, and that "crucifixion is inscribed lengthwise," to borrow a phrase from Irenaeus, over the entire interior odyssey.

The selections reprinted here are Chapters XIX and XX of *The Dark Night of the Soul*. They describe the pathway of mystical ascent according to ten progressive distinguishable steps.

The Dark Night of the Soul

Begins to explain the ten steps of the mystic ladder of Divine love, according to Saint Bernard and Saint Thomas. The first five are here treated

We observe, then, that the steps of this ladder of love by which the soul mounts, one by one, to God, are ten. The first step of love causes the soul to languish, and this to its advantage. The Bride is speaking from this step of love when she says: 'I adjure you, daughters of Jerusalem, that, if ye find my Beloved, ye tell Him that I am sick with love.' This sickness, however, is not unto death, but for the glory of God, for in this sickness the soul swoons as to sin and as to all things that are not God, for the sake of God Himself, even as David testifies, saying: 'My soul hath swooned away'—that is, with respect to all things, for Thy

Dark Night of The Soul, trans. E. Allison Peers (New York: Doubleday, 1959), pp. 167-75. Footnotes have been ommitted.

salvation. For just as a sick man first of all loses his appetite and taste for all food, and his colour changes, so likewise in this degree of love the soul loses its taste and desire for all things and changes its colour and the other accidents of its past life, like one in love. The soul falls not into this sickness if excess of heat be not communicated to it from above, even as is expressed in that verse of David which says: "In thy great goodness, O God, thou didst provide for the needy."*

This sickness and swooning to all things, which is the beginning and the first step on the road to God, we clearly described above, when we were speaking of the annihilation wherein the soul finds itself when it begins to climb this ladder of contemplative purgation, when it can find no pleasure, support, consolation or abiding-place in anything soever. Wherefore from this step it begins at once to climb to the second.

The second step causes the soul to seek God without ceasing. Wherefore, when the Bride says that she sought Him by night upon her bed (when she had swooned away according to the first step of love) and found Him not, she said: 'I will arise and will seek Him Whom my soul loveth.' This, as we say, the soul does without ceasing, as David counsels it, saying: 'Seek ye ever the face of God, and seek ye Him in all things, tarrying not until ye find Him;' like the Bride, who, having enquired for Him of the watchmen, passed on at once and left them. Mary Magdalene did not even notice the angels at the sepulchre. On this step the soul now walks so anxiously that it seeks the Beloved in all things. In whatsoever it thinks, it thinks at once of the Beloved. Of whatsoever it speaks, in whatsoever matters present themselves, it is speaking and communing at once with the Beloved. When it eats, when it sleeps, when it watches, when it does aught soever, all its care is about the Beloved, as is said above with respect to the yearnings of love. And now, as love begins to recover its health and find new strength in the love of this second step, it begins at once to mount to the third, by means of a certain degree of new purgation in the night, as we shall afterwards describe, which produces in soul the following effects.

The third step of the ladder of love is that which causes the soul to work and gives it fervour so that it fails not. Concerning this the royal Prophet says: 'Blessed is the man that feareth the Lord, for in His commandments he is eager to labour greatly.' Wherefore if fear, being the son of love, causes within him this eagerness to labour, what will be done by love itself? On this step the soul considers great works undertaken for the Beloved as small; many things as few; and the long time for which it serves Him as short, by reason of the fire of love wherein it is now burning. Even so to Jacob, though after seven years he had been made to serve seven more, they seemed few because of the greatness of his love. Now if the love of a mere creature could accomplish so much in Jacob, what will love of the Creator be able to do when on this third step it takes possession of the soul? Here, for the great love which the soul bears to God, it suffers great pains and afflictions because of the little that it does for God; and if it were lawful for it to be destroyed a thousand times for Him it would be comforted. Wherefore it considers itself useless in all that it does and thinks itself to be living in vain. Another wondrous effect produced here in the soul is that it considers itself as being, most certainly, worse than all other souls: first, because love is continually teaching it how much is due to God; and second, because, as the works which it here does for God are many and it knows them all to be faulty and imperfect, they all bring it confusion and affliction, for it realizes in how lowly a manner it is working for God, Who is so high. On this third step, the soul is very far from vainglory or presumption, and from condemning others. These anxious effects, with many others like them, are produced in the soul by this third step; wherefore it gains courage and strength from them in order to mount to the fourth step, which is that that follows.

The fourth step of this ladder of love is that whereby there is caused in the soul an habitual suffering because of the Beloved, yet without weariness. For, as Saint Augustine says, love makes all things that are great, grievous and burdensome to be almost naught. From this step the Bride was speaking when, desiring to attain to the last step, she said to the Spouse: 'Set me as a seal upon thy heart, as a seal upon thine arm; for love—that is, the act and work of love—is strong as death, and emulation and importunity last as long as hell.' The spirit here has so much strength that it has subjected the flesh and takes as little account of it as does the tree of one of its leaves. In no way does the soul here seek its own consolation or pleasure, either in God, or in aught else, nor does it desire to seek to pray to God for favours, for it sees clearly that it has already received enough of these, and all its anxiety is set upon the manner wherein it will be able to do something that is pleasing to God and to render Him some service such as He merits and in return for what it has received from Him, although it be greatly to its cost. The soul says in its heart and spirit: Ah, my God and Lord! How many are there that go to seek in Thee their own consolation and pleasure, and desire Thee to grant them favours and gifts; but those who long to do Thee pleasure and to give Thee something at their cost, setting their own interests last, are very few. The failure, my God, is not in Thy unwillingness to grant us new favours, but in our neglect to use those that we have received in Thy service alone, in order to constrain Thee to grant them to us continually. Exceeding lofty is this step of love; for, as the soul goes ever after God with love so true, imbued with the spirit of suffering for His sake, His Majesty oftentimes and quite habitually grants it joy, and visits it sweetly and delectably in the spirit; for the boundless love of Christ, the Word, cannot suffer the afflictions of His lover without succouring him. This He affirmed through Jeremias, saying: 'I have remembered thee, pitying thy youth and tenderness, when thou wentest after Me in the wilderness.' Speaking spiritually, this denotes the detachment which the soul now has interiorly from every creature, so that it rests not and nowhere finds quietness. This fourth step enkindles the soul and makes it to burn in such desire for God that it causes it to mount to the fifth, which is that which follows.

The fifth step of this ladder of love makes the soul to desire and long for God impatiently. On this step the vehemence of the lover to comprehend the Beloved and be united with Him is such that every delay, however brief, becomes very long, wearisome and oppressive to it, and it continually believes itself to be finding the Beloved. And when it sees its desire frustrated (which is at almost every moment), it swoons away with its yearning, as says the Psalmist, speaking from this step, in these words: 'My soul longs and faints for the dwellings of the Lord.' On this step the lover must needs see that which he loves, or die; at this step was Rachel, when, for the great longing she had for children, she said to Jacob, her spouse: 'Give me children, else shall I die.' Here men suffer hunger like dogs and go about and surround the city of God. On this step, which is one of hunger, the soul is nourished upon love; for, even as is its hunger, so is its abundance; so that it rises hence to the sixth step, producing the effects which follow.

Wherein are treated the other five steps of love

On the sixth step the soul runs swiftly to God and touches Him again and again; and it runs without fainting by reason of its hope. For here the love that has made it strong makes it to fly swiftly. Of this step the prophet Isaias speaks thus: 'The saints that hope in God shall renew their strength; they shall take wings as the eagle; they shall fly and shall not faint,' as they did at the fifth step. To this step likewise alludes that verse of the Psalm; 'As the hart desires the waters, my soul desires Thee, O God.' For the hart, in its thirst, runs to the waters with great swiftness. The cause of this swiftness in love which the soul has on this step is that its charity is greatly enlarged within it, since the soul is here almost wholly purified, as is said likewise in the Psalm, namely; 'without fault or guilt.' And in another Psalm: 'I ran the way of Thy commandments when Thou didst enlarge my heart'; and thus from this sixth step the soul at once mounts to the seventh, which is that which follows.

The seventh step of this ladder makes the soul to become vehement in its boldness. Here love employs not its judgment in order to hope, nor does it take counsel so that it may draw back, neither can any shame restrain it; for the favour which God here grants to the soul causes it to become vehement in its boldness. Hence follows that Which the Apostle says, namely: That charity believeth all things, hopeth all things and is capable of all things. Of this step spake Moses, when he entreated God to pardon the people, and if not, to blot out his name from the book of life wherein He had written it. Men like these obtain from God that which they beg of Him with desire. Wherefore David says: 'Delight thou in God and He will give thee the petitions of thy heart.' On this step the Bride grew bold, and said: 'that you would kiss me with the kisses of your mouth.' To this step it is not lawful for the soul to aspire boldly, unless it feel the interior favour of the King's sceptre extended to it, lest perchance it fall from the other steps which it has mounted up to this point, and wherein it must ever possess itself in humility. From this daring and power which God grants to the soul on this seventh step, so that it may be bold with God in the vehemence of love, follows the eighth, which is that wherein it takes the Beloved captive and is united with Him, as follows.

The eighth step of love causes the soul to seize Him and hold Him fast without letting Him go, even as the Bride says, after this manner: 'I found Him Whom my heart and soul love; I held Him and I will not let Him go.' On this step of union the soul satisfies her desire, but not continuously. Certain souls climb some way, and then lose their hold; for, if this state were to continue, it would be glory itself in this life; and thus the soul remains therein for very short periods of time. To the prophet Daniel, because he was a man of desires, was sent a command from God to remain on this step, when it was said to him: 'Daniel, stay upon thy step, because thou art a man of desires.' After this step follows the ninth, which is that of souls now perfect, as we shall afterwards say, which is that that follows.

The ninth step of love makes the soul to burn with sweetness. This step is that of the perfect, who now burn sweetly in God. For this sweet and delectable ardour is caused in them by the Holy Spirit by reason of the union which they have with God. For this cause Saint Gregory says, concerning the Apostles, that when the Holy Spirit came upon them visibly they burned inwardly and sweetly through love. Of the good things and riches of God which the soul enjoys on this step, we cannot speak; for if many books were to be written concerning it the greater part would still remain untold. For this cause, and because we shall say something of it hereafter, I say no more here than that after this follows the tenth and last step of this ladder of love, which belongs not to this life.

The tenth and last step of this secret ladder of love causes the soul to become wholly assimilated to God, by reason of the clear and immediate vision of God which it then possesses; when, having ascended in this life to the ninth step, it goes forth from the flesh. These souls, who are few, enter not into purgatory, since they have already been wholly purged by love. Of these Saint Matthew says: 'Blessed are the pure in heart, for they shall see God.' And, as we say, this vision is the cause of the perfect likeness of the soul to God, for, as Saint John says, we know that we shall be like Him. Not because the soul will come to have the capacity of God, for that is impossible; but because all that it is will become like to God, for which cause it will be called, and will be, God by participation.

This is the secret ladder whereof the soul here speaks, although upon these higher steps it is no longer very secret to the soul, since much is revealed to it by love, through the great effects which love produces in it. But, on this last step of clear vision, which is the last step of the ladder whereon God leans, as we have said already, there is naught that is hidden from the soul, by reason of its complete assimilation. Wherefore Our Saviour says; 'In that day ye shall ask Me nothing,' etc. But, until that day, however high a point the soul may reach, there remains something hidden from it—namely, all that it lacks for total assimilation in the Divine Essence. After this manner, by this mystical theology and secret love, the soul continues to rise above all things and above itself, and to mount upward to God. For love is like fire, which ever rises upward with the desire to be absorbed in the centre of its sphere.

François de Sales

(1567–1622)

The Catholic Church of the early modern era was alive with the ferment of Counterreformation activity. Supporting and informing the massive reforms that swept through that body was an upsurge of vitality in the realm of personal spirituality. During the sixteenth century, Spain was in the forefront of this spiritual renaissance with such figures as Ignatius of Loyola, Teresa of Avila, and John of the Cross. In the seventeenth century, the focus of this activity shifted to France. There we find the seeds of the time-honored Christian contemplative tradition coming once again into flower. Of the many prominent French men and women engaged not only in the practice of the interior life but involved in its propagation and continuing definition was François de Sales—bishop, popular preacher, influential spiritual director, and cofounder of the Order of the Visitation.

Born at the castle of Sales in Savoy, the eldest of ten children, François seemed destined for a brilliant secular career. He studied under the Jesuits at Clermont and then embarked on the study of law in Padua. Soon, however, he announced his intention of entering the priesthood, prompted in part by an intensely painful spiritual experience in which he teetered on the edge of despair only to return to the firm ground of hope after making an act of complete submission to the will of God. The experience was to influence all his later teaching.

Ordained in 1593 and appointed Provost of Geneva the following year, François turned his energies toward reclaiming for Catholicism the Chablis, an area that had been forcibly converted to Calvinism. In this work he was extremely successful, often enduring great hardships and risking his safety to realize his goals. Having gained a reputation for persuasive preaching and personal sanctity, he was made bishop of Geneva in 1602, a post he chose to hold for the rest of his life, despite later offers of more prestigious placement.

For many years he had practiced the Ignatian form of meditation. This method of mental prayer, developed by the great Jesuit leader, was a highly structured and systematic form of mental exercise designed to involve one's intellect, senses, and imagination in influencing the will to order one's life according to God's purpose. This form of guided prayer was characteristic of much Counterreformation spirituality, which tended to be more concerned with psychological processes than with the spirituality espoused in the Medieval world. François de Sales' own work, *Introduction to the Devout Life*, though very different in intent and tone from its Ignatian counterpart, is itself a manual of meditation designed to lead the soul deeper into the life of God by systematic means.

A new and transforming element entered François' spirituality when he came into contact with the works of Teresa of Avila through the medium of the reformed Carmelite order, which was then being introduced into France. Gaining insight into the depths of contemplative prayer, the young bishop began to dream of founding a religious order for women that would be dedicated to the contemplative vision yet allow for the exercise of charitable works among the sick and poor, a practice not ordinarily realizable given the traditional practice of enclosure. It was also to be an order designed for women not sufficiently strong to endure the physical austerities of the Carmelite regime. He was able to realize his dream in 1610 when he cofounded the Order of the Visitation with Jeanne de Chantal, a young widow and fellow traveler on the mystic path whose spiritual director he had become some years before. The Visitation flourished but its original shape was altered in 1618 when, on the insistence of the archbishop of Lyons, the order was made fully enclosed.

The thought of François de Sales is, on the one hand, directly in line with the contemplative tradition and, on the other, distinctively his own. His works contain numerous quotations from the Fathers of the Church, the Cistercians, the Franciscans, the Carmelites, and others; yet there are original views as well. For the bishop of Geneva wrote for a new audience. No longer was the inner life reserved for the monastic world alone. One of the impulses of the Counterreformation was to promote the tradition of Christian spirituality beyond the cloister into the lives of the secular clergy and the laity. François wrote mainly for the sophisticated and cultered audience of the French aristocracy. He taught the possibility of prayer in the secular world of court and salon and the virtue of interior detachment in the midst of luxury. As a result, his language is extremely genteel. It has been described as "sweet" for it was tailored to tastes developed in an atmosphere that favored gracious manners and the elegant turn of a phrase.

Certainly not all of the French aristocracy was outside the monastic world. He also wrote for those fully given over to lives of renunciation and dedicated to the depths of prayer. In *The Treatise on the Love of God*, we see his mature vision of the contemplative life. In his hands the love of God, this familiar refrain of the Christian mystic, takes on new overtones of warmth and reassuring beauty. A deeply optimistic view of human nature pervades his writing. He teaches that inherent in each individual is the impulse to do good and to love God fully, an impulse that comes from God himself. He speaks constantly of the mercy and infinite love of the divine that pervades all life. To respond to this gracious giver, one must accept what is given. The motto of the Visitation as well as of François' own life—"To ask for nothing and refuse nothing"—confirms this view.

He gives much emphasis to "holy indifference," the total and loving abandonment of self-will to the will of God as it is expressed in the events of one's life. In terms of prayer this idea has great meaning. He counseled his spiritual daughters to present themselves before God as statues, content to be shaped by the will of the divine sculptor. This indifference extends to include spiritual experience and even concern for one's own ultimate salvation. It refuses to plumb the mystery of the transcendent with human tools; rather it throws itself headlong into whatever is with profound trust and utter willingness to abandon the self.

The Genevan bishop's stress on human passivity in relation to the divine is somewhat modified by his appreciation of human faculties. Unlike the author of *The Cloud of Unknowing*, he does not preach the abandonment of all mental activity in advanced states of prayer. For him, meditation is not merely a beginner's exercise but is "mystical rumination" in order to find motives for love. It gives birth to contemplation that, in his own words, is a "loving, simple and permanent attention of the spirit to divine things."

The selection reprinted here consists of two chapters from *The Treatise on the Love of God* that treat the contemplative state known in

Teresa of Avila's phraseology as the "prayer of recollection." It is addressed to "Theotimus," François de Sales' imagined reader, a "soul . . . advanced in devotion" who, having successfully navigated the waters of meditation, is ready to embark upon a journey that will take them into the deep waters of the inner life.

The Treatise on the Love of God

Of the loving recollection of the soul in contemplation

I speak not here, Theotimus, of the recollection by which such as are about to pray, place themselves in God's presence, entering into themselves, and as one would say bringing their soul into their hearts, there to speak with God; for this recollection is made by love's command, which, provoking us to prayer, moves us to take this means of doing it well, so that we ourselves make this withdrawing of our spirit. But the recollection of which I mean to speak is not made by love's command but by love itself, that is, we do not make it by free choice, for it is not in our power to have it when we please, and does not depend on our care, but God at his pleasure works it in us by his most holy grace. The Blessed Mother (S.) Teresa of Jesus says: "He who has written that the prayer of recollection is made as when a hedgehog or tortoise draws itself within itself, said well, saving that these beasts draw themselves in when they please, whereas recollection is not in our will, but comes to us only when it pleases God to do us this grace."

Now it comes thus. Nothing is so natural to good as to draw and unite unto itself such things as are sensible of it; as our souls do, which continually draw towards them and give themselves to their treasure, that is, what they love. It happens then sometimes that our Lord imperceptibly infuses into the depths of our hearts a certain agreeable sweetness, which testifies his presence, and then the powers, yea the very exterior senses of the soul, by a certain secret contentment, turn in towards that most interior part where is the most amiable and dearest spouse. For as a new swarm of bees when it would take flight and change country, is recalled by a sound softly made on metal basins, by

St. Francis de Sales, *Treatise on the Love of God*. trans. Henry B. Mackey (Westminster: The Newman Book Shop, 1942), pp. 251-4, 254-6. Footnotes have been omitted.

the smell of honied wine, or by the scent of some odoriferous herbs, being stayed by the attraction of these agreeable things, and entering into the hive prepared for it:—so our Savior,—pronouncing some secret word of his love, or pouring out the odour of the wine of his dilection, more delicious than honey, or letting stream the perfumes of his garments, that is, feelings of his heavenly consolations in our hearts, and thereby making them perceive his most welcome presence,— draws unto him all the faculties of our soul, which gather about him and stay themselves in him as in their most desired object. And as he who should cast a piece of loadstone amongst a number of needles would instantly see them turn all their points towards their well-beloved adamant, and join themselves to it, so when our Saviour makes his most delicious presence to be felt in the midst of our hearts, all our faculties turn their points in that direction, to be united to this incomparable sweetness.

O God! says the soul in imitation of S. Augustine, whither was I wandering to seek thee! O most infinite beauty! I sought thee without, and thou was wast in the midst of my heart. All Magdalen's affections, and all her thoughts, were scattered about the sepulchre of her Savior, whom she went seeking hither and thither, and though she had found him, and he spoke to her, yet leaves she them dispersed, because she does not perceive his presence; but as soon as he had called her by her name, see how she gathers herself together and entirely attaches herself to his feet: one only word puts her into recollection.

Propose to yourself, Theotimus, the most holy Virgin, our Lady, when she had conceived the Son Of God, her only love. The soul of that well-beloved mother did wholly collect itself about that well-beloved child, and because this heavenly dear one was harboured in her sacred womb, all the faculties of her soul gathered themselves within her, as holy bees into their hive, wherein their honey is; and by how much the divine greatness was, so to speak, straitened and contracted within her virginal womb, by so much her soul did more increase and magnify the praises of that infinite loving-kindness, and her spirit within her body leapt with joy (as S. John in his mother's womb) in presence of her God, whom she felt. She launched not her affections out of herself, since her treasure, her loves and her delights were in the midst of her sacred womb. Now the same contentment may be practised by imitation, among those who, having communicated, feel by the certainty of faith that which, not flesh and blood, but the Heavenly Father has revealed, that their Saviour is body and soul present, with a most real presence, to their body and to their soul, by this most adorable sacrament. For as the pearl-mother, having received the drops of the fresh dew of the morning, closes up, not only to keep them pure from all possible mixture with the water of the sea, but also for the pleasure she feels in relishing the agreeable freshness of this heaven-sent germ:—so does it happen to many holy and devout of the faithful, that having received the Divine Sacrament which contains the dew of all heavenly benediction, their heart closes over It, and all their faculties collect themselves together, not only to adore this sovereign King, but for the spiritual consolation and refreshment, beyond belief, which they receive in feeling by faith this divine germ of immortality within them. Where you will carefully note, Theotimus, that to say all in a word this recollection is wholly made by love, which perceiving the presence of the well-beloved by the attractions he spreads in the midst of the heart, gathers and carries all the soul towards it, by a most agreeable inclination, a most sweet turning, and a delicious bending of all the faculties towards this well-beloved, who attracts them unto him by the force of his sweetness, with which he ties and draws hearts, as bodies are drawn by material ropes and bands.

But this sweet recollection of our soul in itself is not only made by the sentiment of God's presence in the midst of our heart, but also by any means which puts us in this sacred presence. It happens sometimes that all our interior powers close and withdraw themselves into themselves by the extreme reverence and sweet fear which seizes upon us in the consideration of his sovereign Majesty who is present with us and beholds us; just as, however distracted we may be, if the Pope or some great prince should appear we return to ourselves, and bring back our thoughts upon ourselves, to keep ourselves in good behaviour and respect. The blue lily, otherwise called the flag, is said to draw its flowers together at the sight of the sun, because they close and unite while the sun shines, but in its absence they spread out and keep open all the night. The like happens in this kind of recollection which we speak of; for at the simple presence of God, or the simple feeling that he sees us, either from heaven or from any other place outside us (even if we are not remembering the other sort of presence by which he is in us), our powers and faculties assemble and gather together within us, out of respect to his divine Majesty, which love makes us fear with a fear of honour and respect.

*   *   *

How this sacred repose is practised

Have you never noted, Theotimus, with what ardour little children sometimes cleave to their mother's breast when hungry? You will see them, with a deep soft murmur, hold and squeeze it with their mouths, sucking so eagerly that they even put their mother to pain; but after the freshness of the milk has in some sort allayed the urgent heat of their little frame, and the agreeable vapours which it sends to the brain begin to lull them to sleep, Theotimus, you will see them softly shut their little eyes, and little by little give way to sleep; yet without letting go the breast, upon which they make no action saving a slow and almost insensible movement of the lips, whereby they continually draw the milk which they swallow imperceptibly. This they do without thinking of it, yet not without pleasure; for if one draw the teat from them before they fall sound asleep, they awake and weep bitterly, testifying by the sorrow which they show in the privation that their content was great in the possession. Now it fares in like manner with the soul who is in rest and quiet before God: for she sucks in a manner insensibly the delights of his presence, without any discourse, operation or motion of any of her faculties, save only the highest part of the will, which she moves softly and almost imperceptibly, as the mouth by which enter the delight and insensible satiety she finds in the fruition of the divine presence. But if one trouble this poor little babe, or offer to take from it its treasure because it seems to sleep, it will plainly show then that though it sleep to all other things yet not to that; for it perceives the trouble of this separation and grieves over it, showing thereby the pleasure which it took, though without thinking of it, in the good which it possessed. The Blessed Mother (S.) Teresa having written that she found this a fit similitude, I have thought good to make use of it.

And tell me, Theotimus, why should the soul recollected in its God be disquieted? Has she not reason to be at peace and to remain in repose? For indeed what should she seek? She has found him whom she sought, what remains now for her but to say: *I found him whom my soul loveth: I held him and I will not let him go.* She has no need to trouble herself with the discourse of the understanding, for she sees her spouse present with so sweet a view that reasonings would be to her unprofitable and superfluous. And even if she do not see him by the understanding she cares not, being content to feel his presence by the delight and satisfaction which the will receives from it. Ah! the mother of God, our Blessed Lady and Mistress, while she did not see her divine child but felt him within her,—Ah! my God! what content had she therein! And did not S. Elizabeth admirably enjoy the fruits of our Saviour's divine presence without seeing him, upon the day of the most holy Visitation? Nor does the soul in this repose stand in need of the memory, for she has her lover present. Nor has she need of the imagination, for why should we represent in an exterior or interior image him whose presence we are possessed of? So that, to conclude, it is the will alone that softly, and as it were tenderly sucking, draws the milk of this sweet presence; all the rest of the soul quietly reposing with her by the sweetness of the pleasure which she takes.

Honied wine is used not only to withdraw and recall bees to their hives, but also to pacify them. For when they stir up sedition and mutiny amongst themselves with mutual slaughter and destruction, their keeper has no better remedy than to throw honied wine amidst this enraged little people; because, when they perceive this sweet and agreeable odour, they are pacified, and giving themselves up to the fruition of this sweetness, they remain quieted and tranquil. O Eternal God! When by thy sweet presence thou dost cast odoriferous perfumes into our hearts, perfumes more pleasing than delicious wine and honey, all the powers of our soul enter into so delightful a repose and so absolute a rest, that there is no movement save of the will, which, as the spiritual sense of smell, remains delightfully engaged in enjoying, without adverting to it, the incomparable good of having its God present.

Marie of the Incarnation

(1599–1671)

A little-known seventeenth-century French writer, Marie of the Incarnation, is a striking example of what can be called "the apostolic orientation of mysticism." She was born Marie Guyart in 1599 in Tours and from an early age exhibited sensitivity to the presence of the divine in her life. She was drawn not only to the rituals and the preaching of the Church but to the interior workings of grace. For example, when she was seven, Christ appeared to her in a dream asking if she wished to belong solely to him. She replied that she did.

Although in her own mind she was destined for the religious life, her parents thought her too gay and lively to be confined to the cloister and so contracted an early marriage for her to which she dutifully assented. The marriage was brief and unhappy. After two years of what Marie referred to as "crosses," her husband died, leaving her with an infant son and the ruins of an unsuccessful business. A few months later, after settling her domestic affairs, she experienced her "conversion," which marked the beginning of her "eternelles fiançelles" with Christ. With her heart set on the expression of this mystic marriage in the form of the vows of a nun, Marie continued to live an exacting life, working for her brother-in-law in his carrier business and raising her son. In private she practiced austerities of the most rigorous kind.

The year 1627 brought the culmination of her interior surrender to her heavenly bridegroom, the sure and simple yet overpowering consciousness of Christ's indwelling presence, a presence that was to direct her life from then on. It was this presence that led her to enter the order of the Ursulines in 1633, leaving her twelve-year-old boy to the care of her sister and under the direction of her own spiritual director. The parting was one of great anguish for both mother and son. Nonetheless, Marie followed what she believed to be her destiny and, for the first years, found peace and joy. Soon, however, she entered a period of spiritual darkness in which the once-desired hours of prayer became intolerable and doubts assailed her as to whether or not she should have left her son.

Yet she persevered and with perseverance came the first intimations of what was to be her unique life's work. She had a mysterious dream in which the Virgin Mary showed her and an unknown lady companion a majestic landscape. She received a profound impression from the sight of this fog-shrouded country and from the smiling countenance of the Mother of God. At the same time she began to discover within herself a zeal for the salvation of souls in foreign lands. In spirit she felt united to the missionaries who labored there, and, while living out the rule of the monastery, gave herself over to these inward journeys of participation.

At that time a woman who was a religious was by definition confined to the cloister. Marie never dreamed that she would be called to carry her apostolic fervor out into the world. Soon, however, she was made aware of the plans of Paul Le Jeune, superior of the Canadian missions, to found a seminary for Indian girls in New France. Originally, it had been intended that the school be a lay venture, but fate would have it that Marie and the Ursulines instead would devote themselves to this mission in the American wilds. In 1638 the "lady" of her dream appeared: a young widow named Marie-Madeleine de la Peltrie with means, an unshakable will and a burning desire to endow the education of little Indian girls. The shape of Marie's emerging vocation was revealed.

The details of the implementation of the school plans are complex and make fascinating reading. Suffice it to say that Marie and a small band of companions, after many months and a perilous ocean voyage, arrived in Quebec in 1639. She lived there until her death in 1671. The history of the founding of the monastery, of the difficulties of mere existence and the colorful and sometimes tragic saga of the relationship between Indians and Europeans forms one of the most interesting chapters in both the history of early Canadian colonization and of the Catholic missionary enterprize. Marie's numerous letters survive and provide an invaluable source of information.

But for us this remarkable and vigorous woman who dealt bravely with great physical hardships, with the task of learning several Indian tongues, with the destruction of the monastery by fire, with the death of many of her young charges in epidemics, with the murder of her fellow missionaries by hostile tribes, was first and foremost a woman of inward orientation. While her letters reveal her active apostolic life, her *Relations* expose the currents that flowed beneath and nourished her activities. We include here a selection dealing with her experience of the "dark night" of the mystic path: that painful desolation of the soul being purged and emptied of self in its ascent to the divine.

Marie's account of this particular phase of her inner drama is characteristically personal and emotional. For her, the stages of the interior life were painted in the vivid hues of her own immediate experience. Many of the other great mystics (Eckhart, John of the Cross, and Catherine of Siena, to name a few) presented the outlines of the mystic path in a more paradigmatic manner. Obviously, they too drew primarily on their own experience, yet in reading their writings one is impressed with the universality of the experience they recounted. Marie's style is more autobiographical and for that reason conveys a lively impression not only of the author's personality but of her circumstances as well. This highly personalized account has the occasional disadvantage of being obscure if one is interested in reading a clearly delineated outline of the mystic path.

At the heart of Marie's mysticism is the assertion that one must gain increasing interior intimacy with Jesus Christ and must practice His precepts as enunciated in the Gospel. This intimacy is effected by means of prayer, a form of prayer that for her was primarily an incessant conversation with the incarnate Word who revealed Himself as Love and Spouse, a conversation that lifted the heart and mind up to the Love it adored. The practice of Christ's precepts is an essential ingredient in this intimacy for it gives one real experiential knowledge of God. His precepts must be carried out in accord with the duties of one's state in life. Prayer, for its part, should turn one toward the practice of virtue and lead to one's transformation into Christ. The ultimate result of this transformation is union with God, and for Marie this union was at its height a union with the sufferings of Christ through one's loving embrace of one's own suffering and pain. The "beautiful gift" of suffering unites one to the deepest mystery of the Christian faith.

Autobiography

I've always experienced that whenever the Divine Majesty has willed to grant me some extraordinary grace He would not only remotely prepare and dispose me for it, but also dispose me in a very particular way when the time for His granting it drew near. This He did by means of a foretaste which, in the peace it begot, was like an experience of paradise. In view of the sublimity of the experience, I'm unable to express myself in any other way regarding it. During these foretastes I would say to Him, "What wilt Thou that I do, my dear Love?" Then I would experience His operation; ordinarily it effected in me a change of state.

Following upon my preceding state (that inaugurated by the impression of the divine attributes), one morning as I was at prayer God absorbed my spirit in Himself by an extraordinarily powerful attraction. I don't know what posture my body assumed at the time. Once again I was granted a vision of the most august Trinity, and its operations were manifested to me in a more elevated and distinct manner than formerly. The impression which I had of the Trinity the first time produced its principal effect in the understanding, and it seemed that the Divine Majesty granted it to me in order to enlighten me and dispose me for what He willed to do to me. But on this present occasion, although the understanding was enlightened and indeed more than on the previous one, it was primarily my will that was involved. For this new grace was granted entirely with a view to love; through love my soul found itself in a state of extreme familiarity with and fruition of the God of love.

The Autobiography of Venerable Marie of the Incarnation, O.S.U. Mystic and Missionary, trans. John J. Sullivan (Chicago: Loyola University Press, 1964), 56–60. Footnotes have been omitted.

Then, while I was engulfed in the presence of this most adorable Majesty, Father, Son, and Holy Spirit, in the acknowledgment and confession of my lowliness and in adoration of the Blessed Trinity, the Second Person of the Divine Word gave me to understand that He was truly the spouse of the faithful soul. I understood this truth with certainty, and the insight into it that was granted me was a proximate preparation for seeing it actualized in myself. At that moment this most adorable Person took possession of my soul and, embracing it with an inexplicable love, united it to Himself and took it for His bride. When I say that He embraced it, this of course was not after the manner of human embraces. Nothing which falls within the scope of the senses is like this divine operation, but it is necessary for me to express myself in terms of our earthly life, since we are composed of matter. This transpired by means of divine touches and of a mutual compenetration in such wise that, no longer being myself, I abided in Him through intimacy of love and of union, so that I was lost to myself and no longer aware of myself, having become Him by participation. Then, for short moments, I was aware of myself and beheld the eternal Father and the Holy Spirit, and then the unity of the divine existence. Being absorbed in the grandeur and in the love of the Word, I found myself impotent to render my homage to the Father and to the Holy Spirit, because the Word held my soul and all its powers captive in Himself, who was my Spouse and my Love, and who desired my soul entirely for Himself. In the excess of His divine love and of His embraces He nevertheless permitted me to cast my glances from time to time to the others, to the Father and to the Holy Spirit, and these glances were expressive of my dependence, although no imagery was here involved, whether symbolic or otherwise. On this occasion my soul knew the distinct operations of each of the three Divine Persons. When the sacred Word was operative in me, the Father and the Holy Spirit contemplated His operation, but at the same time this constituted no obstacle to the unity (of the divine nature), for in a way which I cannot express I perceived separately the unity and the distinction. Each of the Persons was seen to be free in His operation.

I would have need of the powers of the Seraphim and of other blessed spirits to be able to narrate what transpired in this ecstasy and rapture of love which drew the understanding along with it and so made it incapable of regarding anything other than the treasures which it possessed in the sacred Person of the Eternal Word. It would be better to say that the powers of my soul, being engulfed and absorbed and reduced to the unity of the spirit, were all taken up with the Word, who, in the role of Spouse, granted to my soul great intimacy with

Himself and the power to enjoy the dignity of bride. In this state the soul experiences that it is the Holy Spirit who moves it to treat as it does with the Word. It would be impossible for the creature, with all its limitations, to be so bold as to treat in this way with its God. And even if it were so forgetful of itself as to want to undertake to do so, it would not be in its power. Since these operations are entirely supernatural, the soul can only passively receive them and it would be impossible it to distract itself from them or to apply itself to them merely more or less. The effects of these operations show the truth of this. And since the soul has been forestalled in this exalted grace and actually possesses it before perceiving its entry, the suddenness with which this happens shows that only a God of goodness and omnipotence could effect such an impression and operation.

The soul constantly experiences the presence of this gracious Being who has taken possession of her in the spiritual marriage and who inflames and consumes her with a fire so agreeable and pleasant that it is impossible to describe it. He causes her to chant a nuptial song in a manner which delights Him. Neither books nor study can teach the language of this song, which is entirely heavenly and divine. It owes its origin to the mutual embraces of the soul and this most adorable Word who by the kisses of His divine mouth fills her with His spirit and with His life. This nuptial song is the response of the soul to her well-beloved Spouse.

*   *   *

The spiritual marriage completely changes the state of the soul. Prior to this she was in a state of constant tendency toward and expectation of this exalted grace, which was shown her from afar inasmuch as she was made to experience the dispositions and preparations for receiving it. But now she no longer has such a tendency because she actually possesses Him whom she loves. Her being is entirely penetrated and possessed by Him. It is consumed by caresses and acts of love which cause it to expire in Him by suffering deaths the most sweet; moreover, these very deaths constitute the sweetness. I pause to consider whether I might be able to find any suitable comparisons with things of this world, but I can find none which would help me to describe the embraces of the Word and the soul. Although the soul knows that the Word is the great God, equal to the eternal Father, through whom all things have been made and subsist in being, still she embraces Him and speaks to him face to face, knowing that she has been elevated to this dignity of having the Word for her Spouse and of being His bride and hence in a position to say to Him: "Thou art my other self, Thou art all mine. Come, my Spouse, let us be on with the affairs Thou hast committed to me." The soul has no more desires, for she possesses her Beloved. She speaks to Him because He has spoken to her, but it is not by means of words. She performs her duties in order to seek His glory in and through all things, according to the lights He has given her, and to promote His reign as absolute Master of all hearts.

*　　*　　*

To turn now to a more particular account of my interior dispositions and God's dealings with me since the time of our embarking, I began to experience that what His Divine Majesty had made known and intimated to me was being verified in me. This began by the transformation of the peace which I had formerly enjoyed into that which He gave me during the course of our voyage; a peace that was intense and profound but at the same time so subtle that, although it was within me, yet it seemed distant from me. I experienced it as from afar, which is an experience very painful to nature and crucifying to the human spirit. When I was speaking about another state of soul I mentioned that in it the powers of the soul are suspended, because God as it were annihilates them at their very center (that is, the center of the soul) when He takes possession of it, although they actually remain and it merely seems as though they are lifeless. This is, as I then remarked, a crucifying experience. Yet this cross is rendered voluntary by the acquiescence of the soul. Being unable to will or to love anything other than what the Spirit of God operates in it and being unconcerned with the sufferings or the privations of its lower part, the soul finds its profit only in this divine darkness wherein it is lost.

But here, on the contrary, the inferior part experiences both exteriorly and interiorly what it means to serve God at its own expense. It is at this point that one can see whether he really possesses the habit of the virtues. Our Lord gave me the grace to enable me to act in these matters as I previously did. I spoke about the state of my soul to Father Le Jeune, who rendered me every assistance. During the ocean journey I was spiritually on my own, as I had no power to manifest what I experienced because of the subtlety of my interior activity. I could speak only of those things wherein I needed guidance in regard to my exterior activity. This inability to manifest myself was painful for me, for I've always found it easy to do so or at least to say enough to make my disposition clear.

From this state I entered into a much more crucifying one. In it I saw myself despoiled, so it seemed to me, of all the gifts and graces which God had given me, of whatever abilities, interior and exterior, He had endowed me with. I lost confidence in everybody, and the holiest persons and those with whom I'd conversed most intimately were the very ones who caused me to suffer the most, for God permitted them to suffer temptations of constant aversion towards me, as they have since told me. I saw myself as the lowest, most debased, and most contemptible person in the whole world; and, while having these sentiments about myself, I couldn't cease to admire the goodness, the meekness, and humility of my sisters in willing to be submissive to me and to bear with me.

I hardly dared to raise my eyes because of the burden of this humiliation. In this sentiment of the baseness of my spirit I strove to perform the most lowly and abject works, esteeming myself unworthy to perform the others; and at recreation time I hardly dared to speak, thinking myself unworthy to do so. I listened to my sisters with respect; nevertheless I did violence to myself during time of recreation to avoid singularity. In the other functions of my office I carried on in the usual way, and I was able to apply my mind to the study of the language, as all of this was compatible with my interior state at that time. I don't know whether anyone noticed what I was suffering, although at that time it seemed to me that everyone saw my misery as I myself did. I saw myself as so filled with misery that I couldn't discover anything good in myself and could see only that which seemed to have separated me from God and deprived me of His graces and singular mercies towards me.

Jean-Pierre de Caussade

(1675-1751)

The surrender of the will, a prominent theme in Counterreformation French mysticism, became by the early eighteenth century a rich and probing spirituality as fashioned by the Jesuit preacher and spiritual director Jean-Pierre de Caussade. At a time when antimystical tendencies were gaining ground in Europe, de Caussade sought to defend the mystical tradition within his order. To do so he taught the concept of "abandonment," his term for the human will's surrender to divine direction. Abandonment was for him the one sure road to union with God, and it could be practiced by almost anyone, at any time, and in any circumstance.

In de Caussade's view, God presents His will to the individual at every moment. His will may be clearly defined or shrouded in the confusing tumult and tedium of everyday life. But what is sure is that the will is expressed and that it is a loving and knowing will. The individual's response, born of the love for God, can be joyful acceptance. The individual can embrace the present moment in the form it is given, whether pleasurable or onerous, full of promise or stained by suffering, as a sacrament or a channel of God's grace. This is abandonment in its deepest, most Christian sense for it involves accepting not only what is obviously of God or from God, but also what may appear as antithetical to God or "in the way" of one's spiritual progress. It is a view that requires a deep faith in the truth that the Incarnation teaches so well: that the activity of God not only occurs in the soul but reaches out to touch human history, that the wonder of salvation is not achieved in some far-off land of wishful thinking or disembodied spirituality but realized in the present, in the anguish of love, in the creative acceptance of suffering, in the willingness to reach out past what seems meaningless into the chaotic darkness that can teach its own magnificent meaning if only we have the eyes to see.

The small work that conveys these deep insights comes to us with the title *Abandonment to Divine Providence* and though it is from the pen of de Caussade, he was not aware that had authored such a book. He was the spiritual director for a group of Visitation nuns who carefully preserved the letters and recorded the conferences he gave them. These foresighted women collected his diverse statements and had them circulated. Over the period of a century fresh material was added until the book was as we now have it.

The man who unwittingly left posterity such a treasure of spiritual literature was born in 1675 somewhere in the province of Quercy in the south of France. He seems to have spent his childhood in the neighborhood of Toulouse, became a Jesuit novice there in 1693 and a priest in 1704. For a time he held a position as professor of Greek and Latin and seems to have taken a doctorate in theology. But in 1720 he ceased the professorial life and embarked upon a career as a preacher and confessor. It was at this time that he became spiritual director for the convent of nuns at Nancy. He next appears as rector of the Jesuit colleges in Perpignan and Albi. His last five years were spent as director of the theological students in the Jesuit House in Toulouse. Such are the details of the life of this man, about whom we know little more.

A highly educated individual, as were not a few of the great Christian mystics, de Caussade's thought displays none of the pedantry that overintellectualization can produce. Rather, his work is direct, practical, and deeply felt. It appeals to the individual wherever he might find himself on his spiritual journey, whether layperson or religious, whether beginner in the art of prayer or one who has penetrated deep into the recesses of his own soul. It teaches a fundamental principle of the interior life, self-abandonment, that is also found in the writings of other notable figures. In particular, the influences of François de Sales and John of the Cross are recognizable in *Abandonment to Divine Providence*. We recognize François' insistence on "indifference" and "detachment" in de Caussade's formulation of the concept of abandonment, and we recall John in his rendering of the soul proceeding like a blind man enveloped in the darkness of faith that alone can act as his sure guide. But more than this, we see de Caussade's own faith, the certainty of his vision, the wisdom of his counsel, the depth of his union with his God.

Abandonment to Divine Providence

The present moment always reveals the presence and the power of God

Every moment we live through is like an ambassador who declares the will of God, and our hearts always utter their acceptance. Our souls steadily advance, never halting, but sweeping along with every wind. Every current, every technique thrusts us onward in our voyage to the infinite. Everything works to this end and, without exception, helps us toward holiness. We can find all that is necessary in the present moment. We need not worry about whether to pray or be silent, whether to withdraw into retreat or mix with people, to read or write, to

Jean-Pierre de Caussade, *Abandonment to Divine Providence*, trans. John Beevers (New York: Doubleday, 1975). 50–2, 53–6.

meditate or make our minds a receptive blank, to shun or seek out books on spirituality. Nor do poverty or riches, sickness or health, life or death matter in the least. What does matter is what each moment produces by the will of God. We must strip ourselves naked, renounce all desire for created things, and retain nothing of ourselves or for ourselves, so that we can be wholly submissive to God's will and so delight him. Our only satisfaction must be to live in the present moment as if there were nothing to expect beyond it.

If what happens to a soul abandoned to God is all that is necessary for it, it is clear that it can lack nothing and that it should never complain, for this would show that it lacked faith and was living by the light of its reason and the evidence of its senses. Neither reason nor the senses are ever satisfied, for they never see the sufficiency of grace. To hallow the name of God is, according to the Scriptures, to recognize his holiness and to love and adore it in all the things which proceed like words from the mouth of God. For what God creates at each moment is a divine thought which is expressed by a thing, and so all these things are so many names and words through which he makes known his wishes. God's will is single and individual, with an unknown and inexpressible name, but it is infinitely diverse in its effects, which are, as it were, as many as the names it assumes. To hallow God's name is to know, to worship and to love the ineffable being who bears it. It is also to know, to worship and to love his adorable will every moment and all that it does, regarding all that happens as so many veils, shadows and names beneath which this eternal and most holy will is always active. It is holy in all it does, holy in all it says, holy in every manifestation, and holy in all the names it bears.

It is thus that Job blessed the name of God. This holy man blessed the utter desolation which fell upon him, for it displayed the will of God. His ruin he regarded as one of God's names, and in blessing it he was declaring that, no matter how terrible its manifestations, it was always holy under whatever name or form it appeared. And David never ceased to bless it. It is by this continual recognition of the will of God, as displayed and revealed in all things, that God reigns in us, that his will is done on earth as in heaven, and that he nourishes us continually.

The full and complete meaning of self-abandonment to his will is embraced in the matchless prayer given to us by Jesus Christ. By the command of God and the Church we recite it several times a day; but, apart from this, if we love to suffer and obey his adorable will, we shall utter it constantly in the depths of our hearts. When we can utter only through our mouths—which takes time—our hearts can speak instantly, and it is in this manner that simple souls are called to bless God from the depths of their souls. Yet they complain bitterly that they cannot praise him as much as they desire, for God gives to them so much that they feel they cannot cope with such riches. A secret working of the divine wisdom is to pour treasure into the heart whilst impoverishing the senses, so that the one overflows whilst the other is drained and emptied.

The events of every moment are stamped with the will of God. How holy is his name! How right it is to bless it and to treat it as something which sanctifies all it touches. Can we see anything which carries this name without showing it with infinite love? It is a divine warmth from heaven and gives us a ceaseless increase of grace. It is the kingdom of heaven which penetrates the soul. It is the bread of angels which is eaten on earth as well as in heaven. There is nothing trivial about our passing moments, as they enclose the whole kingdom of holiness and the food on which angels feed.

Yes, O Lord, may you rule my heart, nourish it, purify if, make it holy, and let it triumph over all its enemies. Most precious moment! How small it is to my bodily eyes, but how great to the eyes of my faith! How can I think of it as nothing when it is thought of so highly by my heavenly father? All that comes from him is most excellent and bears the imprint of its origin.

*   *   *

The action of God inspires souls to seek the highest degree of holiness. What is required from each soul is complete abandonment to this activity.

Because they do not know how to make use of God's action, many people have recourse to too many means to try to reach holiness. All these could be useful if they were ordained by God, but they are harmful when they hinder the simple, straightforward union of the soul with God. Jesus is our master to whom we do not pay enough attention. He speaks to every heart and utters the word of life, the essential word for each one of us, but we do not hear it. We would like to know what he has said to other people, yet we do not listen to what he says to us. We do not try enough to look at things as having been given a supernatural character by God's action. We should always receive them with the confidence they deserve, generously and with an open heart, for none of them can harm us if we welcome them in this manner. This tremendous activity of God, which never varies from the beginning to the end of time, pours itself through every moment and gives itself in all its vastness and power to every clear-hearted soul which adores and loves it and abandons itself without reserve to it.

You say you would be delighted to be able to die for God. You would find great pleasure in such a violent deed or a life that ended up that way. You long to lose everything, to die abandoned by everybody and to sacrifice your life for others. But as for me, Lord, I give all glory to your will. Obedience to it gives me all the joy of martyrdom, austerity and loving my neighbor. Your will is all-sufficient for me, and I am happy to live and die as it ordains. I delight in it for itself alone, quite apart from all it does, pervading all things and rendering all it touches divine. Because of it, all my life seems lived in heaven, my every moment is part of your activity, and, living or dead, I can know no greater bliss. I shall no longer count the times and the manner of your approach, my beloved. You will always be welcome. It seems to me, dear will of God, that you have revealed to me your greatness and there is now no longer anything I can do outside its embrace, which is the same yesterday, tomorrow and forever. From you, O Lord, pours the unending stream of grace. You ensure that it never fails and that it works unceasingly. So I shall no longer try to find you within the narrow limits of a book, in the life of a saint, or in some high-flown philosophy. All these are only drops of that ocean which flows over us all. God's activity moves through everything, and all else are but mere fragments which disappear within it. I shall no longer try to find God's will in spiritual writings. I shall no longer go begging, as it were, from door to door for food for my soul, nor shall I seek anyting at all from any created being or thing. Dear Lord, I mean to live so that I may honor you as the son of a father who is infinitely wise, good and powerful. I intend to live according to my beliefs; and, as your will governs all things at all times and is always for my benefit, I will live on this vast income, which can never fail, is always present and always available to do me the greatest possible good. Is there any creature whose works can equal those performed by God? Since his uncreated hands do everything for me, why should I run about seeking help from ignorant, helpless creatures who have no real affection for me? I should die of thirst if I rushed from fountain to fountain, from stream to stream when by my side is an immeasurable stretch of water poured out by your hand. Where else do I need to look? You give me bread to feed me, soap to cleanse me, fire to purify me, and a chisel to shape my human form into one worthy of heaven. You give me everything I need. What I seek elsewhere seeks me out and offers itself to me through all creation.

O Love, why should you be so unknown and why should you, as it were, throw yourself and all your delights at everyone whilst people are trying to find you in hidden corners and obscure places where they will never come across you? How foolish they are not to breathe the fresh air, not to wander about the countryside, not to drink the abundant water, not to recognize and seize hold of God and see his holiness in all things.

My dear souls, you are seeking for secret ways of belonging to God, but there is only one: making use of whatever he offers you. Everything leads you to this union with him. Everything guides you to perfection except what is sinful or not a duty. Accept everything and let him act. All things conduct you and support you. Your way is lined with banners as you advance along it in your carriage. All is in the hand of God. His action is vaster and more pervasive than all the elements of earth, air and water. It enters you through every one of your senses so long as you use them only as he directs, for you must never employ them against his will. God's action penetrates every atom of your body, into the very marrow of your bones. The blood flowing through your veins moves only by his will. The state of your health, whether you are weak or strong, lively or languid, your life and death, all spring from his will, and all your bodily conditions are the workings of grace. Every feeling and every thought you have, no matter how they arise, all come from God's invisible hand. There is no created being who can tell you what his action will achieve within you, but continuing experience will teach you. Uninterruptedly your life will flow through this unfathomed abyss where you have nothing to do but love and cherish what each moment brings, considering it as the best possible thing for you and having perfect confidence in God's activities, which cannot do anything but good.

Yes, divine Love, if all souls would only be satisfied with you, what supernatural, sublime, wonderful and inconceivable heights they would scale! Yes, if only we had sense enough to leave everything to the guidance of God's hand, we should reach the highest peak of holiness. Everyone could do it, for the opportunity is offered to everyone. We have, as it were, only to open our mouths and let holiness flow in. In you every soul has a unique model of surpassing holiness and, by your never-wearying activity, may be made to resemble you. If every soul lived, acted and spoke under the guidance of God, they would have no need to imitate anyone else. Each one of them would be a unique and holy being, made so by the most ordinary means.

How, my Lord, can I make people value what I offer them? I possess so great a treasure that I could shower wealth on everyone, and yet I see souls withering like plants in an arid waste.

You simple souls, who are quite without any piety, have no talents, are quite uneducated, understand nothing of the language of spirituality, and are filled with astonished wonder at the eloquence of the learned—come and I will teach you a secret that will put you far ahead of these clever folk. I will make you so well placed for achieving perfection that you will always find yourself in the midst of it. I will unite you to God and you shall go hand in hand with him from the first moment you begin to do what I shall tell you. Come, I say, come, not to study the map of the realms of the spirit, but to possess it so that you can walk freely about it and never be afraid of getting lost. Come, not to study the record of God's grace, not to learn what it has done down all the centuries and is still doing, but come and be the trusting subject of its operation. There is no need for you to understand the lessons it has taught others, nor to repeat them cleverly. You will be taught matters which are for you alone.

10. Modern and Contemporary Masters of the Contemplative Life

---

Simone Weil

(1909–1943)

The twentieth century has produced few spiritual writers whose works resonate with compelling intensity, few too whose unflinching quest for an authentic style of life drove them to such lengths as experienced by Simone Weil. The selection presented here is from her *Waiting for God*, a collection of essays and letters published after her death. This letter, posthumously titled "Spiritual Autobiography" was written to Father Perrin, a priest with whom she had a number of conversations concerning the Catholic faith. In it she describes the process of her unique inner journey and her "possession" by Christ.

This possession is not something Simone sought, nor something she ever expected to happen to her. Indeed, the early course of her life, to all appearances, would not necessarily have prepared her for such an encounter. She was born in 1909 into an upper-middle-class French family. Her father was a doctor, her mother a women of energy and intelligence, and her brother destined to become one of the most gifted mathematicians of his generation. From the beginning Simone was an unusually reflective personality who concerned herself with the plight of the afflicted and underprivileged in the world. She distinguished herself in her philosophical studies in school and went on to become a teacher of philosophy. Of a left-wing political orientation, she was a somewhat unorthodox Marxist who identified with the plight of workers and who studied the problems of industrialization. So great was her identification that she spent time as a factory worker and as a grape harvester to experience firsthand the life of the afflicted. She joined forces with the Loyalists during the Spanish Civil War. And throughout her life she wrote many articles on the political and social ills that she witnessed. She was particularly dismayed by the growing Fascist movement in Germany.

The sense of belonging to the great mass of humanity for whom everyday life was an arduous and often oppressive experience persisted throughout her life. The absolute purity and honesty with which she confronted the fact of being human was often mentioned by those who knew her and, like all persons of spiritual stature, was the context for her inner development. At first her quest for authenticity had a political cast to it. Like many young French intellectuals of the day, she spoke of the revolution to come and of her role in it. However, her orientation became broader. Convinced that such an occurrence was not about to take place, she concerned herself with the implications of industrialization, affliction, and war. In this, she was led into matters of the soul, its relationship both to the world and to God.

Her burgeoning religious introspection was not necessarily apparent to those about her. She outlines its development in the "Spiritual Autobiography" and rightly sees it as the central thread running through her life. Yet she spoke of it to few people. Chief among those to whom she did speak was Father Perrin. A continuing topic of those conversations was the possibility of baptism; for Simone, whose ancestry was Jewish but whose parents were agnostic, was greatly drawn to the Catholic faith. This was in part because she felt that Catholicism was the religion of the "slaves." Yet there were doctrinal obstacles to her becoming a visible part of the Church. The insistence that Jesus was the only incarnation of God, the exclusiveness of doctrine, the fact that the Church claimed the exclusive right to judge truth and to brand persons or ideas as heretical were for her intellectual and ethical leaps she could not make. In the end, she remained on the threshold of the Church, "waiting for God" himself to speak his will. "If," she wrote, "it were conceivable that one might be damned by obeying God and saved by disobeying him: I would nevertheless obey him."

Her short but intensely lived life came to an end in 1943. Always a sickly person, who suffered from excruciating headaches and numerous debilities and whose nature compelled her to lead a life of great austerity, Simone Weil died of semistarvation. For a long time she refused to eat more than the rations allotted to any one person during the war. Her poor health and a diagnosis of tuberculosis made such a regimen unwise. Yet unable or unwilling to violate her moral principles, she succumbed.

Uncompromisingly honest, even skeptical of her own mystical experiences, she brought to the life of the spirit the weapons of a sharply trained, questioning mind, an attitude of disinterested yet open curiosity, an austere sense of the potential inherent in human life, and a compulsion to act in accord with her deeply considered principles. The result was a vivid encounter that speaks urgently to the present day.

Waiting for God

Spiritual autobiography

I may say that never at any moment in my life have I 'sought for God.' For this reason, which is probably too subjective, I do not like this expression and it strikes me as false. As soon as I reached adolescence, I saw the problem of God as a problem the data of which could not be obtained here below, and I decided that the only way of being sure not to reach a wrong solution, which seemed to me the greatest possible evil, was to leave it alone. So I left it alone. I neither affirmed nor denied anything. It seemed to me useless to solve the problem, for I thought that, being in this world, our business was to adopt the best attitude with regard to the problems of this world, and that such an attitude did not depend upon the solution of the problem of God.

This held good as far as I was concerned at any rate for I never hesitated in my choice of an attitude; I always adopted the Christian attitude as the only possible one. I might say that I was born, I grew up, and I always remained within the Christian inspiration. While the very name of God had no part in my thoughts, with regard to the problems of this world and this life I shared the Christian conception in an explicit and rigorous manner, with the most specific notions it involves. Some of these notions have been part of my outlook for as far back as I can remember. With others I know the time and manner of their coming and the form under which they imposed themselves upon me.

For instance I never allowed myself to think of a future state, but I

Simone Weil, "Spiritual Autobiography," in *Waiting for God*, trans. Emma Craufurd (New York: Harper & Row, Publishers, 1973), pp. 62–73.

always believed that the instant of death is the center and object of life. I used to think that, for those who live as they should, it is the instant when, for an infinitesimal fraction of time, pure truth, naked, certain, and eternal enters the soul. I may say that I never desired any other good for myself. I thought that the life leading to this good is not only defined by a code of morals common to all, but that for each one it consists of a succession of acts and events strictly personal to him, and so essential that he who leaves them on one side never reaches the goal. The notion of vocation was like this for me. I saw that the carrying out of a vocation differed from the actions dictated by reason or inclination in that it was due to an impulse of an essentially and manifestly different order; and not to follow such an impulse when it made itself felt, even it if demanded impossibilities, seemed to me the greatest of all ills. Hence my conception of obedience; and I put this conception to the test when I entered the factory and stayed on there, even when I was in that state of intense and uninterrupted misery about which I recently told you. The most beautiful life possible has always seemed to me to be one where everything is determined, either by the pressure of circumstances or by impulses such as I have just mentioned and where there is never any room for choice.

At fourteen I fell into one of those fits of bottomless despair that come with adolescence, and I seriously thought of dying because of the mediocrity of my natural faculties. The exceptional gifts of my brother, who had a childhood and youth comparable to those of Pascal, brought my own inferiority home to me. I did not mind having no visible successes, but what did grieve me was the idea of being excluded from that transcendent kingdom to which only the truly great have access and wherein truth abides. I preferred to die rather than live without that truth. After months of inward darkness, I suddenly had the everlasting conviction that any human being, even though practically devoid of natural faculties, can penetrate to the kingdom of truth reserved for genius, if only he longs for truth and perpetually concentrates all his attention upon its attainment. He thus becomes a genius too, even though for lack of talent his genius cannot be visible from outside. Later on, when the strain of headaches caused the feeble faculties I possess to be invaded by a paralysis, which I was quick to imagine as probably incurable, the same conviction led me to persevere for ten years in an effort of concentrated attention that was practically unsupported by any hope of results.

Under the name of truth I also included beauty, virtue, and every kind of goodness, so that for me it was a question of a conception of the relationship between grace and desire. The conviction that had come to me was that when one hungers for bread one does not receive stones. But at that time I had not read the Gospel.

Just as I was certain that desire has in itself an efficacy in the realm of spiritual goodness whatever its form, I though it was also possible that it might not be effective in any other realm.

As for the spirit of poverty, I do not remember any moment when it was not in me, although only to that unhappily small extent compatible with my imperfection. I fell in love with Saint Francis of Assisi as soon as I came to know about him. I always believed and hoped that one day Fate would force upon me the condition of a vagabond and a beggar which he embraced freely. Actually I felt the same way about prison.

From my earliest childhood I always had also the Christian idea of love for one's neighbor, to which I gave the name of justice—a name it bears in many passages of the Gospel and which is so beautiful. You know that on this point I have failed seriously several times.

The duty of acceptance in all that concerns the will of God, whatever it may be, was impressed upon my mind as the first and most necessary of all duties from the time when I found it set down in Marcus Aurelius under the form of the *amor fati* of the Stoics. I saw it as a duty we cannot fail in without dishonoring ourselves.

The idea of purity, with all that this word can imply for a Christian, took possession of me at the age of sixteen, after a period of several months during which I had been going through the emotional unrest natural in adolescence. This idea came to me when I was contemplating a mountain landscape and little by little it was imposed upon me in an irresistible manner.

Of course I knew quite well that my conception of life was Christian. That is why it never occurred to me that I could enter the Christian community. I had the idea that I was born inside. But to add dogma to this conception of life, without being forced to do so by indisputable evidence, would have seemed to me like a lack of honesty. I should even have thought I was lacking in honesty had I considered the question of the truth of dogma as a problem for myself or even had I simply desired to reach a conclusion on this subject. I have an extremely severe standard for intellectual honesty, so severe that I never met anyone who did not seem to fall short of it in more than one respect; and I am always afraid of failing in it myself.

Keeping away from dogma in this way, I was prevented by a sort of shame from going into churches, though all the same I like being in them. Nevertheless, I had three contacts with Catholicism that really counted.

After my year in the factory, before going back to teaching, I had been taken by my parents to Portugal, and while there I left them to go alone to a little village. I was, as it were, in pieces, soul and body. That contact with affliction had killed my youth. Until then I had not had any experience of affliction, unless we count my own, which, as it was my own, seemed to me, to have little importance, and which moreover was only a partial affliction, being biological and not social. I knew quite well that there was a great deal of affliction in the world, I was obsessed with the idea, but I had not had prolonged and first-hand experience of it. As I worked in the factory, indistinguishable to all eyes, including my own, from the anonymous mass, the affliction of others entered into my flesh and my soul. Nothing separated me from it, for I had really forgotten my past and I looked forward to no future, finding it difficult to imagine the possibility of surviving all the fatigue. What I went through there marked me in so lasting a manner that still today when any human being, whoever he may be and in whatever circumstances, speaks to me without brutality, I cannot help having the impression that there must be a mistake and that unfortunately the mistake will in all probability disappear. There I received forever the mark of a slave, like the branding of the red-hot iron the Romans put on the foreheads of their most despised slaves. Since then I have always regarded myself as a slave.

In this state of mind then, and in a wretched condition physically, I entered the little Portuguese village, which, alas, was very wretched too, on the very day of the festival of its patron saint. I was alone. It was the evening and there was a full moon over the sea. The wives of the fishermen were, in procession, making a tour of all the ships, carrying candles and singing what must certainly be very ancient hymns of a heart-rending sadness. Nothing can give any idea of it. I have never heard anything so poignant unless it were the song of the boatmen on the Volga. There the conviction was suddenly borne in upon me that Christianity is pre-eminently the religion of slaves, that slaves cannot help belonging to it, and I among others.

In 1937 I had two marvelous days at Assisi. There, alone in the little twelfth-century Romanesque chapel of Santa Maria degli Angeli, an incomparable marvel of purity where Saint Francis often used to pray, something stronger than I was compelled me for the first time in my life to go down on my knees.

In 1938 I spent ten days at Solesmes, from Palm Sunday to Easter Tuesday, following all the liturgical services. I was suffering from splitting headaches; each sound hurt me like a blow; by an extreme effort of concentration I was able to rise above this wretched flesh, to leave it to suffer by itself, heaped up in a corner, and to find a pure and perfect joy in the unimaginable beauty of the chanting and the words. This experience enabled me by analogy to get a better understanding of the possibility of loving divine love in the midst of affliction. It goes without saying that in the course of these services the thought of the Passion of Christ entered into my being once and for all.

There was a young English Catholic there from whom I gained my first idea of the supernatural power of the sacraments because of the truly angelic radiance with which he seemed to be clothed after going to communion. Chance—for I always prefer saying chance rather than Providence—made of him a messenger to me. For he told me of the existence of those English poets of the seventeenth century who are named metaphysical. In reading them later on, I discovered the poem of which I read you what is unfortunately a very inadequate translation. It is called "Love" [by George Herbert]. I learned it by heart. Often, at the culminating point of a violent headache, I make myself say it over, concentrating all my attention upon it and clinging with all my soul to the tenderness it enshrines. I used to think I was merely reciting it as a beautiful poem, but without my knowing it the recitation had the virtue of a prayer. It was during one of these recitations that, as I told you, Christ himself came down and took possession of me.

In my arguments about the insolubility of the problem of God I had never foreseen the possibility of that, of a real contact, person to person, here below, between a human being and God. I had vaguely heard tell of things of this kind, but I had never believed in them. In the *Fioretti* the accounts of apparitions rather put me off if anything, like the miracles in the Gospel. Moreover, in this sudden possesion of me by Christ, neither my sense nor my imagination had any part; I only felt in the midst of my suffering the presence of a love, like that which one can read in the smile on a beloved face.

I had never read any mystical works because I had never felt any call to read them. In reading as in other things I have always striven to practice obedience. There is nothing more favorable to intellectual progress, for as far as possible I only read what I am hungry for at the moment when I have an appetite for it, and then I do not read, I *eat*. God in his mercy had prevented me from reading the mystics, so that it should be evident to me that I had not invented this absolutely unexpected contact.

Yet I still half refused, not my love but my intelligence. For it seemed to me certain, and I still think so today, that one can never wrestle enough with God if one does so out of pure regard for the truth. Christ likes us to prefer truth to him because, before being Christ, he is truth.

If one turns aside from him to go toward the truth, one will not go far before falling into his arms.

After this I came to feel that Plato was a mystic, that all the *Iliad* is bathed in Christian light, and that Dionysus and Osiris are in a certain sense Christ himself; and my love was thereby redoubled.

I never wondered whether Jesus was or was not the Incarnation of God; but in fact I was incapable of thinking of him without thinking of him as God.

In the spring of 1940 I read the *Bhagavad-Gita.* Strange to say it was in reading those marvelous words, words with such a Christian sound, put into the mouth of an incarnation of God, that I came to feel strongly that we owe an allegiance to religious truth which is quite different from the admiration we accord to a beautiful poem; it is something far more categorical.

Yet I did not believe it to be possible for me to consider the question of baptism. I felt that I could not honestly give up my opinions concerning the non-Christian religions and concerning Israel—and as a matter of fact time and meditation have only served to strengthen them—and I thought that this constituted an absolute obstacle. I did not imagine it as possible that a priest could even dream of granting me baptism. If I had not met you, I should never have considered the problem of baptism as a practical problem.

During all this time of spiritual progress I had never prayed. I was afraid of the power of suggestion that is in prayer—the very power for which Pascal recommends it. Pascal's method seems to me one of the worst for attaining faith.

Contact with you was not able to persuade me to pray. On the contrary I thought the danger was all the greater, since I also had to beware of the power of suggestion in my friendship with you. At the same time I found it very difficult not to pray and not to tell you so. Moreover I knew I could not tell you without completely misleading you about myself. At that time I should not have been able to make you understand.

Until last September I had never once prayed in all my life, at least not in the literal sense of the word. I had never said any words to God, either out loud or mentally. I had never pronounced a liturgical prayer. I had occasionally recited the *Salve Regina,* but only as a beautiful poem.

Last summer, doing Greek with T——, I went through the Our Father word for word in Greek. We promised each other to learn it by heart. I do not think he ever did so, but some weeks later, as I was turning over the pages of the Gospel, I said to myself that since I had promised to do this thing and it was good, I ought to do it. I did it. The infinite sweetness of this Greek text so took hold of me that for several days I could not stop myself from saying it over all the time. A week afterward I began the vine harvest. I recited the Our Father in Greek every day before work, and I repeated it very often in the vineyard.

Since that time I have made a practice of saying it through once each morning with absolute attention. If during the recitation my attention wanders or goes to sleep, in the minutest degree, I begin again until I have once succeeded in going through it with absolutely pure attention. Sometimes it comes about that I say it again out of sheer pleasure, but I only do it if I really feel the impulse.

The effect of this practice is extraordinary and surprises me every time, for, although I experience it each day, it exceeds my expectation at each repetition.

At times the very first words tear my thoughts from my body and transport it to a place outside space where there is neither perspective nor point of view. The infinity of the ordinary expanses of perception is replaced by an infinity to the second or sometimes the third degree. At the same time, filling every part of this infinity of infinity, there is silence, a silence which is not an absence of sound but which is the object of a positive sensation, more positive than that of sound. Noises, if there are any, only reach me after crossing this silence.

Sometimes, also, during this recitation or at other moments, Christ is present with me in person, but his presence is infinitely more real, more moving, more clear than on that first occasion when he took possession of me.

I should never have been able to take it upon myself to tell you all this had it not been for the fact that I am going away. And as I am going more or less with the idea of probable death, I do not believe that I have the right to keep it to myself. For after all, the whole of this matter is not a question concerning me myself. It concerns God. I am really nothing in it all. If one could imagine any possibility of error in God, I should think that it had all happened to me by mistake. But perhaps God likes to use castaway objects, waste, rejects. After all, should the bread of the host be moldy, it would become the Body of Christ just the same after the priest had consecrated it. Only it cannot refuse, while we can disobey. It sometimes seems to me that when I am treated in so merciful a way, every sin on my part must be a mortal sin. And I am constantly committing them.

I have told you that you are like a father and brother at the same time to me. But these words only express an analogy. Perhaps at bottom they only correspond to a feeling of affection, of gratitude and admiration. For as to the spiritual direction of my soul, I think that God himself has taken it in hand from the start and still looks after it.

Dag Hammarskjöld

(1905–1961)

Dag Hammarskjöld is best known as the second Secretary General of the United Nations. He served in this capacity from 1953 to 1961, when he was killed in an airline crash during a peace mission to President Moise Tshombe of Katunga in the Congo.

Not until the posthumous publication of his book *Markings*, which he described as "a sort of white book concerning my negotiations with myself and with God," did the world learn of another side of his personality. Always regarded as a man of gentleness, keen moral sensitivity, and exceptional negotiating and peacemaking abilities, Hammarskjöld disclosed his more private self to be deeply contemplative, and religiously—indeed, cosmically—attuned.

He descended on his mother's side from generations of scholars and pastors. His father, Hjalmar Hammarskjöld, was prime minister of Sweden, and known chiefly for keeping his nation neutral during World War I. Hjalmar also played key roles in various international peace organizations and conferences following the war. From his father, Dag became acquainted early with the techniques of diplomacy and the dynamics of statesmanship. He also perpetuated the religious sensitivities of his mother.

As a student in the University of Uppsala, Hammarskjöld majored in law and economics. Before becoming a civil servant in Sweden, he taught political economics in Stockholm University from 1933 to 1936. Thereafter he was involved in various forms of governmental work in Sweden, from the Ministry of Finance to the Ministry of Foreign Affairs. In 1951 he became a deputy foreign minister. In the same year he was made vice chairman of Sweden's delegation to the United Nations General Assembly. As noted, he became Secretary General in

1953. During the early part of his administration the United Nations was involved in the Korean War. It was also engaged in dealing with disturbances in the Middle East and with revolutions in Africa. It was a time of large and widespread international political upheaval and sociocultural transition.

The contemplative disposition disclosed in *Markings*, a portion of Hammarskjöld's diary, exhibits a combination of intriguing components. There is a near preoccupation with the reality and imminence of death. Hammarskjöld does not appear morbid in this respect; rather, his concerns about death seem to invoke a constellation of convictions and sensitivities about human destiny, the worth of a person's work, and the responsibilities human beings have toward one another to bear one another's burdens. Because Hammarskjöld was always somewhat mistrustful of dogmatic formulations, one cannot be confident that this is the way he would have put it. But it is clear that he understood the pathway of service to require a subordination of self-interest. It is also manifestly apparent that he interpreted this relinquishment to involve death to the ego. This renunciation is an enactment of the way of the cross *(via crucis)* and, because it implies self-sacrifice, it may include martyrdom.

At the same time, Hammarskjöld finds human involvement and divine interest to be so intimately interwoven that human beings— servants, he calls them—actually carry the responsibility "for God." But the theological translation oversimplifies the subtlety of his insight. He himself chose to phrase the idea in aphoristic, poetic language. As one reads *Markings*, one hears echoes of the Medieval mystics, perhaps Meister Eckhart most of all, together with elements of a spirit of piety and gentleness.

Running through all of it is a persistent and profound melancholy that has been exhibited in Swedish art and letters since the mid-nineteenth century. There is Lutheran piety in it, an awareness that victory implies suffering, a yearning for harmony among human beings, nations, and political entities, a conviction that human affairs ought to be mannerly. But deep within it is the other strain, a haunting sound, a quest for a more profound peace that seems elusive and inaccessible, almost as if Hammarskjöld is saying—as Eckhart surely did—that beyond the highest orders of known interdependency there is something more, impenetrably mysterious.

Markings

Oedipus, the son of a king, the winner of a throne, fortunate and innocent, is compelled to recognise the possibility and, in the end, the fact that he, too, is guilty, which makes it just that he should be sacrificed to save the city.

Success—for the glory of God or for your own, for the peace of mankind or for your own? Upon the answer to this question depends the result of your actions.

How am I to find the strength to live as a free man, detached from all that was unjust in my past and all that is petty in my present, and so, daily, to forgive myself?

Life will judge me by the measure of the love *I myself* am capable of, and with patience according to the measure of my honesty in attempting to meet its demands, and with an equity before which the feeble explanations and excuses of self-importance carry no weight whatsoever.

What has Life lost by the happiness which might have been his, had he been allowed to go on living? What has it gained by the suffering he has escaped?

What nonsense I'm talking! Life is measured by the living, and the number of a man's days are reckoned in other terms.

Not to brood over my pettiness with masochistic self-disgust, not to take a pride in admitting it—but to recognise it as a threat to my integrity of action, the moment I let it out of my sight.

How selfish and aesthetic our so-called 'sympathy' usually is. There come times when, momentarily, we can serve as the foundation for somebody else's faith in himself—a faith which is constantly being threatened in all of us. When this happens, what we do to make it possible for him to 'go on', we make the foundation for our own life-preserving self-esteem.

In this matter—as in many others—realism is the opposite of desecra-

Dag Hammarskjöld, *Markings*, trans. Leif Sjöberg and W. H. Auden (New York: Alfred A. Knopf, 1964), pp. 149–54, 159–60, and 165–6.

tion. The truth we have to endure is our present reality without the justifications which time may provide.

For the sacrificed—in the hour of sacrifice—only one thing counts: faith—alone among enemies and sceptics. Faith, in spite of the humiliation which is both the necessary precondition and the consequence of faith, faith without any hope of compensation other than he can find in a faith which reality seems so thoroughly to refute.

Would the Crucifixion have had any sublimity or meaning if Jesus had seen himself crowned with the halo of martyrdom? What we have later added was not there for Him. And we must forget all about it if we are to hear His commands.

We have to acquire a peace and balance of mind such that we can give every word of criticism its due weight, and humble ourselves before every word of praise.

There is no history but that of the soul, no peace but that of the soul. *(St John Perse)*

Clad in this 'self', the creation of irresponsible and ignorant persons, meaningless honours and catalogued acts—strapped into the straitjacket of the immediate.

To step out of all this, and stand naked on the precipice of dawn—acceptable, invulnerable, free: in the Light, with the Light, of the Light. *Whole*, real in the Whole.

Out of myself as a stumbling-block, into myself as fulfilment.

'Why', you ask, 'deny yourself something which does nobody else any harm and does you good?'

Yes, why—provided it does not conflict with the path you have chosen. Your subsequent reaction to your behaviour when you have forgotten this proviso—as one reacts to a lie or a humiliating weakness—is sufficient answer to your question.

Everything in the present moment, nothing for the present moment. And nothing for your future comfort or the future of your good name.

Suddenly—without your help—some impasse or other you have dared your all to break, disappears. But you are tempted to 'keep yourself well to the fore'—whether this helps the cause or doesn't, even, perhaps, without caring if it might do harm.

Do you wish to forfeit even that little to which your efforts may have entitled you? Only if your endeavours are inspired by a devotion to duty in which you forget yourself completely, can you keep your faith in their value. This being so, your endeavour to reach the goal should have taught you to rejoice when others reach it.

'—a lie or a humiliating weakness—' One consequence among others: you suffer under criticism which is *not* justified. Yes, and let it sap your strength to meet your task.

For he maketh the storm to cease; so that the waves thereof are still. Then are they glad, because they are at rest: and so he bringeth them unto the haven where they would be. (Psalm CVII. vv29–30)

'The flutes of exile' *(St John Perse)*—For ever among strangers to all that has shaped your life—*alone.* For ever thirsting for the living waters—but not even free to seek them, a *prisoner.*
The answer—the hard straight brutal answer: in the One you are never alone, in the One you are always at home.

*   *   *

'The Uncarved Block'—remain at the Centre, which is yours and that of all humanity. For those goals which it gives to your life, do the utmost which, at each moment, is possible for you. Also, act without thinking of the consequences, or seeking anything for yourself.

Do not seek death. Death will find you. But seek the road which makes death a fulfilment.

Your body must become familiar with its death—in all its possible forms and degrees—as a self-evident, imminent, and emotionally neutral step on the way towards the goal you have found worthy of your life.

As an element in the sacrifice, death is a fulfilment, but more often it is a degradation, and it is never an elevation.

The arête that leads to the summit separates two abysses; the pleasure-tinged death-wish (not, perhaps, without an element of narcissistic masochism), and the animal fear arising from the physical instinct for survival. Only he can conquer vertigo, whose body has learned to treat itself as a means.

No choice is uninfluenced by the way in which the personality regards its destiny, and the body its death. In the last analysis, it is our conception of death which decides our answers to all the questions that life puts to us. That is why it requires its proper place and time—if need be, with right of precedence. Hence, too, the necessity of preparing for it.

Courage and love: equivalent and related expressions for your bargain with Life. You are willing to 'pay' what your heart commands you to give. Two associated reflexes to the sacrificial act, conditioned by a self-chosen effacement of the personality in the One. One result of 'God's marriage to the Soul' is a union with other people which does not draw back before the ultimate surrender of the self.

*   *   *

In the faith which is 'God's marriage to the soul', you are one in God, and
God is wholly in you,
just as, for you, He is wholly in all you meet.
With this faith, in prayer you descend into yourself to meet the Other,
in the steadfastness and light of this union,
see that all things stand, like yourself, alone before God,
and that each of your acts is an act of creation, conscious, because you are a human being with human responsibilities, but governed, nevertheless, by the power beyond human consciousness which has created man.
You are liberated from things, but you encounter in them an experience which has the purity and clarity of revelation.
In the faith which is 'God's marriage to the soul', everything, therefore, has a meaning.
So live, then, that you may use what has been put into your hand. . . .

Only in man has the evolution of the creation reached the point where reality encounters itself in judgement and choice. Outside of man, the creation is neither good nor evil.
Only when you descend into yourself and encounter the Other, do you then experience goodness as the ultimate reality—united and living—in Him and through you.

Did'st Thou give me this inescapable loneliness so that it would be easier for me to give Thee all?

Still a few years more, and then? The only value of a life is its content—for *others*. Apart from any value it may have for others, my life is worse than death. Therefore, in my great loneliness, serve others. Therefore: how incredibly great is what I have been given, and how meaningless what I have to 'sacrifice'.

> Hallowed be Thy Name,
> Thy kingdom come,
> Thy will be done—

You wake from dreams of doom and—for a moment—you *know*: beyond all the noise and the gestures, the only real thing, love's calm unwavering flame in the half-light of an early dawn.

The fire of the body
burns away its dross and, rising in a flame of self-surrender,
consumes its closed microcosm.

The ultimate surrender to the creative act—it is the destiny of some to be brought to the threshold of this in the act of sacrifice rather than the sexual act; and they experience a thunderclap of the same dazzling power.

Pierre Teilhard de Chardin
(1881–1955)

Teilhard de Chardin, French theologian, philosopher, and paleontologist, has had large influence in the Christian world in the current era. Throughout his career, he exhibited a passion for conceiving religious affirmations in a scientific language, via categories fashioned by evolutionist thinking. Based on a combination of religious and scientific reflection, he proposed a point of view in which the human being is depicted as moving toward individual fulfillment in harmony with the general disposition of all things natural, psychic, and cosmological.

Born in Sarcenat, in the Auvergne district of central France, a few miles from Clermont, of a devoutly Catholic mother and a Christian father described as a "gentleman farmer," Teilhard joined the Jesuit order at the age of eighteen. Six years later, for a three-year term, he taught physics and natural history at the Jesuit college in Cairo. He was ordained a priest on August 24, 1911. During these years he was also working to complete his doctoral studies in natural sciences in Paris. When the war broke out in 1914, Teilhard chose to be a stretcher bearer rather than a chaplain. His courage in war won him several medals of honor. After the war he returned to Paris, finished his doctoral work by 1921 and, in 1923, made his first visit to China. There he was involved in the discovery of Palaeolithic Man. From here on his work was established. The chronicle finds him returning to Paris, writing and publishing scientific papers on his work in China, planning articles and books on the religious implications of what he envisioned, and experiencing perpetual, though not dramatic, difficulty with his superiors in the Jesuit order and with ecclesiastical authorities in Rome. In intellectual terms, the controversy focused on the support his lectures and writings seemed to be giving to a pantheistic position. He returned to China, was caught there prior to the beginning of World War II, and remained there throughout the war.

Following the war he returned to Paris, became active again lecturing and giving papers to conferences. He became involved in the work of UNESCO and found ample opportunity to test his convictions in well-established intellectual circles.

Partly through the resistance of ecclesiastical authorities—resistance that was lifelong and created much frustration and some bitterness—he was denied a professorial appointment at the Collège de France. He left Paris in 1951, first on an archeological expedition to South Africa, then for New York, where he became associated with the Wenner Gren Foundation as a research scholar. On behalf of the foundation, he made a second journey to South Africa, spent his remaining days conducting research and organizing a portion of the foundation's research program, and died on Easter Sunday, April 10, 1955. At the time of his death he was relatively unknown. Twelve persons attended his funeral in New York City. He was buried in a simple ceremony in the cemetery of the Jesuit novitiate for the New York Province, at Saint Andrew on the Hudson.

Teilhard's reflections were novel in a variety of respects. They exhibit his penchant for viewing the entire course of created life, from the beginning through the present into the future, in one grand, comprehensive sweep. The beginning of life to its culmination: this was the scope of his queries. Within this framework he sought to be more than descriptive; he also intended to interpret the entire sequence creatively, distinguishing the various stages in the evolutionary process as progressive advances toward the realization of a final synthesizing "omega point."

His views were designed to support the thesis that the universe is dynamic through and through. From this he believed a corollary followed: any defensible religious apprehension of reality must keep this dynamic quality very prominently in mind; any religious view that bases itself upon a static view of the universe is obsolete and irresponsible.

Included within his perception of the world is an analysis of the reasons for the widespread irreligion in the twentieth century. Teilhard believed that the imagery, both religious and cosmological, that had been fostered by the Church was neither compelling nor attractive because it presumed a world view that was indefensible scientifically. As an alternative, he stressed the reality of process. As he explained it, he found it necessary to make up his own language, develop his own version of cosmology, though all the while with intended scientific verification.

At bottom is a mystical apprehension. Teilhard understood that the reality of God courses through all things, urging them toward fulfillment. As the process works itself out, the invisible realities become visible, and the imperfect reaches beyond itself to the time of harmonious fulfillment. The distinctiveness of the vision is that the description of the process is correlated with shifts in evolutionary cycles. It is as if Teilhard were pleading, "If only you could perceive the world this way." He sensed that fundamental alterations would occur in the way in which human priorities are established.

He called it science. It stimulated theology. But it was mystical before it was either of these. And because that is what it was, it drew both science and theology onto its own intrinsic base.

Hymn of the Universe

The Offering.

Since once again, Lord—though this time not in the forests of the Aisne but in the steppes of Asia—I have neither bread, nor wine, nor altar, I will raise myself beyond these symbols, up to the pure majesty of the real itself; I, your priest, will make the whole earth my altar and on it will offer you all the labours and sufferings of the world.

Over there, on the horizon, the sun has just touched with light the outermost fringe of the eastern sky. Once again, beneath this moving sheet of fire, the living surface of the earth wakes and trembles, and once again begins its fearful travail. I will place on my paten, O God, the harvest to be won by this renewal of labour. Into my chalice I shall pour all the sap which is to be pressed out this day from the earth's fruits.

My paten and my chalice are the depths of a soul laid widely open to all the forces which in a moment will rise up from every corner of the earth and converge upon the Spirit. Grant me the remembrance and the mystic presence of all those whom the light is now awakening to the new day.

One by one, Lord, I see and I love all those whom you have given me to sustain and charm my life. One by one also I number all those who make up that other beloved family which has gradually surrounded me, its unity fashioned out of the most disparate elements, with affinities of the heart, of scientific research and of thought. And again one by one— more vaguely it is true, yet all-inclusively—I call before me the whole vast anonymous army of living humanity; those who surround me and support me though I do not know them; those who come, and those who go; above all, those who in office, laboratory and factory, through their vision of truth or despite their error, truly believe in the progress of earthly reality and who today will take up again their impassioned pursuit of the light.

This restless multitude, confused or orderly, the immensity of which terrifies us; this ocean of humanity whose slow, monotonous wave-flows trouble the hearts even of those whose faith is most firm: it is to this deep that I thus desire all the fibres of my being should respond.

Pierre Teilhard de Chardin, *Hymn of the Universe* (New York: Harper and Row, 1965), 19–21 and 23–6.

All the things in the world to which this day will bring increase; all those that will diminish; all those too that will die: all of them, Lord, I try to gather into my arms, so as to hold them out to you in offering. This is the material of my sacrifice; the only material you desire.

Once upon a time men took into your temple the first fruits of their harvests, the flower of their flocks. But the offering you really want, the offering you mysteriously need every day to appease your hunger, to slake your thirst is nothing less than the growth of the world borne ever onwards in the stream of universal becoming.

Receive, O Lord, this all-embracing host which your whole creation, moved by your magnetism, offers you at this dawn of a new day.

This bread, our toil, is of itself, I know, but an immense fragmentation; this wine, our pain, is no more, I know, than a draught that dissolves. Yet in the very depths of this formless mass you have implanted—and this I am sure of, for I sense it—a desire, irresistible, hallowing, which makes us cry out, believer and unbeliever alike: 'Lord, make us one.'

Because, my God, though I lack the soul-zeal and the sublime integrity of your saints, I yet have received from you an overwhelming sympathy for all that stirs within the dark mass of matter; because I know myself to be irremediably less a child of heaven than a son of earth; therefore, I will this morning climb up in spirit to the high places, bearing with me the hopes and the miseries of my mother; and there—empowered by that priesthood which you alone (as I firmly believe) have bestowed on me—upon all that in the world of human flesh is now about to be born or to die beneath the rising sun I will call down the Fire.

Fire in the Earth.

It is done.

Once again the Fire has penetrated the earth.

Not with sudden crash of thunderbolt, riving the mountain-tops: does the Master break down doors to enter his own home? Without earthquake, or thunderclap: the flame has lit up the whole world from within. All things individually and collectively are penetrated and flooded by it, from the inmost core of the tiniest atom to the mighty sweep of the most universal laws of being: so naturally has it flooded every element, every energy, every connecting-link in the unity of our cosmos; that one might suppose the cosmos to have burst spontaneously into flame.

In the new humanity which is begotten today the Word prolongs the unending act of his own birth; and by virtue of his immersion in the world's womb the great waters of the kingdom of matter have, without even a ripple, been endued with life. No visible tremor marks this inexpressible transformation; and yet, mysteriously and in very truth, at the touch of the supersubstantial Word the immense host which is the universe is made flesh. Through your own incarnation, my God, all matter is henceforth incarnate.

Through our thoughts and our human experiences, we long ago became aware of the strange properties which make the universe so like our flesh:

like the flesh it attracts us by the charm which lies in the mystery of its curves and folds and in the depths of its eyes;

like the flesh it disintegrates and eludes us when submitted to our analyses or to our fallings off and in the process of its own perdurance;

as with the flesh, it can only be embraced in the endless reaching out to attain what lies beyond the confines of what has been given to us.

All of us, Lord, from the moment we are born feel within us this disturbing mixture of remoteness and nearness; and in our heritage of sorrow and hope, passed down to us through the ages, there is no yearning more desolate than that which makes us weep with vexation and desire as we stand in the midst of the Presence which hovers about us nameless and impalpable and is indwelling in all things. *Si forte attrectent eum.**

Now, Lord, through the consecration of the world the luminosity and fragrance which suffuse the universe take on for me the lineaments of a body and a face—in you. What my mind glimpsed through its hesitant explorations, what my heart craved with so little expectation of fulfilment, you now magnificently unfold for me: the fact that your creatures are not merely so linked together in solidarity that none can exist unless all the rest surround it, but that all are so dependent on a single central reality that a true life, borne in common by them all, gives them ultimately their consistence and their unity.

Shatter, my God, through the daring of your revelation the childishly timid outlook that can conceive of nothing greater or more vital in the world than the pitiable perfection of our human organism. On the road to a bolder comprehension of the universe the children of this world day by day outdistance the masters of Israel; but do you, Lord Jesus, 'in whom all things subsist', show yourself to those who love you as the

---

*"That they [all humankind] should seek God, if happily they may feel after him or find him . . . ' (Acts 17–27).

higher Soul and the physical centre of your creation. Are you not well aware that for us this is a question of life or death? As for me, if I could not believe that your real Presence animates and makes tractable and enkindles even the very least of the energies which invade me or brush past me, would I not die of cold?

I thank you, my God, for having in a thousand different ways led my eyes to discover the immense simplicity of things. Little by little, through the irresistible development of those yearnings you implanted in me as a child, through the influence of gifted friends who entered my life at certain moments to bring light and strength to my mind, and through the awakenings of spirit I owe to the successive initiations, gentle and terrible, which you caused me to undergo: through all these I have been brought to the point where I can no longer see anything, nor any longer breathe, outside that *milieu* in which all is made one.

At this moment when your life has just poured with superabundant vigour into the sacrament of the world, I shall savour with heightened consciousness the intense yet tranquil rapture of a vision whose coherence and harmonies I can never exhaust.

What I experience as I stand in face of—and in the very depths of—this world which your flesh has assimilated, this world which has become your flesh, my God, is not the absorption of the monist who yearns to be dissolved into the unity of things, nor the emotion felt by the pagan as he lies prostrate before a tangible divinity, nor yet the passive self-abandonment of the quietist tossed hither and thither at the mercy of mystical impulsions. From each of these modes of thought I take something of their motive force while avoiding their pitfalls: the approach determined for me by your omnipresence is a wonderful synthesis wherein three of the most formidable passions that can unlock the human heart rectify each other as they mingle: like the monist I plunge into the all-inclusive One; but the One is so perfect that as it receives me and I lose myself in it I can find in it the ultimate perfection of my own individuality . . . .

Thomas Merton

(1915–1968)

Thomas Merton is one of the most significant persons in the Christian world in the twentieth century. If he isn't recognized as such yet, he will be eventually, based upon the impetus and guidance he has given to the revival of monasticism in the modern world. In stimulating monastic renewal, Merton has demonstrated that this ancient religious institution can play an important contemporary religious, social, and cultural role. Not only does its presence testify to the perennial vitality of a classical mode of self-knowledge and wisdom in a postclassical, indeed, post-Enlightenment age. But Merton also found monasticism to be an effective instrument of social reform, by virtue of its ability to offer an alternative to more prevalent ways of living and being. Furthermore, the monastic revival with which he is associated occurred at the very time that avenues for rapprochement were opened between Eastern and Western religions and cultures. Merton not only participated in these initial "dialogues" and discussions, but was in the vanguard. For these purposes, he traveled to Asia in 1968—during the course of which he was the tragic victim of an accidental electrocution—and recorded his aspirations and impressions in a posthumously published book, *The Asian Journal of Thomas Merton.*

The earlier portion of his life story was recorded in his autobiography, *The Seven Storey Mountain,* first published in 1948. Here the reader is given Merton's impressions and interpretations regarding his birth and ancestry in the United States, his early years in France, his education in England and then in New York at Columbia University, his early critical attitude toward religion, and his ultimate rejection of religious skepticism as witnessed by his becoming a Trappist monk. He entered Gethsemani Abbey in 1944. His religious awakening appears to have occurred in stages. First he realized that he believed in God as interpreted by Christians, next that he was indeed a Catholic Christian, and finally that he was called to the monastic vocation in a place where spirituality was practiced in an austere fashion.

Merton was a prolific writer. Trained under Mark van Doren at Columbia University, he had a sensitivity to letters and literary expression. This enabled him to interpret the rudiments of monastic life to those outside as well as to his fellow monks. His writings reflect the characteristics of the monastic impulse in a manner others could understand and with which the monks themselves could identify. And his acquaintance with the dominant tendencies in modern literature as well as with the fundamental development of modern thought provides his writing with a range of applicability and a degree of quality unmatched in the modern monastic genre. In addition to his receptivity to Asian religious experience, he also grasped the intentions of the counterculture early in its development. He understood some of that movement's objectives to be consonant with monastic goals, both of which sought to provide an alternative to the dominant way of living and being in the Western world. Merton was taken by the writings of Herbert Marcuse, was well-versed in Marxist ideology—particularly those portions critical of Western capitalism—and was also fascinated with the similarities between Marxist analyses and monastic intentions. His interpretation of historical and cultural development was also influenced by the vision of Teilhard de Chardin.

In his final address, in Bangkok, Thailand, on December 10, 1968, a few hours before he died, Merton said:

Both Christianity and Buddhism agree that the root of man's problems is that his consciousness is all fouled up and he does not apprehend reality as it fully and really is; that the moment he looks at something, he begins to interpret it in ways that are prejudiced and predetermined to fit a certain wrong picture of the world, in which he exists as an individual ego in the center of things. This is called by Buddhism *avidya*, or ignorance. From this basic ignorance, which is our experience of ourselves as absolutely autonomous individual egos—from this basic wrong experience of ourselves comes all the rest. This is the source of all our problems.[1]

He continued on to speak about the remedy the two religions prescribe:

Christianity and Buddhism alike, then, seek to bring about a transformation of man's consciousness. And instead of starting with matter itself and then moving up to a new structure, in which man will automatically develop a new consciousness, the traditional religions begin with the consciousness of the individual, seek to transform and liberate the truth in each person, with the idea that it will communicate itself to others. Of course, the man par excellence to whom this task is deputed is the monk. And the Christian monk and the Buddhist monk—in their sort of ideal setting and the ideal way of looking at them—fulfill this role in society.[2]

This comes close to the heart of his vision.

[1] *The Asian Journal of Thomas Merton*, edited by Naomi Burton, Brother Patrick Hart, and James Laughlin (New York: New Directions, 1973), p. 332.
[2] *Ibid.*, p. 333.

Contemplation
in a World of Action

... What does the contemplative life or the life of prayer, solitude, silence, meditation, mean to man in the atomic age? What can it mean? Has it lost all meaning whatever?

When I speak of the contemplative life I do not mean the institutional cloistered life, the organized life of prayer. This has special problems of its own. Many Catholics are now saying openly that the cloistered contemplative institution is indefensible, that it is an anachronism that has no point in the modern world. I am not arguing about this—I only remark in passing that I do not agree. Prescinding from any idea of an institution or even of a religious organization, I am talking about a special dimension of inner discipline and experience, a certain integrity and fullness of personal development, which are not compatible with a purely external, alienated, busy-busy existence. This does not mean that they are incompatible with action, with creative work, with dedicated love. On the contrary, these all go together. A certain depth of disciplined experience is a necessary ground for fruitful action. Without a more profound human understanding derived from exploration of the inner ground of human existence, love will tend to be superficial and deceptive. Traditionally, the ideas of prayer, meditation and contemplation have been associated with this deepening of one's personal life and this expansion of the capacity to understand and serve others.

*   *   *

... The real point of the contemplative life has always been a deepening of faith and of the personal dimensions of liberty and apprehension to the point where our direct union with God is realized and "experienced." We awaken not only to a realization of the immensity and majesty of God "out there" as King and Ruler of the universe (which He is) but also a more intimate and more wonderful perception of Him as directly and personally present in our own being. Yet this is not a pantheistic merger or confusion of our being with His. On the contrary, there is a distinct conflict in the realization that though in

Thomas Merton, *Contemplation in a World of Action* (New York: Doubleday, 1973), pp. 171, 175–9.

some sense He is more truly ourselves than we are, yet we are not identical with Him, and though He loves us better than we can love ourselves we are opposed to Him, and in opposing Him we oppose our own deepest selves. If we are involved only in our surface existence, in externals, and in the trivial concerns of our ego, we are untrue to Him and to ourselves. To reach a true awareness of Him as well as ourselves, we have to renounce our selfish and limited self and enter into a whole new kind of existence, discovering an inner center of motivation and love which makes us see ourselves and everything else in an entirely new light. Call it faith, call it (at a more advanced stage) contemplative illumination, call it the sense of God or even mystical union: all these are different aspects and levels of the same kind of realization: the awakening to a new awareness of ourselves in Christ, created in Him, redeemed by Him, to be transformed and glorified in and with Him. In Blake's words, the "doors of perception" are opened and all life takes on a completely new meaning: the real sense of our own existence, which is normally veiled and distorted by the routine distractions of an alienated life, is now revealed in a central intuition. What was lost and dispersed in the relative meaninglessness and triviality of purposeless behavior (living like a machine, pushed around by impulsions and suggestions from others) is brought together in fully integrated conscious significance. This peculiar, brilliant focus is, according to Christian tradition, the work of Love and of the Holy Spirit. This "loving knowledge" which sees everything transfigured "in God," coming from God and working for God's creative and redemptive love and tending to fulfillment in the glory of God, is a contemplative knowledge, a fruit of living and realizing faith, a gift of the Spirit.

*   *   *

This inner awareness, this experience of love as an immediate and dynamic presence, tends to alter our perspective. We see the prayer of petition a little differently. Celebration and praise, loving attention to the presence of God, become more important than "asking for" things and "getting" things. This is because we realize that in Him and with Him all good is present to us and to mankind: if we seek first the Kingdom of Heaven, all the rest comes along with it. Hence we worry a great deal less about the details of our daily needs, and we trust God to take care of our problems even if we do not ask Him insistently at every minute to do so. The same applies to the problems of the world. But on the other hand, this inner awareness and openness makes us especially sensitive to urgent needs of the time, and grace can sometimes move us to pray for certain special needs. The contemplative life does not ignore the prayer of petition, but does not overemphasize it either. The contemplative prays for particular intentions when he is strongly and spontaneously inspired to do so, but does not make it his formal purpose to keep asking for this and that all day long.

Now, prayer also has to be seen in the light of another fundamental experience, that of God's "absence." For if God is immanently present He is also transcendent, which means that He is completely beyond the grasp of our understanding. The two ("absence" and "presence") merge in the loving knowledge that "knows by unknowing" (a traditional term of mysticism). It is more and more usual for modern people to be afflicted with a sense of absence, desolation, and incapacity to even "want" to pray or to think of God. To dismiss this superficially as an experience of "the death of God"—as if henceforth God were completely irrelevant—is to overlook one significant fact: that this sense of absence is not a one-sided thing: it is dialectical, and it includes its opposite, namely presence. And while it may be afflicted with doubt it contains a deep need to believe.

*   *   *

This experience of struggle, of self-emptying, "self-naughting," of letting go and of subsequent recovery in peace and grace on a new level is one of the ways in which the *Pascha Christi* (the death and resurrection of Christ) takes hold on our lives and transforms them. This is the psychological aspect of the work of grace which also takes place beyond experience and beyond psychology in the work of the Sacraments and in our objective sharing of the Church's life.

I am of course not talking about "mystical experience" or anything new and strange, but simply the fullness of personal awareness that comes with a total self-renunciation, followed by self-commitment on the highest level, beyond mere intellectual assent and external obedience.

Real Christian living is stunted and frustrated if it remains content with the bare externals of worship, with "saying prayers" and "going to church," with fulfilling one's external duties and merely being respectable. The real purpose of prayer (in the fully personal sense as well as in the Christian assembly) is the deepening of personal realization in love, the awareness of God (even if sometimes this awareness may amount to a negative factor, a seeming "absence"). The real purpose of meditation—or at least that which recommends itself as most relevant for modern man—is the exploration and discovery of new dimensions in freedom, illumination and love, in deepening our awareness of our life in Christ.

What is the relation of this to action? Simply this. He who attempts to act and do things for others or for the world without deepening his own self-understanding, freedom, integrity and capacity to love, will not have anything to give others. He will communicate to them nothing but the contagion of his own obsessions, his aggressiveness, his ego-centered ambitions, his delusions about ends and means, his doctrinaire prejudices and ideas. There is nothing more tragic in the modern world than the misuse of power and action to which men are driven by their own Faustian misunderstandings and misapprehensions. We have more power at our disposal today than we have ever had, and yet we are more alienated and estranged from the inner ground of meaning and of love than we have ever been. The result of this is evident. We are living through the greatest crisis in the history of man; and this crisis is centered precisely in the country that has made a fetish out of action and has lost (or perhaps never had) the sense of contemplation. Far from being irrelevant, prayer, meditation and contemplation are of the utmost importance in American today. Unfortunately, it must be admitted that the official contemplative life as it is lived in our monasteries needs a great deal of rethinking, because it is still too closely identified with patterns of thought that were accepted five hundred years ago, but which are completely strange to modern man.

But prayer and meditation have an important part to play in opening up new ways and new horizons. If our prayer is the expression of a deep and grace-inspired desire for newness of life—and not the mere blind attachment to what has always been familiar and "safe"—God will act in us and through us to renew the Church by preparing, in prayer, what we cannot yet imagine or understand. In this way our prayer and faith today will be oriented toward the future which we ourselves may never see fully realized on earth.

Ernesto Cardenal

(1925–   )

A Nicaraguan poet and social philospher, Ernesto Cardenal is known in the United States both through his writings and because of his associations with Thomas Merton. Cardenal lived for a time in Gethsemani, the Trappist Abbey near Louisville, Kentucky, Merton's monastic home. In addition to being Cardenal's novice master, Merton wrote about Cardenal and introduced his essays and poems in several publications.

As a student in Nicaragua, Cardenal was involved in various revolutionary activities, though his participation seems to have been carried out most effectively through a serious of sharply worded sayings and epigrams. He was educated in the University of Mexico in Mexico City, and then in the United States at Columbia University. During his formative years, he was influenced by Ezra Pound, which encounter helped shape his literary talents. Along the way he also developed a talent for ceramics and clay modeling, and some of his work was exhibited.

Cardenal entered Gethsemani in 1957, but remained only a few years, because of poor health. Furthermore, he felt compelled to return to Central America to identify with those who were seeking liberation from oppression. There, in Nicaragua, he has continued his vocation as priest, contemplative, and poet and has given his efforts toward establishing an experimental religious community committed to finding a way between capitalist and communist forms of government.

Fidel Castro regards Cardenal as his favorite poet. Ivan Illich remains close to him. Thomas Merton took deliberate steps to bring him to other persons' attention. And Jürgen Moltmann, the contemporary German theologian, has a very high regard for him.

Cardenal commands attention because of the combination of interests and talents he brings and fits together. For example, one finds in his writings a marked influence of Teilhard de Chardin coupled with a re-enunciation of Franciscan spirituality together with a rather sensuous rendering of The Song of Songs. As if these features were not enough, one also perceives more than a fleeting acquaintance with the writings of Martin Buber. Further, because of his participation in and support of revolutionary political activity, Cardenal is also identified with the theology of liberation, the successor "school" to the theology of hope. Somehow he has found a way to blend all of these influences and interests in a view that takes reality to be dynamic, multilayered, forward-tending, personal, and, most importantly, sacramentally ordered.

In Cardenal's view, everything visible reflects invisible realities. God animates all things, motivating them toward fulfillment. In the process, God is drawing all things unto himself: all of reality's processes reflect a searching and sighing for God. But God is also affected by the process, and can have no rest until the entire creation is brought to its true identity and culmination.

Blended with the vision of a creation in process of fulfilling itself is a very clever use of light imagery. Cardenal sometimes likens reality to a sun. This enables him to view the world as being flooded with light, as being luminous, and thus as mirroring or reflecting the source of light. These light-motifs are drawn upon in his frequent references to St. Paul's text, "but now we see as in a mirror, but then face to face."

In his poetry and prose, Cardenal is attentive to the ways in which human beings participate in rhythms and processes that give shape to what will be. Perceiving the cosmos as a harmony of light and sound, he describes the promise of the human voyage in the following depiction: "We are not yet partakers of the feast, but we have been invited, and we see the light and hear the music in the distance." What is yet to be is described in joyful wedding imagery: the culmination of love, the union of interior self-knowledge with awareness of the presence of God, and the manifestation of the luminous presence throughout the whole of reality. Many of these themes are enunciated in the selection from the concluding paragraphs of To Live Is to Love, a modern commentary on The Song of Songs, which follows.

To Live Is to Love

When you contemplate the vastness of the universe in a star-lit night (our own galaxy with its three hundred thousand million stars, and the stars which shine with a brightness of three hundred thousand suns, and the one hundred million galaxies in that part of the universe which is accessible to exploration), you ought not to be conscious of your own smallness and insignificance but rather of your grandeur. For the spirit of man is much greater than all these universes, because man can contemplate, comprehend and be conscious of all of these, whereas all these worlds cannot comprehend man. All these worlds are composed of simple molecules such as the hydrogen molecule, which consists only a nucleus and an electron, whereas the human body consists of much more complex molecules and, in addition, possesses the gift of life, a life whose complexity transcends by far that of the molecular

Ernesto Cardenal, *To Live Is to Love*, trans. Kurt Reinhardt (New York: Herder and Herder, 1972), pp. 148-50, 152, 155-6.

world. Man, moreover, possesses consciousness and love. And when a lover says that the eyes of his beloved shine more brightly than the stars, he is not using a hyperbole (even though the Dorado Sigma shines three hundred thousand times brighter than the sun), because in the eyes of the beloved is the sheen of understanding and love, a light which is not found in either the Lyra Alpha or in Antares. Although the radius of the universe measures one hundred thousand million light years, it has definite limits, and even the most inferior of men is greater than the entire material universe; he has a greatness of a different order, which surpasses any mere quantitative greatness. For the entire material universe circulates like a small point in the human intellect which speculates on it in its understanding.

And all these worlds are silent. They are praising God, but with an unknowing, mindless praise. But you, oh man, are the voice and the consciousness of these worlds. And while these worlds are incapable of love, you are matter aflame with love.

Your understanding, however, is not separated from all these worlds. You yourself are this immense universe, its conscience and its heart. You yourself are a vast universe that thinks and loves.

According to Plato, the soul completes and perfects the universe and has been created to endow the cosmos with an intellect. Man represents the perfection of visible creation, and therefore we cannot regard him as of little worth and significance (as "a vile earth worm"), for to do so would be to regard as worthless and insignificant the entire work of God.

The vastness of the universe which you contemplate in a star-lit night becomes even vaster when you look at yourself as part of this universe and when you begin to realize that it is you who are this universe, contemplating itself, a universe which, in addition to its spatio-temporal dimensions, acquires a new dimension of even greater magnitude within your own self.

We are the consciousness and the conscience of the cosmos. And the incarnation of the Word in a human body signifies its incarnation in the entire cosmos.

The entire cosmos is in communion. The calcium in our bodies is the same calcium that we find in the sea (and which we have drawn from the sea, for our life itself has had its origin in the sea), and both the calcium of our body and that of the sea derive from heaven, from the calcium that is contained in the stars and that floats in the interstellar oceans and from which have sprung the stars (for the stars are a condensation of the brittle matter of the interstellar spaces and derive from them as our body derives from the sea). Actually, there are no interstellar and intergalactic empty spaces, since the entire cosmos is one single material mass, more or less rarefied or condensed, and thus the entire cosmos forms one single body. The constitutive elements of the meteorites (such as calcium, iron, copper, phosphorus) that have split off from distant stars are the same elements which are found in our planet, in our bodies and in the interstellar spaces. Thus we are made of the matter of the stars or, to say it more accurately, the entire cosmos is made of our own flesh. And when the Word became flesh and dwelled among us, what Adam said to Eve became applicable to all nature: "This is flesh of my flesh and bone of my bones." In the body of Christ, as in our own body, is incarnate the entire creation.

In our body commune all living animals, all fossils, all metals and all the other elements of the universe. The sculptor who sculpts in stone consists of the same matter that is in the stone; he is, as it were, the consciousness and the conscience of the stone, the stone become artist, besouled matter. And when man loves God and enters into union with Him, the whole of creation, with its mineral, plant and animal kingdoms, loves God and enters into union with Him.

* * *

. . . This is why St. Paul says that all creatures—plants and animals included—are groaning, waiting for the resurrection of our body. And therefore the resurrection of one single body heralds the resurrection of all bodies. And thus the resurrection of Christ—"the first-born among the dead"—suffices to bring about the resurrection of the entire creation . . . .

The entire cosmos is a song, a choral chant, a festive song and a marriage feast (" . . . a king prepared a wedding feast for his son"). We ourselves are not yet partakers of the feast, but we have been invited, and we see the light and hear the music in the distance. "At midnight there was a cry, 'The bridegroom is here! Go out and meet him' " (Matthew 25, 6). The Baptist had already announced his coming with the words,

> The bride is only for the bridegroom;
> and yet the bridegroom's friend,
> who stands there and listens,
> is glad when he hears the bridegroom's voice.
> (John 3, 29)

The liturgy is the daily commemoration, on this earth and in time, of this wedding feast that was prepared in eternity. For the Catholic Church, therefore, all days are festive days, and in the liturgy all days are called *feria*, that is feast days (the feast of Monday, the feast of Tuesday, and so on), and all the days of the year of the zodiac and of the liturgical year are for us symbols of that eternal feast that never ends. And our song, joined with the choruses of the stars and the atoms, is the same song that is sung by the choir of angels, the same song that is sung perhaps by countless human species and by countless planets, a song to which reference is made in the Book of Job, when Job spoke of the joyful shouts of the morning stars which blend with the jubilant voices of the sons of God. We are now still far away in the dark, waiting for the bridegroom, but we can already see a light in the distance and hear a choral chant at midnight.

Suggestions for Further Readings

Armstrong, E. A. *Saint Francis, Nature Mystic: The Derivation and Significance of the Nature Stories in the Franciscan Legend* (Berkeley: University of California Press, 1973).

Bacovcin, Helen, translator. *The Way of a Pilgrim, and The Pilgrim Continues His Way* (Garden City: Doubleday, 1978).

Bakan, David. *Sigmund Freud and the Jewish Mystical Tradition* (Princeton: Van Nostrand, 1958).

Baker, Eve. *The Mystical Journey. A Western Alternative* (London: Wildwood House, 1977).

Bastide, Roger. *The Mystical Life*, trans. H. F. Kynaston-Snell and David Waring (London: Jonathan Cape, 1934).

Baumgardt, David. *Great Western Mystics, Their Lasting Significance* (New York: Columbia University Press, 1961).

Benz, Ernst, and others. *Man and Transformation*. Selections from the Eranos-Jahrbücher (New York: Pantheon Books, 1964).

Bergson, Henri. *The Two Sources of Morality and Religion* (New York: H. Holt, 1935).

Bharati, Agehananda. *The Light at the Center* (Santa Barbara: Ross-Erikson, 1976).

Blakney, Raymond B. *Meister Eckhart* (New York: Harper and Row, Publishers, 1941).

Bolle, Kees W. *The Freedom of Man in Myth* (Nashville: Vanderbilt University Press, 1968).

Bouyer, Louis. *The Cistercian Heritage* (London: A. R. Mowbray, 1958).

Bridges, Hal. *American Mysticism. From William James to Zen* (New York: Harper and Row, Publishers, 1970).

Brinton, Howard H. *Friends for 300 Years: The History and Beliefs of the Society of Friends since George Fox Started the Quaker Movement* (New York: Harper and Row, Publishers, 1952).

Brown, Peter. *Augustine of Hippo* (Berkeley: University of California Press, 1967).

Burnaby, John. *Amor Dei. A Study of the Religion of St. Augustine* (London: Hodder and Stoughton, 1938).

Butler, Dom Cuthbert. *Western Mysticism* (New York: Harper Torchbooks, 1966).

Capps, Donald and Walter H. Capps, eds. *The Religious Personality* (Belmont: Wadsworth Publishing Company, 1970).

Capps, Walter H. *Hope Against Hope. From Moltmann to Merton in One Theological Decade* (Philadelphia: Fortress Press, 1976).

———. "Religious Renewal," in *The Center Magazine.* Vol X, No. 2 (March/April 1977), pp. 13–19.

——— and Wendy M. Wright. "The Contemplative Mode," in *Studia Mystica.* Vol. I, No. 2 (Spring, 1978), pp. 68–74.

Cardenal, Ernesto. *Apocalypse and Other Poems* (New York: New Directions Books, 1977).

Chesterton, G. K. *St. Francis of Assisi* (New York: Doubleday, 1924).

Clark, James M. *The Great German Mystics: Eckhart, Tauler and Suso* (Folcroft, Pa.: Folcroft Press, 1969).

Clark, Walter Houston. "Mysticism as a Basic Concept in Defining the Religious Self," in *Lumen Vitae,* 19 (1964), pp. 221–32.

———. "The Mystical Consciousness and Its Contribution to Human Understanding," in *Humanitas* 6 (1971), pp. 311–24.

Cohen, J. M. *The Life of Saint Teresa* (London: Penguin, 1957).

Crookall, Robert. *The Interpretation of Cosmic and Mystical Experiences* (Cambridge, England: James Clarke, 1969).

D'Arcy, Martin C. *The Meeting of Love and Knowledge: Perennial Wisdom* (New York: Harper and Row, Publishers, 1957).

Davy, Marie-Magdeleine. *The Mysticism of Simone Weil* (London: Rockliff, 1951).

Dillard, Annie. *Holy the Firm* (New York: Harper and Row, Publishers, 1977).

———. *Pilgrim at Tinker Creek* (New York: Harper and Row, Publishers, 1974).

Dunne, John S. *A Search for God in Time and Memory* (New York: Macmillan, 1969).

———. *The Reasons of the Heart. A Journey into Solitude and Back Again into the Human Circle* (New York: Macmillan, 1978).

———. *The Way of All the Earth: Experiments in Truth and Religion* (New York: Macmillan, 1972).

Dupre, Louis. *The Other Dimension: A Search for the Meaning of Religious Attitudes* (New York: Doubleday, 1973).

Elder, E. Rozanne, editor. *The Spirituality of Western Christendom* (Kalamazoo: Cistercian Publications, 1976).

Etten, H. Van. *George Fox and the Quakers*, translated and revised by E. Kelvin Osborn (New York: Harper Torchbooks, 1959).

Feuerstein, G. "Meister Eckhart-Mystic or Yogin," in his *Yoga and Beyond* (New York: Schoken Books, 1972), pp. 152–69.

Francis, Saint of Assisi, *The Little Flowers of St. Francis: The Mirror of Perfection: the Life of St. Francis*, by St. *Bonaventura* (New York: E. P. Dutton, 1951).

Freeman, D. H. *John of Ruysbroeck. His Mysticism and Influence upon Gerhardt Groote and John Tauler.* Ph.D. dissertation, Boston University Graduate School, 1959.

Fremantle, Anne J. *The Protestant Mystics* (Boston: Little, Brown, 1964).

Frost, A. E. *Saint John of the Cross. An Introduction to his Philosophy, Theology and Spirituality* (London: Hodder and Stoughton, 1937).

Furst, Margaret Lewis. *Mysticism. Window on a World View* (Nashville: Abingdon, 1977).

Gilson, Etienne. *The Mystical Theology of St. Bernard* (New York: Sheed and Ward, 1940).

Graef, Hilda C. *Mystics of Our Times* (Garden City: Hanover House, 1962).

────. "St. Gertrude. Mystical Flowering of the Liturgy," in *Orate Fratres.* 20 (February 24, 1946), pp. 171–4.

────. *The Story of Mysticism* (Garden City: Doubleday, 1965).

────. *The Way of the Mystics* (Westminster: Newman Bookshop, 1948).

Grant, F. C. "St. Paul's Mysticism," in *Biblical World.* 44 (December, 1941), pp. 375–87.

Graham, Dom Aelred. *Zen Catholicism. A Suggestion* (New York: Harcourt, Brace, Jovanovich, 1965).

Greeley, Andrew M. *Ecstasy: A Way of Knowing* (Englewood Cliffs: Prentice-Hall, 1974).

Happold, F. C. *Mysticism. A Study and an Anthology* (London: Penguin 1963).

────. *Religious Faith and Twentieth-Century Man* (London: Penguin, 1966).

Harkness, Georgia E. *The Dark Night of the Soul. A Modern Interpretation* (London: E. Melrose, 1966).

────. *Mysticism: Its Meaning and Message* (Nashville: Abingdon Press, 1973).

Hillman, James. *The Myth of Analysis. Three Essays in Archetypal Psychology* (New York: Harper and Row, Publishers, 1978).

────. *Re-Visioning Psychology* (New York: Harper and Row, Publishers, 1975).

Inge, William R. *Christian Mysticism* (London: Methuen, 1948).

────. *Mysticism in Religion* (Chicago: University of Chicago Press, 1948).

────. *Outspoken Essays.* 2 vols (New York: Longmans, Green and Company, 1927).

James, William. "Pluralistic Mystic," in *Hibbert Journal.* 8 (July, 1910), pp. 739–59.

────. "Suggestions about Mysticism," in his *Collected Essays and Reviews*

(New York: Longmans, Green, and Company, 1920), pp. 599–13.

———. *The Varieties of Religious Experience. A Study in Human Nature* (New Hyde Park: University Books, 1963).

Johnston, William. "Defining Mysticism. Suggestions from the Christian Encounter with Zen," in *Theological Studies.* 28 (March, 1967), pp. 94–110.

———. *Silent Music. The Science of Meditation* (New York: Harper and Row, Publishers, 1974).

———. *Still Point. Reflections on Zen and Christian Mysticism* (Bronx: Fordham University Press, 1970).

Jones, Rufus M. *The Flowering of Mysticism* (New York: Macmillan, 1939).

———. *New Studies in Mystical Religion* (New York: Macmillan, 1927).

———. *Studies in Mystical Religion* (New York: Macmillan, 1909).

Jung, Carl G. *Archetypes and the Collective Unconscious,* trans. R. F. C. Hull (New York: Routledge and Kegan Paul, 1955).

———. *Memories, Dreams, Reflections* (New York: Random House, 1961).

Kelsey, Morton T. *Dreams: The Dark Speech of the Spirit. A Christian Interpretation* (New York: Doubleday, 1968).

Knowles, David. *Christian Monasticism* (London: World University Library, 1969).

———. *Cistercians and Cluniacs: The Controversy Between St. Bernard and Peter the Venerable* (London: Oxford University Press, 1955).

———. *The Nature of Mysticism* (New York: Hawthorn Books, 1966).

———. "Saint Bernard of Clairvaux, 1090–1153," in *Dublin Review.* 227 (1953), pp. 104–21.

———. *What is Mysticism?* (London: Burns and Oates, 1967).

Lawrence, Brother. *The Practice of the Presence of God,* trans. D. Attwater (London: Orchard Books, 1926).

Leclercq, Jean. *Bernard of Clairvaux and the Cistercian Spirit,* trans. Claire Lavoie (Kalamazoo: Cistercian Publications, 1976).

Leonard, A. "Phenomenological Inquiries into Mystical Experience," trans. E. W. Geissmann in *Cross Currents.* 3 (1953), pp. 231–50.

———. "Phenomenological Introduction to Catholic Mysticism," in *Church History.* 40 (December, 1971), pp. 397–411.

Leuba, James H. *The Psychology of Religious Mysticism* (New York: Harcourt, Brace, Jovanovich, 1926).

Levasti, A. "St. Catherine of Siena and Dame Julian of Norwich," in *Life of the Spirit.* 7 (February, 1953), pp. 332–4.

Lewis, H. D. "Mysticism," in *London Quarterly and Holborn Review.* 189 (July, 1964), pp. 190–7.

Lovat, Lady Alice. *The Life of St. Teresa* (London: Herbert and Daniel, 1911).

Maes, B. *Franciscan Mysticism* (London: Sheed and Ward, 1928).

Marechal, Joseph. *Studies in the Psychology of the Mystics* (London: Burns, Oates, and Washbourne, 1977).

Maritain, Jacques. "Magic, Poetry, and Mysticism," in his *Situation of Poetry* (New York: Philosophical Library, 1955), pp. 23–36.

———. "Natural Mystical Experience and the Void," in his *Ransoming the Time*

(New York: Scribner's, 1941), pp. 255-89.

Mascall, E. L. *A Guide to Mt. Carmel. Being a Summary and an Analysis of the Ascent of Mt. Carmel by St. John of the Cross* (London: Dacre Press, 1939).

Maslow, Abraham H. *Religion, Values, and Peak-Experiences* (Columbus: Ohio State University Press, 1964).

———. *Toward a Psychology of Being* (Princeton: Van Nostrand, 1962).

Merton, Thomas. *The Asian Journal of Thomas Merton*, eds. Naomi Burton, Patrick Hart, and James Laughlin (New York: New Directions Books, 1973).

———. *The Ascent to Truth* (New York: Harcourt, Brace, Jovanovich, 1951).

———. *Bread in the Wilderness* (New York: New Directions Books, 1953).

———. *Contemplation in a World of Action* (New York: Doubleday, 1973).

———. *Emblems of a Season of Fury* (New York: New Directions Books, 1961).

———. "Is Mysticism Normal?" in *Commonweal*. 51 (November 4, 1949), pp. 94-8.

———. *Life and Holiness* (New York: Herder and Herder, 1963).

———. "The Monk as Marginal Man," in *The Center Magazine*. Vol. II, No. 1 (1969), p. 33.

———. *Mystics and Zen Masters* (New York: Farrar, Straus and Giroux, 1967).

———. *The New Man* (New York: Farrar, Straus and Company, 1961).

———. *New Seeds of Contemplation* (New York: New Directions Books, 1961).

———. *No Man is an Island* (New York: Harcourt, Brace, Jovanovich, 1955).

———. "The Sacred City," in *The Center Magazine*. Vol. I, No. 3 (March, 1968), pp. 73-77.

———. *The Seven Storey Mountain* (New York: Harcourt, Brace, Jovanovich, 1948).

———. *The Sign of Jonas* (New York: Harcourt, Brace, Jovanovich, 1953).

Merton, Thomas. *Silence in Heaven. A Book of the Monastic Life* (New York: Thomas Y. Crowell Company, 1956).

———. *The Silent Life* (New York: Farrar, Straus, and Cudahy, 1957).

———. *Thoughts in Solitude* (New York: Farrar, Straus, and Cudahy, 1958).

———. *The Waters of Siloe* (New York: Harcourt, Brace, Jovanovich, 1949).

———. *What are these Wounds?* (Milwaukee: Bruce Publishing Company, 1950).

———. "The Wild Places," in *The Center Magazine*. Vol. I, No. 5 (1968), pp. 40-4.

———. *The Wisdom of the Desert* (New York: New Directions Books, 1960).

Molinos, M. De. *The Spiritual Guide which Disentangles the Soul* (London: Methuen, 1908).

Moller, Herbert. "Affective Mysticism in Western Civilization," in *Psychoanalytic Review*. 52 (1965), pp. 259-72.

Morris, C. W. "Mysticism and its Language," in Ruth N. Anshen, editor, *Language: An Inquiry into its Meaning and Function* (New York: Harper and Row, Publishers, 1957), pp. 179-87.

Naranjo, Claudio. *The One Quest* (New York: Viking Press, 1972).

——— and Robert Ornstein. *On the Psychology of Meditation* (New York: Viking Press, 1971).

Needleman, Jacob and Dennis Lewis, eds. *On the Way to Self Knowledge* (New

York: Alfred A. Knopf, 1976).

————. *Sacred Tradition and Present Need* (New York: Viking Press, 1975).

Needleman, Jacob. *A Sense of the Cosmos. The Encounter of Modern Science and Ancient Truth* (New York: Doubleday, 1975).

————. *The Sword of Gnosis* (Baltimore: Penguin Books, 1974).

Nouwen, Henri. *The Genesee Diary. Report from a Trappist Monastery* (New York: Doubleday, 1976).

————. *The Living Reminder. Service and Prayer in Memory of Jesus Christ* (New York: Seabury Press, 1977).

Oberman, Heiko A. "Gabriel Biel and the Late Medieval Mysticism," in *Church History*. 30 (September, 1961), pp. 279-87.

O'Brien, Elmer, ed. *Varieties of Mystic Experience* (New York: Mentor Books, 1965).

Ornstein, Robert E., ed. *The Nature of Human Consciousness* (San Francisco: W. H. Freeman, 1973).

Otto, Rudolf. *The Idea of the Holy*, trans. John W. Harvey (New York: Oxford University Press, 1958).

————. *Mysticism East and West* (New York: Meridian, 1932).

Owen, H. P. "Christian Mysticism. A Study in Walter Hilton's 'The Ladder of Perfection.' " in *Religious Studies*. (7 March, 1971), pp. 31-42.

Ozment, Stephen E. *Mysticism and Dissent. Religous Ideology and Social Protest in the Sixteenth Century* (New Haven: Yale University Press, 1973).

Panikkar, Raymond. "The Contribution of Christian Monasticism in Asia to the Universal Church," in *Cistercian Studies*, 2 (1975), pp. 73-84.

————. *The Trinity and World Religions. Icon-Person-Mystery* (Madras: The Christian Literature Society, 1970).

Parrinder, Geoffrey. *Mysticism in the World's Religions* (New York: Oxford University Press, 1976).

Passmore, John A. *The Perfectibility of Man* (New York: Scribner's, 1971).

Peers, E. Allison. *Mother of Jesus. A Portrait of St. Teresa of Jesus* (London: S.C.M. Press, 1945).

————. *Mystics of Spain* (New York: Fernhill Press, 1951).

————. *Saint Teresa of Jesus, and Other Essays and Addresses* (London: Faber and Faber, 1953).

————. *Spirit of Flame. A Study of St. John of the Cross* (New York: Morehouse-Gorham Company, 1944).

————. *Studies of the Spanish Mystics* (New York: Macmillan, 1951).

Pennington, M. Basil. *Daily We Touch Him* (New York: Doubleday, 1976).

Pickering, F. P. "German Mystic Miscellany of the Late Fifteenth Century in the John Rylands Library," in *John Rylands Library Bulletin*. 22 (October, 1938), pp. 455-92.

Poulain, Auguste F. *The Graces of Interior Prayer. A Treatise on Mystical Theology* (St. Louis: Herder, 1950).

Prenter, Regin. *Spiritus Creator. Luther's Concept of the Holy Spirit* (Philadelphia: Muhlenberg Press, 1953).

Rahner, Karl. *Encounters with Silence* (New York: Newman Press, 1960).

_____. *Spiritual Exercises* (New York: Herder and Herder, 1965).

Reinhold, H. A. *The Soul Afire. Revelations of the Mystics* (Garden City: Doubleday, 1973).

Roszak, Theodore. *The Making of a Counter-Culture: Reflections on the Technocratic Society and its Youthful Opposition* (New York: Doubleday, 1969).

Rugg, Harold. *Imagination* (New York: Harper and Row, Publishers, 1963).

Russell, Bertrand. *Mysticism and Logic and Other Essays* (London: George Allen and Unwin, 1917).

Scholem, Gershom G. *Major Trends in Jewish Mysticism* (New York: Schocken Books, 1961).

_____. *On the Kabbalah and Its Symbolism* (New York: Schocken Books, 1970).

_____. *Sabbatai Sevi: The Mystical Messiah.* Bollingen Series, 93 (Princeton: Princeton University Press, 1973).

Schweitzer, Albert. *The Mysticism of Paul the Apostle*, trans. William Montgomery (New York: Seabury Press, 1968).

Smart, Ninian. "Interpretation and Mystical Experience," in *Religious Studies.* 1 (October, 1965), pp. 75–87.

Smith, Huston. *Forgotten Truth. The Primordial Tradition* (New York: Harper and Row, Publishers, 1976).

_____. *The Religions of Man* (New York: Harper and Row, Publishers, 1965).

Smith, Margaret. *An Introduction to Mysticism* (New York: Oxford University Press, 1977).

_____. *The Way of the Mystics. The Early Christian Mystics and the Rise of the Sufis* (New York: Oxford University Press, 1978).

Soderblom, Nathan. "Chrstian Mysticism in an Indian Soul: Sundar Singh," in *International Review of Missions.* 11 (April, 1922), pp. 226–38.

_____. "Holiness," in *Encyclopedia of Religion and Ethics*, ed., James Hastings (1913), VI, pp. 731–41.

Sommerfeldt, John R. "Abelard and Saint Bernard of Clairvaux," in *Papers of the Michigan Academy of Science, Arts, and Letters.* 46 (1961), pp. 493–501.

Staal, Frits. *Exploring Mysticism. A Methodological Essay* (Berkeley: University of California Press, 1975).

Stace, W. T. *Mysticism and Philosophy* (Philadelphia: J. B. Lippincott, 1960).

Steer, Douglas V. "Meaning of Mysticism within Christianity," in *Religion in Life.* 22 (1953), pp. 515–26.

Steiner, George. *Language and Silence* (London: Penguin Books, 1969).

Stendahl, Krister. "Religion, Mysticism, and the Institutional Church," in *Daedalus.* 96 (1967), pp. 854–9.

Suzuki, Daisetz Teitaro. *Mysticism: Christian and Buddhist. The Eastern and Western Way* (New York: Collier Books, 1962).

Symposium on Mysticism, Turku, Finland, 1968. *Mysticism.* Based on papers read at the symposium on mysticism held at Abo on September 7–9, 1968. (Stockholm: Almquist and Wiksell, 1970).

Tart, Charles T. *Altered States of Consciousness. A Book of Readings* (New York: John Wiley and Sons, 1969).

Thurman, Howard. *Deep is the Hunger: Meditations for Apostles of Sensitive-*

ness (New York: Harper and Row, Publishers, 1951).

———. *Disciplines of the Spirit* (New York: Harper and Row, Publishers, 1963).

———. *Footprints of a Dream. The Story of the Church for the Fellowship of all Peoples* (New York: Harper and Row, Publishers, 1959).

———. *The Inward Journey* (New York: Harper and Row, Publishers, 1961).

———. *Meditations of the Heart* (New York: Harper and Row, Publishers, 1953).

Tyrrell, George. "Mystical Element of Religion," in *Edinburgh Review.* Vol. 210 (July, 1909), pp. 34–56.

Underhill, Evelyn. *Essentials of Mysticism and Other Essays* (New York: Dutton, 1972).

———. *The Mystic Way* (London: Dent, 1913).

———. *Mysticism: A Study in the Nature and Development of Man's Spiritual Consciousness* (New York: Noonday Press, 1955).

———. *The Mystics of the Church* (New York: Schocken Books, 1964).

Von Hugel, Baron Friedrich. *Eternal Life* (Edinburgh: T. and T. Clark, 1912).

———. *The Mystical Element of Religion as Studied in Saint Catherine of Genoa and Her Friends* (London: Dent, 1923).

Waddell, Helen. *The Desert Fathers* (Ann Arbor: University of Michigan Press, 1957).

Walsh, James, ed. *Pre-Reformation English Spirituality* (New York: Fordham University Press, 1965).

———. *Spirituality through the Centuries. Ascetics and Mystics of the Western Church* (New York: P. J. Kenedy, 1964).

Watts, Alan W. *Behold the Spirit: A Study in the Necessity of Mystical Religion* (New York: Pantheon Books, 1950).

———. *Beyond Theology: The Art of Godmanship* (New York: Pantheon Books, 1964).

———. *The Joyous Cosmology: Adventures in the Chemistry of Consciousness* (New York: Pantheon Books, 1962).

———. *The Supreme Identity: An Essay on Oriental Metaphysics and the Christian Religion* (New York: Pantheon Books, 1950).

Wienpahl, Paul. *The Matter of Zen. A Brief Account of Zazen* (New York: New York University Press, 1964).

Yeats, William B. *A Vision. A reissue with the Author's Final Revisions* (New York: MacMillan, 1956).

Zaehner, Robert C. *Mysticism, Sacred and Profane. An Inquiry into Some Varieties of Praeter-Natural Experience* (Oxford: Clarendon Press, 1957).

———. *Zen, Drugs and Mysticism* (New York: Pantheon, 1973).

Index